THE GUNSMITH'S MANUAL

by J. P. Stelle

and

Wm. B. Harrison

Skyhorse Publishing books may be purchased in bulk at special discounts for sales promotion, corporate gifts, fund-raising, or educational purposes. Special editions can also be created to specifications. For details, contact the Special Sales Department, Skyhorse Publishing, 307 West 36th Street, 11th Floor, New York, NY 10018 or info@skyhorsepublishing.com.

Skyhorse® and Skyhorse Publishing® are registered trademarks of Skyhorse Publishing, Inc.®, a Delaware corporation.

Visit our website at www.skyhorsepublishing.com.

10 9 8 7 6 5 4 3

Library of Congress Cataloging-in-Publication Data is available on file.

ISBN: 978-1-62087-720-3

Printed in the United States of America

EDITOR'S NOTE

J. P. STELLE AND WM. B. HARRISON'S

THE GUNSMITH'S MANUAL

by Dr. Jim Casada

First published in 1883, *The Gunsmith's Manual* is generally reckoned to be the first substantive work dealing with gunsmithing exclusively and in detail. As staff for *American Gunsmith* note in "The Gunsmith's Reference Library," published in 2009, this volume, while well over a century old, is more than a mere historical curiosity. "The book's first 18 pages present one of the most concise histories of the gun, from the discovery of gunpowder to the breechloader, we've ever read." They also recommend its coverage of mundane matters, such as removal of rusted screws, as a way of gaining full familiarity with muzzleloader nomenclature, and for insight when it comes to restoration work on black powder guns.

Thomas G. Samworth, the publishing genius who created and owned the Small-Arms Technical Publishing Company, was also enthusiastic about the book's merits when he reprinted it in 1945. His promotional for the work gives an excellent assessment of its value at the time. "Back in 1882, when any town and village of any size whatever had its own hardworked gunsmith, J. P. Stelle and William B. Harrison wrote *The Gunsmith's Manual* — one of the very few early American works on firearms, and a book immediately recognized and accepted as the standard textbook of the gunsmithing profession. This publication held that position of eminence for several decades; in fact, it was the authority until the coming of smokeless powder."

Ray Riling, in his *Guns and Shooting: A Bibliography*, offers a useful summation of the book's wide-ranging contents: "Hints, recipes, and practical suggestions to the individual craftsman and gunsmith. Descriptions of guns and pistols, stocks, barrels, breeching tools, chambering of breech-loading barrels, gun-ribs, thimbles, rifling, locks, gun-hammers and their fitting, nipples, cones, springs, rods, bullet-moulds, etc." In other words, the work's coverage is comprehensive. None of these sources provides appreciable biographical information on the authors, and my own researches have been similarly fruitless. Internal evidence in the book does suggest that one if not both men were working gunsmiths, and there is no doubt whatsoever that they knew their subject matter intimately. The book is rightly considered a landmark in the field of gunsmithing and should be reckoned the cornerstone of any library on the subject.

Some indication of its enduring appeal is offered by the fact that Samworth's reprint of the Excelsior Publishing original (many listings of the Samworth reprint wrongly give Excelsior as the 1945 publisher) was but the first of a series. A decade later, Pioneer Press, a small specialty publisher in Harriman, Tennessee, produced another reprint. In 1972, the Gun Room Press of Highland Park, New Jersey, continued the trend. Then in 1993, there was yet another reprint, by the Border Press. All these reprints notwithstanding, the book is quite difficult to find. Indeed, the original edition and the Samworth reprint are highly collectible, the latter thanks in part to its lovely dust jacket. The dust jacket, Gayle Hoskins' painting *Trade from the Mononngahela*, depicts frontiersmen gathered outside a gunsmithing shop in the Lancaster, Pennsylvania, area. Samworth also offered the painting as a separate print. It is, like the book, in considerable demand in collectors' circles.

For most members of the Firearms Classics Library, this book's primary appeal will be its historic merits. Yet anyone who putters with or shoots muzzleloaders will also find it valuable from a factual standpoint, and savvy black powder gunsmiths still use it as a go-to reference work. Those considerations, not to mention the fact that the book, whether in original or reprinted form, is missing from most collections, make it a logical and welcome addition to the Firearms Classics Library.

Jim Casada

ROCK HILL, SOUTH CAROLINA

Trade from the Monongahela

THE

GUNSMITH'S MANUAL;

A COMPLETE HANDBOOK

FOR THE

AMERICAN GUNSMITH,

BEING A

PRACTICAL GUIDE TO ALL BRANCHES OF THE TRADE.

BY J. P. STELLE AND WM. B. HARRISON.

Skyhorse Publishing

PREFACE.

THE GUNSMITH'S MANUAL is designed to furnish in convenient form such information as shall be of most use in the actual every-day work of the shop, and for such demands or emergencies as are liable to challenge the knowledge or skill of the workman. It is manifestly not the province of such a book to assume to guide a manufacturer in the conduct of a great factory. Were such a work at all feasible, it could not also properly meet the wants of the ordinary gunsmith, and the scope of his little shop. He is the man whose case has been kept steadily in mind in the preparation of the following pages, and whatever the book contains has been included because it was believed to be useful to him. No pains have been spared to make every detail full, explicit and reliable, and it is believed that any intelligent man will find but little trouble in understanding and successfully applying the instructions.

In the confident hope that this work will maintain and enhance the favorable reputation which MESSRS JESSE HANEY & Co. have acquired by their Trade Manuals and Useful Handbooks, it is respectfully submitted to the verdict of the American Gunsmiths by

THE AUTHORS.

INDEX.

CHAPTER I.

CHAPTER II.

CHAPTER III.

PAGE

CHAPTER IV.

CHAPTER V.

CHAPTER VI.

CHAPTER VII.

CHAPTER VIII.

CHAPTER IX.

CHAPTER X.

CHAPTER XI.

CHAPTER XII.

CHAPTER XIII.

CHAPTER XIV.

CHAPTER XV.

CHAPTER XVI.

CHAPTER XVII.

CHAPTER XVIII.

CHAPTER XIX.

CHAPTER XX.

PAGE

CHAPTER XXI.

CHAPTER XXII.

CHAPTER XXIII.

CHAPTER XXIV.

CHAPTER XXV.

PAGE

CHAPTER XXXI.

CHAPTER XXXII.

CHAPTER XXXIII.

PAGE

CHAPTER XXXIV.

CHAPTER XXXV.

CHAPTER XXXVI.

CHAPTER XXXVII.

CHAPTER XXXVIII.

CHAPTER XXXIX.

PAGE

CHAPTER XL.

CHAPTER XLI.

CHAPTER XLII.

THE GUNSMITH'S MANUAL.

CHAPTER I.

HISTORY OF THE GUN.

Discovery of Gunpowder.—No authentic records have been left to show when or by whom was discovered the wonderful properties of the chemical compound now known as gunpowder; nor have we any information concerning the uses to which it was originally applied. There is little probability that it was at once employed as an agent in fire-arms; indeed, we have pretty strong evidence to show that it was not, for Roger Bacon refers to it in his famous treatise, *De Nullitate Magiœ*, published A. D., 1216, while fire-arms are mentioned by no writer as having been known earlier than about 1338.

The First Fire-Arms.—The first fire-arms, or guns, as we now call them, are said to have been rude cannon, formed by banding together flat iron bars, something on the plan of our wooden casks or barrels of to-day. These guns were fired with a "slow match," the gunners retiring to a safe distance while the match was burning to the priming. Their earliest use was as engines of war. The writers of ancient history tell us that they were so employed by the Moors at the noted siege of Algesiras, Spain, in 1341, and at the battle of Calais, in 1346. At the latter battle, Edward III is credited with having had four pieces, which made him victorious.

Earliest Hand-Guns.—It is claimed by Spanish historians that to Spain belongs the honor of having been the first power to furnish her soldiers with fire-arms so small that they could be transported by a single person. They were unwieldy affairs at the beginning, however; really small cannon lashed upon wooden scantlings. The soldier could not fire his piece off-hand, but was forced to carry a "rest" with him wherever he went. Being ready to discharge his arm he balanced it upon the rest, steadied it by holding the scantling under his arm, and then "touched it off" with a live coal of fire, while he sighted along the barrel to take aim at his object. What happened immediately after the coal came in contact with the powder the historian saith not, but a modern writer, who has been examining one of these old guns in a museum, jumps to the conclusion that the soldier, with the scantling under his arm, must have been launched suddenly into an impressive dream of first-class earthquakes, or something else "like unto the combined kicking of about fifty mules."

Prejudice Against Fire-Arms.—For about two centuries after the invention of hand fire-arms they were so inefficient that the cross-bow, then in general use, was able to quite successfully hold its own against them. It was not until 1596 that Queen Elizabeth, by a proclamation, directed that cross and other bows used in the army should be discarded entirely in favor of muskets. And thereat there arose much murmuring of dissatisfaction throughout the English Empire, according to Michael Montaigne, a most prominent man of his time, who narrates the fact, and adds: "Except the noise in our ears, to which we will be henceforth accustomed, I think the fire-arm is one of very little effect, and I hope that we shall one day give up its use." Could he return to earth at this age, and see the wonderful fire-arms that have developed from the humble beginning of which he was then treating, he would speedily lose his hope to the effect that one day its use would be entirely given up.

The First Rifle.—The first rifle is said to have been made about the close of the fifteenth century, by one Gaspard Zollner, of Vienna. It was a simple barrel with straight grooves; the only object of the grooves being to prevent its becoming so "dirty" from continued use, as did the smooth-bore. Spiral grooving does not seem to have been thought of until many years later.

The Arquebus.—The earliest noted improvement in the hand-gun, making it lighter and giving it a longer barrel, was called the arquebus; but even this was so heavy that a "rest" was necessary while discharging it. This rest was a single staff armed with a steel point which went into the ground like the Jacob-staff of a surveyor, but which fitted it for use as a pike when not employed in connection with the gun. It was called the *schweine feder*, which rendered into English means the "hog's bristle."

The arquebus was a regular "match-gun;" that is, it had a "pan" or receptacle at the side of the breech for the priming powder, which communicated with the interior of the barrel by a small perforation called the "touch-hole." The priming was lighted by a match, which consisted of a coil of small rope saturated with some kind of chemical, which caused it to burn readily and hold fire for a long time. The soldier using the arquebus carried the match in his hand and kept it buring during an action. The manner of setting off the piece was about the same as with the live coal—he secured his sight and then touched the priming with his lighted match.

The Match Lock.—Later, the serpent-match was invented and looked upon as a startling improvement. It was a simple S-shaped piece of iron or wire hinged to the side of the gun just back of the priming pan. The upper end was provided with a beak which gripped the lighted fuse, while the lower end played the part of a modern trigger. With this contrivance the gunner had only to take sight and them pull with his finger upon the lower end of the S until the lighted fuse was brought down into the priming. After many years of use an improvement was made upon the S, consisting of a small spring which threw it back into an erect position so soon as the pressure upon the lower end was discontinued.

The powder employed with the old arquebus was of two grades as to size of grain; a coarse grade for the charge, and a fine grade for the priming. Its chemical composition does not seem to have differed materially from that of our modern gunpowder.

The serpent match, so called because the upper end holding the fuse was often shaped to represent the head of a serpent, was the first actual step taken towards a gun-lock. It was thought to be perfection itself, especially after the returning spring had been added, and so strong a hold did it take upon all nations that only a few years has elapsed since it was wholly abandoned in some of the most benighted regions, as in China, for instance, where it is known to have been used in the army at a date as late as 1860.

Musket-Petronel.—Next in order to the arquebus came the musket, a Spanish invention. It was heavier than its predecessor, and carried a charge twice as large. Almost simultaneously with this appeared the first cavalry fire-arm, which was called the petronel. It was shorter than the musket and larger in bore; the horseman rested its breech against his breast and communicated the fire by means of the serpent match.

The Wheel-Lock.—In 1517 the Germans astonished the world by inventing and bringing into use the "wheel-lock," which was a regular gun-lock, entirely doing away with the lighted match. It consisted of a small disk of steel fluted on the edges, set in close contact with the priming pan, and made to revolve with great rapidity by means of a spiral spring arranged somewhat on the plan of the spring of a spring-clock. In contact with its fluted edge, and held there by a spring, was arranged a sharp flint; hence when the steel disk was set in motion a train of sparks was thrown off as it revolved over the edge of flint. These sparks fell into the priming pan and ignited the powder, discharging the piece. The spring was wound up like winding a clock or watch, and a slight pressure upon a trigger under the breech set the wheel in motion. The pressure was continued until the gun was discharged, when it was discontinued, the result of which was an immediate stopping of the wheel. A single winding would usually discharge the gun about half a dozen times.

The Pistol.—The wheel-lock went into quite general use, finally leading to the invention of the pistol, about 1544. The first pistols were single barrel, and very short. The stock was heavy, and the breech or handle, instead of leaving the barrel with a curve, as in later days, dropped at right angles to the iron. It was put into use as a cavalry arm, first by the Germans and afterwards by the people of many other nations. In 1607 the German horse soldiers were all regularly armed with double-barrel wheel-lock pistols.

The Snaphaunce.—After the date just mentioned modifications and improvements in fire-arms were rapid and constant. The wheel-lock was finally followed by the "snaphaunce," which was a straight piece of furrowed steel brought to bear upon the flint instead of the disk. It was more simple in its construction than the wheel-lock, and hence less liable to get out of order. Of course it worked in obedience to the action of a spring, but the spring was not a spiral—it was more on the plan of the mainspring in modern gun-locks.

The Flint-Lock.—About 1630 Spain again popped to the surface; this time with the regular flint-lock, embracing precisely the same mechanism as the flint-lock used in our Revolutionary war, and familiar to very many of the older people of the present day. Its advantges over the wheel-lock and the snaphaunce were so marked that France at once adopted it for use in her armies, but England held back, contending that the wheel-lock was the better invention, till 1690, when she gave up the contest, and adopted the flint-lock.

Important Improvements.—Rapidly following the invention of the flint-lock came important improvements in the musket. The stock was lightened and put into better shape, and sights were invented and placed upon the barrels. Up to this time the soldier had been forced to carry his ammunition in bulk, but now cartridges were brought into use, carried in convenient and neatly made cartridge-boxes. Steel bayonets to set over the muzzle of the gun also appeared, the first in 1693. Prior to this time a rude kind of bayonet had been more or less in use—it was a sort of dagger set into a wooden handle, the latter to be thrust into the muzzle of the gun in case of a hand-to-hand charge, where loading and firing could not be attended to. Iron ramrods took the place of the inconvenient and unsafe wooden ones formerly in use, which was regarded as a long stride in the efficiency of the musket. With the old wooden ramrods, clumsy and easily broken, the loading of a musket was a slow and laborious task, but the iron rod secured comparative ease and rapidity.

Advance of the Rifle.—With the general improvement of fire-arms the rifle had worked gradually into favor and use. Its main drawback, as an army gun, laid in the difficulty experienced in loading it. But it was admirably adapted to the wants of the people settling the wilds of the American continent, hence they adopted it almost to the entire exclusion of any other kind of fire-arm. In the armies its use was limited to a few corps of sharpshooters, usually on the frontiers where it was advantageous to harass the enemy by picking off his men at long range. England seems to have been rather prejudiced against the rifle until after our war with her for Independence. In that war she appears to have had so striking a demonstration of its efficiency that she soon after adopted it as a military arm; and other nations, having faith in her superior judgment, finally followed her example, bringing the rifle rapidly upward in rank as an effectual implement of war.

The Percussion Lock.—In 1807 a Scotch clergyman by the name of Alexander Forsyth, invented a new method of igniting the charge in fire-arms, which, after various changes and improvements, settled down to what is now known as the percussion cap. The percussion lock was a simultaneous invention, of course; though it did not differ materially, in point of construction, from the old flint-lock already in use. The main difference consisted in the substitution of a cylinder and tube for the priming pan and frizzen, and a hammer for the cock.

A strong current of prejudice set at once against the percussion lock, though nobody could tell why. All declared it would not do, but none attempted to give a reason for the faith that was in them. As a result the new invention was pretty effectually held in the background until 1834, when its opponents accepted a challenge for a public test of its merits against those of the flint-lock. The test extended to 6,000 rounds. In the course of these the percussion lock (afterwards more commonly known as the cap-lock), gave but six mis-fires, while the flint-lock scored nine hundred and twenty-two misses.

This astounding defeat at once sealed the fate of the flint-lock; still it was a long time before the prejudice existing against the other could be entirely removed. Even as far down as the date of our Mexican war, General Scott flatly objected to its use in his army, and had his men armed with the flint-lock, although there were then in our arsenals percussion-lock muskets enough to have armed all his forces more than twice over.

But facts are such stubborn things that even the strongest prejudice must give way to them sooner or later. So it proved in this instance; one by one the manufacturers of flint-lock fire-arms adopted the improvements resulting from the discoveries of the Scotch clergyman, until finally no more flint-locks were made, and the percussion lock was in undisputed possession of the field.

The Breech-Loader.—When the percussion-lock had been fully adopted by the public, and all the "latest improvements" had been added to it, people thought that the fire-arm had attained to such a degree of perfection as to preclude any further change in the future; but how mistaken! The fate of the percussion-lock is now as much sealed as was that of the flint-lock at the test-trial of 1834. It is going the way of all its predecessors, and its entire extinction is only a matter of time. The breech-loader, with charge and ignition combined in the same cartridge, is rapidly taking its place, and, until some new and wonderful discovery comes to the surface, must, undoubtedly, stand paramount as the gun of the future.

While springing into general favor at one leap, as it were, the breech-loader is no new and sudden appearance. In truth it is of great antiquity. In the Tower of London, the Woolwich Museum, and in the Museum of Paris, may be seen hundreds of breech-loaders that were made centuries ago. Of course they were not made to use the percussion cartridge peculiar to many such guns of modern make, nevertheless they were veritable breech-loaders, and the real suggestors, no doubt, of the modern arm of that character.

In the Museum of Artillery, at Woolwich, there is a breech-loading pierrier, or paterera, of the time of Edward IV. (1471). It consists of a directing barrel, terminating in a square bar or frame of iron, and a separate loading chamber, with handle, which was fastened in its place for firing by an iron wedge. There are also found in the museums many breech-loading pistols, that were evidently in use about cotemporaneous with this gun.

The records kept at St. Etienne, France, show that the French monarch, Henry II, shot with a breech-loading gun in 1540. And the English records show that the Marquis of Worcester took out a patent in that country for a breech action on the "cut-screw" principle in 1661. A portion of the specification reads as follows:

"An invencione to make certain guns or pistols which in the tenth part of one minute of an hour may be re-charged; the fourth part of one turne of the barrell, which remains still fixt, fastening it as foreceably and effectually as a dozen shrids of any screw, which, in the ordinary and usual way require as many turnes."

There are several specimens of the breech-loader made on this plan, now in the Woolwich Museum. There are also other specimens, on a plan entirely different, made at a date but a little more recent, for it seems that then, as in modern days, one invention was very apt to suggest another. Three years after the Marquis of Worcester had taken out his patent, one Abraham Hill, of London, patented some six different systems of breech-loaders. In his specification concerning one of them he says:

"It is a new way of making a gun or a pistoll, the breech whereof rises on a hindge, by a contrivance of a motion under it, by which it is also let down and bolted fast by one of the same motion."

This, as will be readily seen, was rubbing pretty close upon the breech-loader of the present day.

Since the dates of the patents just referred to, the breech-loading fire-arm is known to have been in uninterrupted existence; but so strong was the current turned against it by popular prejudice, that it was little known to the people in general. A want of scientific training among the masses was the cause which held it back; they were unable to clearly understand all the whys and wherefores connected with its workings, and, therefore, rejected it on the plea that it was dangerous, without really knowing whether it was or not.

Great improvements in the breech-loader now succeeeded each other with astonishing rapidity up to the time when M. Lefaucheux, of France, capped the climax by inventing the cartridge containing within itself the cap, or means of igniting the charge. This made it available as a sporting gun, and hence promptly set it forward into public attention; and finally, after a score or so of improvements, usually at the hands of the English, into public favor. It is, at last, the gun of the period, and the old muzzle-loader, with all its good qualities (and they were certainly many), is rapidly surrendering the field to the more successful candidate, and retiring in the footsteps of its honored predecessors, the wheel-lock and the flint-lock.

CHAPTER II.

HOW GUNS ARE MADE.

Gunsmith—Gunmaker.—The modern gunsmith is not necessarily a gunmaker, but rather a repairer of guns that have happened to get out of order. In earlier days the devotees to his calling may, in their little shops, have made guns entire, but now, if the gunsmith *makes* them at all, that making consists in merely finishing up the parts and putting them together—generally making the stock entire. All gun parts can now be bought as "gunsmith's materials," either finished or in the rough, as may be desired. They are made by a variety of workmen, the business of each man being to make a single part, and nothing more. There is at present too much in a good gun to admit of all being made advantageously by one man; he would need to be a kind of "Jack-of-all-trades," and, like the traditional Jack, it is but reasonable to suppose that he would be really first-class at none.

In some of the large establishments where guns are made all these different workmen are employed, hence such an establishment is really a collection of workers in many trades. The gunsmith who has his shop for repairing purposes, or for putting together materials under the name of gunmaking, will not be specially concerned with reference to any of these trades; still it is but reasonable to suppose that he would like to know something of how the implements, or parts of implements, that he will be constantly handling, were put up; and, besides, there will exist something akin to a necessity for his possession of such knowledge, owing to the fact that his customers will often call upon him to answer many a question as to how this or that gun was made, etc. With this view of the case, it is really necessary to give a brief outline of gunmaking, following the work from the rough material to the final finish.

Gun-Barrels—Best Materials for.—The barrels of the finest and best guns, either Damascus, or other steel, or iron, are formed, as made in Europe and England, of scraps of iron suited to the purpose, and selected with great skill and the greatest possible care. These scraps, which are usually bought up about the country, are placed in what is called a "shaking tub"—a vessel which is violently shaken and rocked about by machinery or otherwise (depending upon the particular locality) for the purpose of scouring and brightening the scraps. This done, they are carefully picked over by adepts, who cull out the unsuitable pieces. So rigid is the culling that it often happens that out of a ton of scoured scraps not more than one hundred pounds weight of them are chosen as suitable for going into the best barrels.

Among the scraps usually thought to be best are old chains that have been used for many years, the wear and rust of time having left only the best elements of the iron. The Damascus steel, which has attained to so high a reputation, got it by being manufactured out of old coach springs. Of course it is not all made of coach springs now, but it was in years ago; agents then traveled all over the country hunting and buying them up, paying a much higher price for an old broken spring than a new one would cost its owner.

On Making Gun-Barrels.—The selected scraps to be worked into gun-barrel material are cut into small pieces and thrown into a furnace, where they are exposed to intense heat until fused, after which they are brought forth an adhering mass and placed under a hammer, which drives them together and forges them into bars. The bars are next rolled into thin plates, and then cut into strips twelve inches long and six inches wide. The *very best* guns are made of a combination of iron and steel. Both materials having been rolled and cut into sheets of exactly the same size, these sheets (one-fourth of an inch thick) are piled upon each other alternately to the number of thirty, and subjected to a welding heat; they are then driven together under a five-ton hammer into a consolidated slab. The slabs so formed are next worked down into one-fourth inch square rods. The more the material is hammered and worked the better it is. The rods are next twisted until they present the appearance of a strand of rope, some rods being twisted to the right and others to the left. Two rods, with opposite twist,

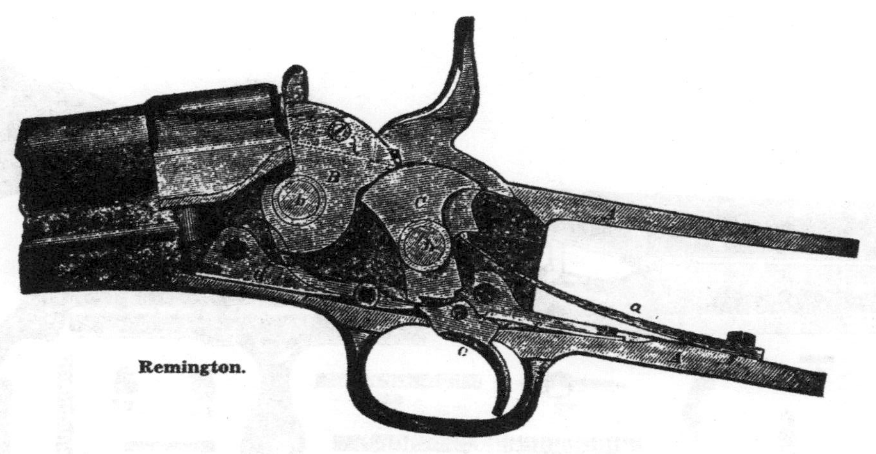

Remington.

Remington—Keene's Patent.

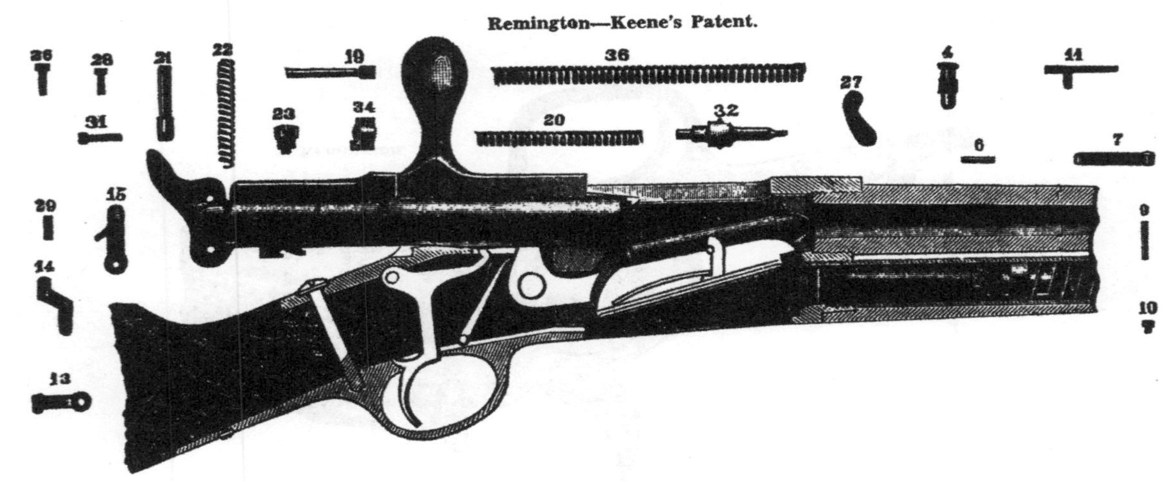

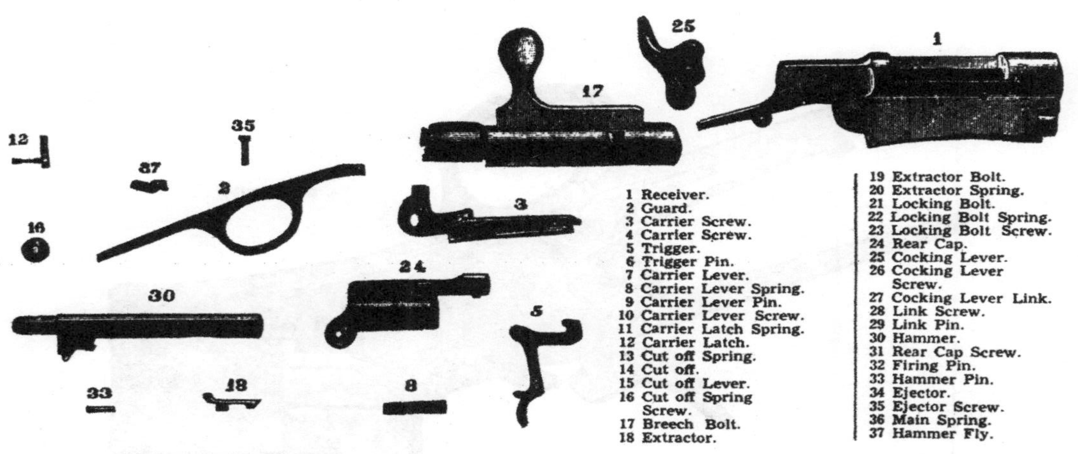

1 Receiver.
2 Guard.
3 Carrier Screw.
4 Carrier Screw.
5 Trigger.
6 Trigger Pin.
7 Carrier Lever.
8 Carrier Lever Spring.
9 Carrier Lever Pin.
10 Carrier Lever Screw.
11 Carrier Latch Spring.
12 Carrier Latch.
13 Cut off Spring.
14 Cut off.
15 Cut off Lever.
16 Cut off Spring Screw.
17 Breech Bolt.
18 Extractor.
19 Extractor Bolt.
20 Extractor Spring.
21 Locking Bolt.
22 Locking Bolt Spring.
23 Locking Bolt Screw.
24 Rear Cap.
25 Cocking Lever.
26 Cocking Lever Screw.
27 Cocking Lever Link.
28 Link Screw.
29 Link Pin.
30 Hammer.
31 Rear Cap Screw.
32 Firing Pin.
33 Hammer Pin.
34 Ejector.
35 Ejector Screw.
36 Main Spring.
37 Hammer Fly.

Remington.

are heated to the welding degree, placed upon each other, and rolled together; they are now in a narrow slab, presenting that fine curl of "grain" peculiar to the Damascus, or that beautiful wavy figure peculiar to the laminated steel, as the case may be. The next operation is to coil one of these slabs around a mandrel in a spiral form, and weld it securely under the blows of hand-hammers. It is now a gun-barrel in the rough.

Finishing and Proving.—The rough barrel goes from the welder to the borer, where it is put through the process of "rough boring." From the "rough borer" it goes into the hands of the "fine borer," who bores it out smoothly and to near the size it is to be when finished. Another operator then takes it in charge and dresses it to smoothness externally, then the "tester" takes it and dips it into strong acid, which soon shows any imperfection in either twist or welding that might exist. If not perfect, it is sent back to be worked over; if all right, it passes to the next department, where it is straightened inside. This part of the work is governed entirely by the eye, and hence demands the services of a workman of great skill, and experience.

Having been "passed on" by the "straightener," the barrel goes to the "turner," who turns it in a lathe until the outside is true and correspondingly straight with the interior, and is of exactly the required weight. If the arm is to be a double-barrel shot gun, the barrel next goes into the hands of a workman who joins it to another barrel with the utmost nicety; to attain which, levels and other suitable instruments are brought into requisition. Like the man who straightens the bore, the man who joins the barrels must be a workman of great skill.

The next operation is to braze on the "lumps;" then, next in order, the ribs are put on. Now comes the "proving." The rear ends having been securely plugged, they go to the proof department, where is placed into each barrel fully four ordinary charges of gunpowder; then, atop of this, a wad of strong brown paper, rammed securely down, then a leaden bullet large enough to exactly fit the bore, and then another wad of brown paper. The charge is fired, and if the barrels stand the ordeal unfazed, they are ready to be fitted to the action; otherwise, they go back to be worked over. In some houses the "proving" is done before the barrels are joined together.

Action, Stock and Final Finish.—The "action man" now takes the perfect barrels in hand and performs his part of the work. In the meantime the stock-maker has not been idle. A stock is already in waiting, and next must come a series of fittings of the most exquisite nicety, until the gun is actually a gun and ready for its final test. This is applied by the "targeteer," who passes upon it according to its merits. If his report comes in favorable, the gun goes to the proper department for final finish. The stock is dressed up, finished in oil or varnish and chequered, and its mountings put on. Every piece of metal is polished and burnished to the highest possible degree, and all the needed engraving is done. Next comes the case-hardening, coloring. and the browning or bronzing; and this having been well and satisfactorily performed, the gun is ready for market.

On Making the Rifle.—The processes employed in making the modern rifle do not differ materially from those named in the foregoing. Of course there are some processes employed on the shot gun that are not called for in the manufacture of the rifle, and some on the rifle not needed on the shot gun. The general principle is the same, however, and therefore it is not necessary to consume time in further description. The great care mentioned is only done to make a good gun; only the cheap and inferior guns are pitched together in an easier and more irregular way. But the gunsmith would not thank any one for a treatise on cheap and bad guns. They are legion, more's the pity, and his extensive dealings with them will afford annoyance sufficient to do away with any desire on his part to fight his battles over in a book.

Plain Steel-Barrel Guns.—Of course there are guns with "plain steel barrels," as they are called, which pass muster as fair; and the barrels of these are made by a process differing materially from that described in the foregoing; all else connected with the making is the same. These plain steel barrels are made of round bars of steel two inches in diameter. The bars are first cut into lengths of nine inches each; a hole or bore three-fourths of an inch in diameter is drilled through the centre. They are now called moulds, and the next step is to pass them through rolls, which reduce them to the required size for barrels and stretch them out to the required length, holding them, at the same time, in the proper shape, externally. Having been thus rolled, they are bored out internally, turned and ground externally, until they have attained to the shape and proportions of correctly-formed barrels. After this comes the fitting up and "proving," as in the case of the finer guns.

CHAPTER III.

GUNS NOW IN USE.

Guns Defined.—Excepting the pistol, and the mortar, perhaps, all fire-arms now in use are classed under the name of guns. The cannon or artillery ordnance in all its sizes and forms, is simply a large gun. It is variously divided off, according to character, into heavy siege-guns, field-pieces, rifled-cannon and smooth-bores. These again are sub-divided into a large number of different kinds, as the Armstrong, the Dahlgren, the Columbiad, the Paixhan, the Parrot, the Whitworth, etc. But with guns of this class the practical gunsmith will have nothing to do, and hence it is but reasonable to suppose that he feels no particular concern about them. It is with the small-arms that his concern will mainly lie, and therefore from this page to the conclusion of this work the gun mentioned will be some instrument classing with the small fire-arms, and liable to be brought to a gunsmith's shop for repairs.

The small arms, or hand guns are muskets, rifles, carbines, fowling-pieces and pistols. These may be properly divided into three classes: the flint-lock, the percussion-lock and the cartridge breech-loader.

The Old Flint-Lock Guns.—Of the old flint-locks, only a few are now in existence within the United States. Here and there one has been kept as a kind of heirloom by some family, and occasionally these drop in upon the gunsmith for repairs, but not often. They are more common along the Mexican border in Texas, perhaps, than in any other portion of the country.

A minute description of the old flint-lock-gun need not be given, as, in general characteristics it does not differ materially from all other muzzle-loaders. The barrel is usually longer than that of the more modern gun; and, in the case of the rifle, the stock (all wood) extends nearly to the muzzle. It is what, in later days, when half-stocks had been invented, was called a full-stock. As already intimated the interior mechanism of the lock differs very little from that of the more modern cap or percussion-lock. On the outside, in place of the cap-hammer is a cock arranged with two lips for holding a flint. The lips are brought together firmly upon the flint by means of a screw which passes down immediately back of it. In the top of the lock-plate, directly in front of the cock, is set the priming-pan; a small iron receptacle made to contain, say the fourth of a teaspoonful of gunpowder. When the lock is in position the butt or open end of the pan comes squarely up against the barrel of the gun where a small hole called the "touch-hole" communicates with the interior, and with the charge, when the gun is loaded. Over the priming-pan a cover fits nicely, lying horizontally when the pan is closed, and turning up at right angles on the edge nearest the cock, and standing erect, a small plate of steel, immediately in front of the flint. This cover, with its vertical plate is called the frizzen. It works on a hinge, and is held into whatever position set, by means of a small spring called the heel spring. When the cock is set in motion by drawing upon the trigger and releasing the check to the mainspring, the flint comes in contact with the steel plate of the frizzen, throwing it back upon its hinge and scraping down its face directly towards the priming-pan. As the frizzen flies back the pan is uncovered, of course, enabling the flint to end its journey directly in the priming powder of the pan. In its scrape over the steel plate of the frizzen it causes many brilliant sparks of fire, which descending with it into the priming sets off the charge.

The Percussion-Lock Gun.—As has already been stated, the immediate successor of the old flint-lock was the percussion or cap-lock. While now far beyond its zenith, it is still the prevailing gun in many portions of the country; especially in out-of-the-way districts South and West. In the oldest make of these guns a small plug of iron is screwed into the barrel at the point where the touch-hole of the flint-lock was located. It is called the cylinder. The end passing into the barrel is drilled to communicate with the powder-bed of the gun, and with a cap-tube, which is screwed into the cylinder, to stand erect near the side of the barrel. In more modern guns the cylinder has been discarded, the tube going directly into the barrel and communicating with the powder-bed.

The oldest percussion-lock rifles are set in whole-stock, on the plan of the flint-lock gun; and on account of the fact that all the old-fashioned folks are not yet dead, some factories put up new guns after the same model, calling them Kentucky rifles. The stock reaches the full length of the barrel, which is heavy and about four feet long. It is octagon in shape. But in most of the more modern rifles the barrel is shorter, say from 32 to 36 inches in length, and comparatively light; and the stock extends only half the length of the barrel, joining to a rib affixed to the barrel for the purpose of holding the ramrod-thimbles.

The "patent-breech" may be mentioned as another peculiarity of the percussion-lock gun, since it was not known in the days ere the flint-lock had lost its prestige. In those early days the breech end of the barrel was closed by a plug of iron, screwed in and called the breech-pin. From its upper side there extended backward along the stock a thin plate or strap, through which screws passed at right angles to hold the barrel in place. This method of securing the breech-end of the barrel into the stock has been done away with by the patent breech, which secures it by means of a short hook on the end of the breech-pin; or, rather, on the end of the short plug screwed into the barrel in place of the old breech-pin. It is much more convenient than the old fashioned arrangement, as it enables the barrel to be taken from the stock in a moment, doing away with the labor of drawing the breech-pin screws.

On the Muzzle-Loaders. — The percussion-lock muzzle-loaders all work upon about the same principle. The charge must go in at the muzzle and be put down to the breech. In the case of army guns it is usually contained in a paper cartridge. The soldier bites off the end of the cartridge in which the powder is inclosed, to admit of a communication with the cap, and then forces it down with the ramrod. But in the case of rifles and fowling pieces, or shotguns, as the latter are most commonly called in this country, cartridges are seldom employed. In loading a rifle the powder is first measured in a "charger," and then poured down the barrel; next comes the patch, which is usually a piece of new and strong cotton cloth, most commonly the kind known as white drilling. This, having been tallowed upon one side, the tallowed side is spread over the muzzle of the gun, and the bullet is pressed upon it into the muzzle, the side from which the "neck," formed in moulding, has been cut, must be directly downward. Generally with the handle of a knife the bullet is pressed into the bore as far as it can be sent by such means; then the patch is gathered around it and cut smoothly off exactly flush with the muzzle end of the barrel. The next operation is to draw the ramrod, throw the gun under the left arm, with its breech resting upon the ground and its muzzle in front of the breast, and then having set the butt end of the ramrod upon the bullet and grasped it in both hands, the bullet is gradually, and by main strength, forced downward into position.

To make sure that it is entirely down the gun is taken from under the arm, by some, and set with the breech resting upon the ground more in front, after which the ramrod is raised up a foot or so and pitched down the bore like throwing a pike. If it does not bound back the bullet is not down solid upon the powder, and the pitching is repeated until it does bound. The upward bound of a few inches is sufficient to settle it that the bullet is down.

In the early times the bullet of the rifle was patched with dressed deer-skin exclusively.

Charging the shot-gun muzzle-loader is an operation somewhat different. First comes the powder poured down the bore from a charger, as in the case of the rifle. Next comes a wad, usually of paper, which must fit tightly, and be rammed down solid upon the powder. Following this comes the shot, measured in the same charger, or in one of the same capacity. The measure of powder and the measure of shot usually made about the same. Over the shot is rammed a loose wad—it needs only to be tight enough to prevent the shot from rolling out when the muzzle of the gun happens to come lower than the breech. Disk-like wads of pasteboard or felt cloth are the latest invention.

The Breech Loaders.—The breech-loading gun is now before the public in considerable variety; and being really the gun of the day, and, consequently, engaging the best thought of inventors, it is constantly appearing in new forms. This being the case, about all that could be expected in this work, is a mere mention of the general principles upon which it works.

Taking a double-barrel shot-gun for illustrating these general principles, it may be stated that the barrels are movable at the breech or rear end, and butt upon the face of the standing breech peculiar to the latest and best muzzle-loaders. The face of these barrels fits smoothly against that of the standing breech. There is nothing in the way of a breech-pin to resist the backward force of the ignited powder, or hold the barrels in place. The hooks mentioned as peculiar to the patent breech muzzle-loader are not there—nothing at all like them. But the barrels, when put into place for shooting are held there by means of a solid piece of iron attached to them underneath, called the "lump." To effect this, it descends into an iron bed on the stock called the "action," its projections fitting into suitable recesses in the action and being held there by the agency of keys, wedges, bolts or grips.

There are many devices for gripping, bolting or wedging up the gun, as it is called; and also many for attaching the barrels to the stock. In all cases the barrels play upon a hinge pin, which admits of their dropping down at the muzzle and rising at the breech, the latter to reject the empty cartridge and receive the loaded one. At every discharge the gun is opened and closed by throwing up the barrels for the purpose just named, and then letting them down again into position for shooting. The means by which this opening and closing is effected vary greatly in the guns of different makers.

Variety of Breech-Loaders.—This gives the general idea of about all there is of it. There are a few breech-loaders made in both this country and in Europe whose barrels are fixed, the cartridge being inserted through some other device; and there are still a few others whose barrels slide forward or sideways in the stock to receive the load—do not tilt on a hinge-pin—but neither of these kinds are so common as the kinds just referred to.

CHAPTER IV.

PISTOLS NOW IN USE.

Old-Style Pistols.—Pistols, the smallest of fire-arms, were originally plain implements of a single barrel; but, as improvements advanced, a second barrel was added to many of them, presenting what is known as the double-barreled pistol. Some of these old-fashioned single and double-barreled pistols will still occasionally find their way into the shop of the gunsmith, though their numbers, as now in use, are comparatively small, especially the muzzle-loaders. In rare instances a flint-lock "horse pistol" or holster may put in an appearance, though none such are now on sale at any house dealing in fire-arms. Some few houses are still offering the old cap-lock army holster, always a second-hand article that once belonged to the Government, and was bought up by dealers when the Government had discarded it for the adoption of more modern and better arms. A description of this kind of weapon is unnecessary as it is simply a small musket with side-lock, and all on the usual plan, differing only in being short and having a turned-down handle, to be held in one hand, instead of the usual breech. The single or double-barrel muzzle-loaders, outside the line of army holsters, will usually have the central lock, which is next to no lock at all; simply a mainspring working in the handle and throwing the cap-hammer, which is fitted in the middle of the piece immediately behind the breech end of the barrel. Some very cheap pistols for boys are still made on this plan.

The Derringer.—The old Derringer, though not now much manufactured in this country, is still among the people in considerable numbers. It is a muzzle-loader, with side-lock and full-stock in wood; and, by the way, it is a very good pistol of its kind.

The Pepper Box.—There are quite a number of little breech-loading cartridge-pistols, with single barrels, now in use, but the pistol of the day is a repeater, of which there are kinds in great variety. One of the oldest and now rarest of these is the "pepper-box," so called. It has a single barrel containing from five to seven bores, which are loaded from the muzzle. A tube for percussion caps communicates with each bore at the breech, and upon these a hammer strikes, having an automatic action, rising up and striking in response to pressure upon a trigger underneath, which pressure also revolves the barrel, bringing the caps into proper position for receiving the blow. It was never a popular pistol, people objecting to a kind of way it had of sometimes letting off its seven charges simultaneously, when the person operating it had intended to fire but one.

Old Colt's Revolver.—Next among the repeaters, in point of scarcity, is the Colt's revolver of the earliest patent. It has a stationary single barrel and revolving cylinder, the latter containing from five to seven chambers for receiving the charges. It is not a muzzle-loader, though the charges must be put into the chambers at the breech, somewhat on the muzzle-loading plan. It is fired by means of percussion caps. The cylinder revolves, throwing the chamber to be discharged into proper position at the breech of the barrel when the cap-hammer is drawn back. Though inconvenient, compared to the cartridge pistol of more modern make, the old Colt's revolver is yet an excellent arm. There are houses still making revolvers on the same plan.

Sharp's Four Shooter.—Next to the old Colt's revolver may be placed the Sharp's four shooter. It is a neat and strong-shooting, little breech-loading pistol, using a No. 22 cartridge. The barrel has four bores but does not revolve; but the hammer has a revolving point, for striking the cartridge, which moves into proper position for a new discharge every time it is drawn back to full cock. The barrel slides forward upon the stock for receiving new cartridges.

The Breech-loading Cartridge Revolvers.—Next comes the regular breech-loading cartridge revolver, which is the pistol now most common and most popular. To attempt a detailed description of every style of this weapon would be to swell our book to unwieldy proportions, and even were the multitudinous styles at present before the public described, it would be impossible to keep pace with the number which would be constantly introduced. But, even were it possible to do so, no good purpose would be subserved. Various as the styles appear, they all embrace devices and combinations which are substantially covered by our several chapters, and the intelligent workman will not require minute descriptions to recognize or understand the individual weapon when well grounded in a knowledge of the class of fire-arms to which it belongs. It is our purpose to give such descriptions, directions and illustrations as shall make everything sufficiently clear and explicit to enable the reader, with careful attention thereto, to handle successfully and satisfactorily any job likely to come to his hands.

CHAPTER V.

ON GENERAL GUNSMITHING.

The Gunsmith and his Trade.—Few trades present so little regular routine as does that of the gunsmith. In most trades it is the same thing over and over again; but, with the exception of taking the gun to pieces and putting it together; and, perhaps, of tempering, case-hardening and the like, the gunsmith may work regularly for a long time without being called upon to do precisely the same thing twice. As a consequence, the gunsmith must be merely an ingenious mechanic or worker in metals, capable of thinking deeply and searching out causes and requirements—there is little need of his being anything more. The gun, in all its forms, is only a machine, and a simple one at that—so simple as to be easily understood by any one capacitated for making an intelligent study of machinery.

Fitting up a Shop.—The specialties to claim the attention of the gunsmith in fitting up his shop if his means are limited may be few. It will be about like fitting up the shop of any general worker in metals. He will need a forge, an anvil and a vise ; in a word he will need a light but complete set of blacksmith's tools, to begin with. This outfit will be his foundation, so to speak ; and he can add to it such smaller tools as judgment and experience may suggest as wanted; such, for instance, as a hand-vise or two, cutting-pliers, bending-pliers, holding pliers, small files of various shapes, small drills, a screw-plate or two, a few gravers, and so on. He might have many special tools, such as could not be bought at the ordinary hardware store, or at any house dealing in outfits for the general worker in metals, but for ordinary repairing, he will not have much need of them. Among the special tools that he will be compelled to have will be a rifle-guide, a few sets of rifle-saws and a few mould-cherries. These with proper instructions he can make himself if he finds he cannot buy them cheaper than he can make them. There are a few specialties in the way of tools or machines for gunsmiths that are offered to the trade by houses dealing in gunsmith's materials, and some of them may be found very useful as labor-savers, but the gunsmith *can* get along without them if he does not wish to buy. Prominent among these is a mainspring-vise or clamp, which has several advantages over the common hand-vise sometimes employed for clamping the mainspring. It would be well to look after these things, and to adopt them in every case where it appeared beyond question that they could be made to pay. There is no occasion to speak against any of the specialties that may be presented to the attention of the trade —of their merits the party most concerned must be his own judge.

CHAPTER VI.

TAKING APART, CLEANING AND PUTTING GUNS TOGETHER.

To Take the Gun Apart.—With the muzzle-loading guns now in common use this is an operation so simple as to be scarcely worthy a mention. If the gun is an old-fashioned breech-pinned muzzle-loader, the first thing is to push out the small wire pins or bolts which pass through the stock, under the barrel, and through the barrel-loops. The next thing is to draw the breechpin screw; this lets the barrel out of the stock. If it is desirable to unbreech the gun, it is done by clamping the breechpin in a vise, and then turning the barrel by hand until it is screwed off the pin.

The patent-breech muzzle-loader comes apart the same way in every particular, with the exception that there is no breechpin screw to draw; the barrel can be easily lifted from the stock by simply raising the muzzle and unhooking the patent breech, so soon as the pins or bolts before mentioned as holding it down have been removed. The unbreeching is done at the vise much the same as in the other case.

To take apart the ordinary breech-loader, begin by setting the hammer at half-cock. Open the lever, then draw the bolt, starting it with a tap from the handle of the screwdriver. Next detach the fore-piece, and the barrel will come out without further resistance. Instructions to take down and assemble different kinds of breech-loading guns will be found in Chapter XL.

To Clean the Gun when Apart.—In olden times a bucket of water and a wisp of tow and a stout "wiper" had to be brought into requisition, particularly for the interior of the barrel, but now these things are mainly obsolete, so far as relates to the outfit of the gunsmith. The owner of a muzzle-loader, who does not wish to remove the breechpin, may still resort to the old plan of washing out the barrel, though there is now really no necessity for it. A little benzine poured down the muzzle, after stopping the tube, will do the work of cleaning effectually and in a few minutes. Let stand a short time, then remove the plug from the tube and force the benzine out by running down a tow wad on the wiper—all the dirt will go out through the tube with it, leaving you nothing to do but wipe the benzine from the bore with the tow.

In the case of a gun unbreeched, or a breech-loader, all that is necessary is to saturate a bit of cotton flannel with benzine and run it through the barrel a few times. If the gun is a fine one, well finished, this process will leave the interior as shining and bright as a mirror.

With the same arrangement rub thoroughly any of the metal parts that happen not to be clean, and all impurities will promptly leave them. After this, oil and wipe with a chamois skin, and the work is done.

Benzine may be had at any drug store at about the price of kerosene. It is especially valuable as a gun cleaner for two reasons : its peculiar fitness for detaching and carrying away dirt, and its highly volatile properties, which cause it to evaporate and entirely leave the metal in a short time after the application has been made. Its adoption has completely done away with the necessity of ever using a drop of water upon a gun, in any case, which is a matter of decided importance and advantage.

To Put the Gun Together.—With the muzzle-loaders the operation of putting together is simply a work directly in reverse to that of taking apart. In case of the common make of breech-loaders a little more variation may be regarded as necessary. Take the grip of the stock in the left hand, having the lever open. Hook on the barrel and turn the gun over with the hammers underneath, still holding the stock at the grip. The weight of the barrel will keep it in place. With the right hand attach the forepiece and push in the bolt.

Of course there are guns of peculiar make, now and then to be met with, which will require a different routine, both in taking apart and putting together. The details, with full directions for taking down and assembling nearly all the breech-loading guns now made, will be found explained, with cuts of their mechanism and working parts, in Chapter XLII.

A careful study will soon show the gunsmith how they come apart and how they go together. The main thing is to work with extreme care, and to never act until you clearly understand what you are doing.

CHAPTER VII.

TOOLS REQUIRED FOR WORK, THEIR COST, ETC.

GIVEN in alphabetical order are some of the tools that will be required by the gunsmith, and in connection a very brief sketch is given of their approximate cost at hardware stores. This list is intended only as a sort of guide in purchasing, and is by no means intended as a complete list of what may be wanted.

The Alcohol Lamp.—This lamp, shown in Fig. 1, is useful for small soldering, tempering small taps,

FIGURE 1.

drills, etc. Glass or brass lamps with caps to prevent evaporation, are sold for about 50 cents each.

Alcohol Lamp, Self-Blowing.—This lamp, shown in Fig. 2, very convenient when continued blowing is required, or when the "knack" of using the common plow-pipe cannot be readily acquired. It may be used for soldering, brazing small articles, or hardening small tools, Size 2½ inches diameter and 5 inches high, $2; about 3 inches diameter and 6 inches high, $3.

Anvil.—An anvil weighing about ninety or one hundred pounds is heavy enough. An Eagle anvil of this weight will cost about $9 or $10. The body of this kind of anvil is cast iron with steel face and horn. Price per pound is about ten cents.

Barrel Planes.—These planes are now but little used, except for stocking guns or rifles which are to

FIGURE 2.

be fitted with full-length stocks. As this form of gun is somewhat going out of use, so the stocker's planes are getting to be cast to one side. They are made similar to a narrow rabbet plane, but have the iron set close to the fore end. Any narrow plane with the fore end cut off to within half an inch of the opening in which the iron is placed will make a substitute for the stocker's plane. The plane with round face is used to let in round barrels, and one with a face equal in width to the sides of an octagon barrel, for letting in such barrels. A narrow plane is used to let in the ramrod, by cutting a groove centrally in the bottom of the barrel groove. The planes used are about four in number and the cost is about seven or eight dollars for the set as sold by dealers.

Bevel.—Bevels for ascertaining and forming surfaces, not at a right angle with some certain line, can be had from one dollar upward in price. The four inch is very good size. The blade is held in position by a screw, which forms part of the joint on which the blade turns. Shown in Fig. 3.

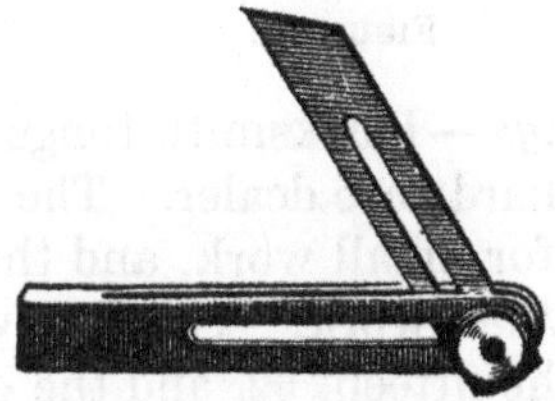

FIGURE 3.

Beveling Clamp.—These tools are generally made of about three sizes, and are used for holding hammers when filing the bevel upon the sides. They are also useful for holding lock-plates while filing the bevel on them. In the vise, work can only be conveniently held at a vertical or horizontal position; this clamp is designed to furnish a means to hold it so as to file an angle of about 45 degrees. The tool is shown in Fig. 4. It is held in the vise, the shoulders resting on the vise jaws. The spring between the jointed portions opens the tool when the vice jaws are opened, the closing of the vise jaws, of course, closing the clamp upon the work that is placed in it. The cost of these tools is from two to three dollars, according to size and quality.

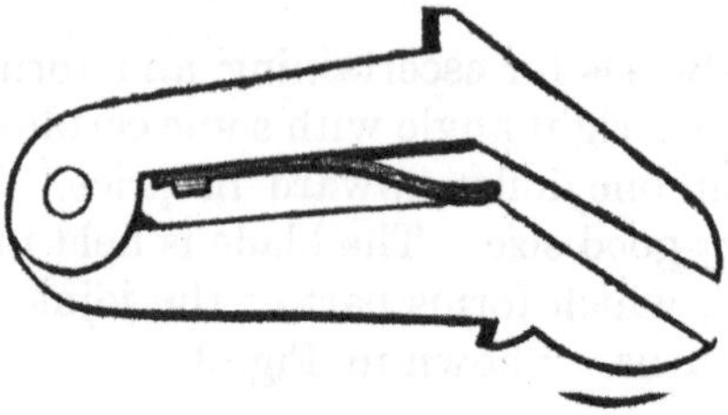

FIGURE 4.

Blacksmith Tongs.—Blacksmith tongs can now be purchased of the hardware dealer. The twelve inch length are used for small work, and the fifteen or eighteen for heavier work. The twelve inch cost about 50 cents; the fifteen, 62, and the eighteen, 75 cents each.

Blow-Pipe.—Select a blow-pipe eight or ten inches in length, with bulb or without, as fancy may dictate. If the end where the mouth comes in contact be silver or nickle-plated, it will not taste of brass. If it be difficult to get one plated, tin it with soft solder by wetting with soldering acid, and melting the solder on it by holding it over the lamp. Wipe off all superfluous solder with a rag. The cost of plain eight or ten inch pipe is about 25 cents. Add about one-third or one-half this price for pipes with bulb.

Breeching Taps.—Breeching taps ought to be obtained in pairs, one to enter first and another to follow, cutting a full thread at the bottom. The prices per pair are for the 3/8 inch $2.25; 1/2 inch, $2.50; 5/8 inch, $2.75. For shot gun taps, 3/4 inch, $3.00; 7/8 inch, $3.25. A stock with dies will cost about a like sum, but if the stock be fitted with only two sets of dies, it will be much less. The two threads used for rifle pins are 14 and 16 to the inch.

The 14 and 16 threads are not always adhered to. A house in Philadelphia say they use taps of 18 threads, and a firm in Pittsburg advertise taps of 20 threads per inch.

Calipers and Dividers.—The best length of spring calipers and dividers, for common bench work, is about four inches. The cost is from 50 cents to $1.50, according to quality.

Chisels.—The chisels, as used by stockers, are about half a dozen in number. The narrowest is about one-eighth of an inch wide, and the widest about half inch. The set of six will cost about a dollar or a dollar and a half.

Cutting Pliers.—A pair of cutting pliers, six inches in length, for cutting wire, are indispensable. Select those of good quality. Poor pliers of this description are poor, indeed. The cost will be from 75 cents to $1.50. There are patented pliers of this kind in market that are recommended by many who use them.

Drill Stock.—Many kinds are in market, from eight inches in length upward. Some are termed hand drills, and the larger ones, used against the breast, are called breast drills. The hand drills can be obtained as low as 50 cents and upward; the price of breast drills from two to three dollars. Select a drill stock, if one be required, of a size and strength to suit the work to which it will be used.

File Card.—This is for cleaning filings, dirt, etc., that may collect in files. It consists of a strip of common cotton card tacked to a piece of wood con-

FIGURE 5.

veniently shaped to handle. It is also useful to clean the dirt and debris that will collect in screw taps. The cost is about 25 cents. Shown in Fig. 5.

Fitting Square.—A fitting square with a four, five or six-inch blade is required for many purposes, not only for laying out iron stocks and marking off "square work," but other work that will come into a gun shop. The gun squares used by carpenters and cabinet makers are very good. If the stock be of iron, or an iron frame filled with wood, they are better than those with wooden stocks. The cost of the six, inch may be about 75 cents. The other somewhat less.

Floats.—For half-stocking, the gouge and floats are used for letting in barrels. The floats are made with a handle bent at an angle so that the hand will not hit the work. The round float in form resembles a gouge with teeth like a coarse file cut on the rounded or bottom surface. Floats have been made by drawing the temper of a thick gouge and cutting teeth in it, or taking a half-round file and drawing the temper, and then cutting teeth on the round side. Floats for octagon barrels are flat, like a chisel with teeth cut on one of the flat sides. A thin float for letting in cross bolts is made in the same manner. A float for fitting ramrods may be made of a steel rod with teeth cut on one end, and a handle fixed to the other. The bolt float will cost about 50 cents. The rod float about $1.00 each for two sizes. Rifle, two sizes, about $1.25 each. Shot gun, two sizes, about $1.50 each.

Forge.—Little advice can be given respecting a forge. Some prefer the bellows forge, while others select the fan blower. The great requirement of the gunsmith is portability and occupying little space. It should also be so enclosed as to prevent escape of dust, and be free from accident of fire escaping if left with the fire lighted. The cost of either form of portable forge will be from $20, upward.

Glue Pot.—Glue pots can be purchased with kettle fitting inside the pot and tinned on inside, quart size about 75 cents. A glue pot may be extemporized by selecting a common round fruit can, cutting out the cover so as to allow a smaller can to fit and be held in place. Where economy is desired or a pot cannot be purchased, the can glue pot will answer every purpose.

Gouges.—About six gouges are needed. The sizes

are about one-eighth for the smallest, and increasing to three-quarters for the largest. The cost of the set will be about one dollar and a quarter.

Grind Stone.—An Ohio stone, about 20 inches diameter and 2½ inches thick, mounted plain, can be got up for about three or four dollars. The iron fixtures will cost about a dollar, and the stone a cent and a half or more per pound, according to locality.

Hack Saw.—A hack saw shown in Fig. 6, with iron frame, to hold a blade of eight or ten inches in

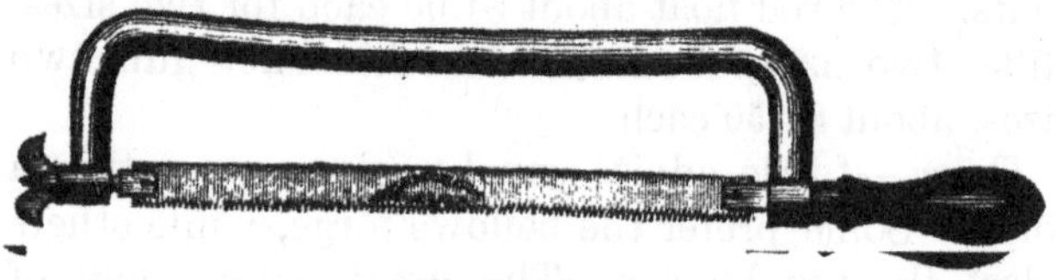

FIGURE 6.

length is required for cutting off barrels, slotting screws, cutting off rods of iron, brass, etc., besides many other uses. The eight inch with blade will cost about $1.25, the ten inch about $1.50. If at any time a blade be broken they can be replaced at from 25 to 50 cents.

Hammers.—In choosing hammers select the plain riveting hammer with cross pein. The sizes generally most used are a four ounce, a twelve ounce and a heavier one for use at the forge. The four ounce costing about 30 cents, the twelve ounce about 50 cents, and the larger one according to weight. In selecting hammers try the pein with a fine file to learn the temper. In many cases the pein is left too soft for riveting steel.

Handles.—Handles for files or screwdrivers are best when made of maple or apple wood. Maple is generally preferred. Some mechanics like soft wood, as bass-wood or white birch, for file handles, but they are not so neat as those made of maple. Get those with ferrules made from sheet brass, raised to form. Soft wood handles are worth about 25 cents per dozen, and the hard wood about 50 cents.

Hand Shears.—For cutting sheet tin, brass, thin sheet steel, small springs, etc., select a pair of hand shears about nine or ten inches in length, costing

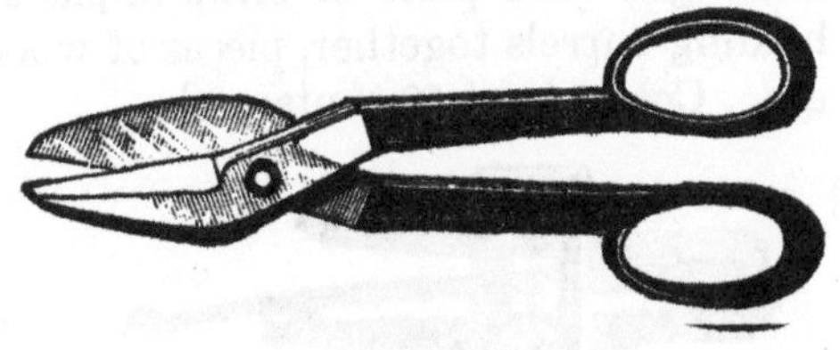

FIGURE 7.

about $1.50. With these, common watch-springs can be cut lengthwise, for making small springs for pistols. The temper need not be drawn to cut them. (Shown in Fig. 7.)

Hand-vise.—A hand-vise for holding wire, screws, etc., is needed. About four or four and a half inches in length is most convenient. For holding small wire, cut a groove with a three-square file across the jaws toward the jointed end. The cost will be from 50 cents to $1.00, according to quality.

Iron Clamps.—A pair of malleable iron clamps (shown in Fig. 8), opening about four inches, are

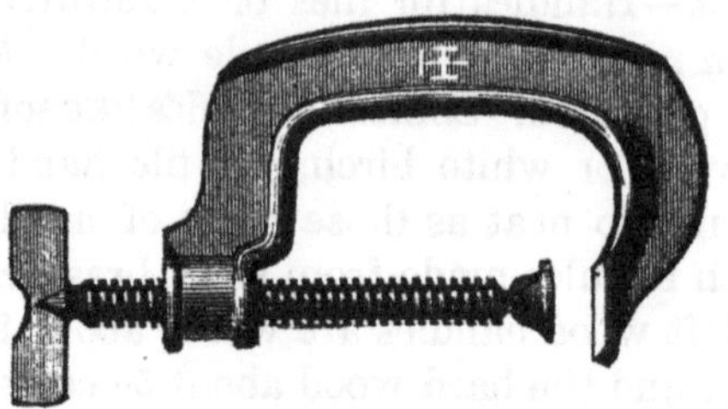

FIGURE 8.

useful for holding barrels into the stock during stocking, holding a lock plate or strap in place for marking, holding barrels together, pieces of wood to be glued, etc. Cost, about 50 cents each.

FIGURE 9.

Mainspring Vise.—This tool (shown in Fig. 9, as clamping a spring) is used to clamp the mainspring, preparatory to removing it from the lock. The hammer is set at full cock, and the vise applied, the screw tightened until the spring can be lifted from place. In taking down double guns, a vise for each lock spring is very convenient, as the springs can then rest in the vise, being cramped in place, until ready to be put back into their respective places. The cost of these vises is from 25 cents to $2 each, according to quality and make. For a left-side lock, reverse the sliding piece, so that the short end will bear on the bend of the mainspring.

Marking Gauge.—A wood marking gauge is used for laying out lines parallel to a surface already formed. If made of beech wood, and plain, it is generally sold for about 25 cents each.

Screw-cutting Tools.—A small die stock and dies, with taps for lock work, will cost about $2.50. A plate and ten taps, suitable for all sizes of nipples, English and German, can be had for about $8.00.

Screw Wrench.—One of Coe's patent wrenches, about twelve-inch size, costing about a dollar, is the best make and the most durable size for all purposes. This wrench is generally known as a "monkey wrench."

Soldering Copper.—A copper for soldering, similar to the kind used by tinners, is the kind to get. A good size—No. 3—will weigh about a pound and a half, costing about 75 cents.

Screw drivers.—Several screw-drivers are required, and of several widths, to fit different sized screw heads. The narrowest may be about one-eighth inch, and the widest, say, half inch to five-eighths inch. If the mechanic desires to make these himself, select octagon steel, about one-quarter inch diameter, draw one end to form the tang, and the other to form the screw-driving part. Get good apple, beech or maple wood handles. Let the length project about six or seven inches from the handle. For the larger size screw-drivers get steel three-eighths diameter. Old files, with the temper drawn and the points ground to shape, make a passable screw-driver. Screw-drivers purchased at the store, are generally not so satisfactory as those made from rods. Stub's round steel wire rod makes good screwdrivers.

Pliers—Three kinds of pliers are used by gunsmiths ; flát nose, round nose, and long flat nose or clock-makers' pliers. Six inch is about the right length for general use. The round nose are useful for bending wire or metal into circular forms. The long flat nose for holding work for soldering and handling work at the forge. Of the flat nose a five inch pair are useful in many cases. The cost of pliers (six inch), is from about 50 cents to $1.00 per pair according to quality.

Wing Dividers—A pair of wing dividers, about eight inches in length, will be found the best size for general use. The cost will be about 75 cents. In purchasing see that the screw that binds the leg to the arc or wing is well fitted. The thread, either in the leg or the screw, is sometimes stripped or worn out after a little using.

CHAPTER VIII.

TOOLS, ETC., AND HOW TO MAKE THEM.

THE tools given in this chapter are such as are needed by the gunsmith, and as directions are given for making them, they can be made by almost any ingenious person during leisure hours.

The Alcohol Lamp.—A lamp for this kind of work is easily made. A common gum or mucilage bottle with a tube inserted in the cork has been used, so has a small tin spice-box, with a tube soldered into the cover. A common copper or brass cartridge, with the head filed off, can be used for a tube. A common oil can, such as is used for oiling sewing machines, with about half of the taper tube cut off, will make a serviceable lamp. These appliances are small, unsightly and not to the taste of the mechanic who has a pride in the appearance of his tools.

The best form of lamp, shown in Fig. 10, may be made by obtaining a small glass kerosene hand lamp, which will cost only a trifle of two or three shillings. Cut off that portion of the burner above the screw, where it is held to the socket that is fastened to the lamp. Remove the tube that holds the lamp-wick and also the little contrivance made to raise and lower the wick. In the place where the tube was inserted, generally a flat one, file out with a round file, a place which is large enough to receive a common brass 44-cartridge that has had the head cut off or removed by filing; this is the tube for the wick. Fasten it in place with soft solder. Let this tube project a little into the lamp, and solder it on the under side. The greater portion of the tube projects above the place where soldered.

FIGURE 10.

The wick is made of common cotton wicking, letting the end inside touch the bottom of the lamp. Fill with alcohol, and the lamp is ready for use. Be careful that the wick is not too tight in the tube, or in other words, do not fill the tube with too much wick, as it will prevent the alcohol from rising and the lamp from burning. To prevent evaporation of the alcohol and to have the wick always ready for lighting, cover the tube with a cap that fits it quite closely and has the upper end closed. A brass cartridge that will go over the tube makes a good cover. Remove the primed cap or see that the cap has been exploded before using it to cover the lamp tube.

A Self-blowing Lamp.—A very good form of this lamp is shown in Fig. 11. It consists of a lamp en-

FIGURE 11.

closed in a kind of cup which has an open place at the bottom to admit the lamp and a small boiler, fitting loosely, and held by a flange on its top. A small pipe is soldered to the top of this boiler and extends downward, and has an end like a blow-pipe that passes through one side of the cup and ends near or a little above the lamp wick. The operation is as follows: the lamp being lighted, heats alcohol placed in the boiler, and the steam thereby made produces a jet that blows the lamp flame the same as is done with the mouth.

The size of the cup may be from three inches to three and a half in diameter, and about five inches high. The opening at the bottom may extend about half of the height. The lamp is made of less diameter than the interior of the cup to admit of moving to get a good flame from the blow-pipe. The lamp may be $1\frac{3}{4}$ inches in diameter and an inch high. The boiler is about two inches high and has the bottom made a little convex, as shown by dotted lines, and is some smaller than at the top where a flange is formed to admit of its resting on the top of the cup. The top of the boiler is also convex, and has a short tube in which a cork is fitted, for the purpose of filling it. The blowing tube is about three-sixteenths of an inch in diameter. There is a long slot in the cup near its handle which readily admits of its being put in position for blowing. There are several small holes near the top of the cup to insure draft to the lamp, and there is a large hole about an inch in diameter opposite the end of the blow-pipe through which the flame issues where the work is held.

For silver soldering, small brazing, tempering, or any similar small work, this lamp is most excellent. To make the small blowing-pipe, drill a smooth hole through a piece of iron or steel and ream out one side of it. Cut a strip of thin copper or soft brass of a width just enough to fill the hole if it were made into a tube. Point one end of the strip and roughly form it into a tube, insert in the hole and pull it through. Or the strip can be rolled around a piece of iron wire forming it to a tube by hammering. Soft solder it after being formed to shape.

Breech Wrenches.—In many shops the monkey wrench is made to do duty in removing breech-pins,

FIGURE 12.

but at the expense of marring the pin where the wrench engages it. If many guns with breech-pins like those used in army guns are handled, it is worth while to have solid wrenches forged of iron like Fig. 12. The length may be about fifteen inches, with an opening to fit the shoulder of the breech-pin. The width at this place may be about one and a half inches; thickness, about half an inch; diameter at end of handle, about three-quarters of an inch, and at the small portions near the centre, about half an inch.

A wrench for removing patent breeches or nuts from double guns is made like Fig. 13. It consists of a steel bar about fifteen or sixteen inches long and about three-quarters of an inch diameter. At a little to one side of the center is fastened a steel collar that has four projections made at one end. A similar piece is fitted opposite to it, but is made to move back and forth to fit the work by means of a screw that is formed behind where it is fitted. A slot is made in the extension of the piece and a key fitted to prevent its turning around as the nut is turned to advance it toward its fellow piece.

The only substitute to answer for this tool is to file down the jaws of a monkey wrench so that they will turn between the extensions of a patent breech while the first breech is being removed. This is a poor substitute, as there is only one handle to turn with, and when force is applied to remove the breech

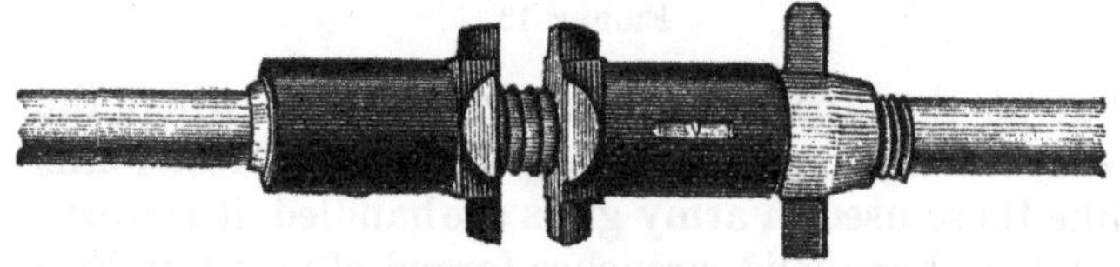

FIGURE 13.

it does not have the force applied equally to each side as in the other kind of wrench, consequently it is not as effective nor so easy to remove the breech. If an extension to form another handle could be improvised it would make it much better.

The Bit Stock.—Even if the gunsmith have a lathe there is much work that can be done to advantage with a common bit-stock. But as the drills and tools used in the lathe generally have round shanks by which to hold them in the chuck, the square hole where bits and tools are held in the bit stock must be filled by brazing or soldering a piece of iron into it and boring a hole to fit the shank of the lathe tools. It is advisable to have these shanks about seven-sixteenths diameter, as explained under the heading "Shanks of Tools."

In holding small drills made of steel wire or twist drills a small drill chuck must be fitted to the bit stock.

A small solid chuck with a quarter inch hole may be made with a shank to fit the seven-sixteenth hole. A set screw must be fitted to hold the shanks of the two sizes mentioned.

Bottoming Tools.—Bottoming tools are used for letting in locks, cutting out for escutcheons, and are useful in other places where a chisel cannot be made

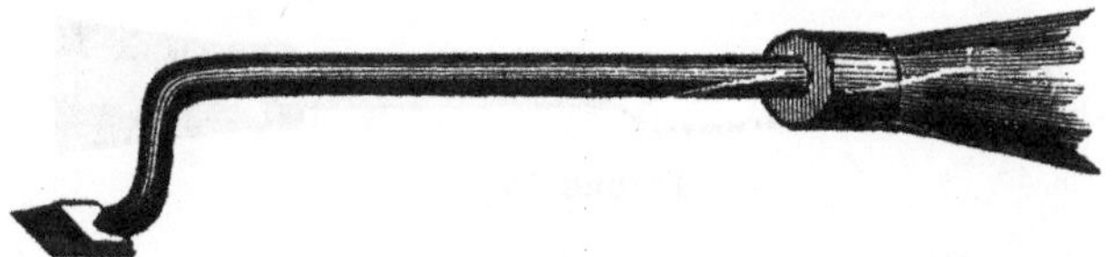

FIGURE 14.

to operate. The form of this tool is shown in Fig. 14. It consists of a square or round shank about three-sixteenths or a quarter-inch in diameter and about six inches long. At one end a wooden handle is attached, and the other end is bent at an angle which is about half an inch or perhaps a little more, and on this angle is another one turned parallel with the shank and which is about three-eighths of an inch long. This is the cutting end and is fashioned like the cutting edge of a chisel, and is about a quarter of an inch wide. The bottom side, as it would be held for use, is ground flat and the upper side bevelled like a chisel. The cutting edge may be square or rounded to suit round places as letting in the bridle of a lock. The size given is that generally used, but if it be made about twice this size it will be found very useful in letting in octogon rifle barrels; if the tool be made larger and hollow like a gouge it is very useful in letting in round gun barrels. In letting in break off straps it will be found to take the place of a chisel to some advantage.

Chequering Tools.—The tools used for chequering are very simple. Imagine a small saw, or rather

FIGURE 15.

two small saws about one inch or more long, made at the end of a straight steel shank. The form is given in Fig. 15. The double saw can be made by filing it as one thick saw and then cutting a groove lengthwise with it. In using, one blade first forms a groove and the other blade works the next cut; as the first cut is finished, another mark is being made while so doing. This insures equal width of the cuts. Care must be exercised in using them so as not to tear the wood. A fine cut, sharp edged, three square or a small half round file may be used to finish the work if desired.

Nipple Wrenches.—Two forms of nipple wrenches are used, one for square and the other for two sided nipples. The most serviceable of these are made from a straight rod of steel, with a cross handle and an opening at the opposite end to correspond with the square on the nipple. For the two-sided, a hole to receive the round part of the nipple where the cap goes on, may be drilled in a rod of steel and a slot filed across to receive the shoulders of the sides. The square shouldered kind must have a hole drilled of the diameter of the square, and then being heated a square punch of the size of the square is driven in. The nipples used for Government or military arms have the squares larger than sporting guns, and the wrenches are generally made of a flat piece of steel with a square hole made through from side to side at one end and squared to fit the tube. When made, harden and draw to a blue color for temper.

Portable Forge.—The following description of a "home made" portable forge shown in Fig. 16 is given by a contributor to the *Blacksmith and Wheelwright:* "In size it is two feet square and three feet high ; it is made entirely of wood ; the bellows are round and are sixteen and a half inches in size, covered then with the best sheep skins. The bed of the forge consists of a box six inches deep. It is supported by corner posts, all as shown in the sketch. Through the centre of the bottom is a hole six inches in diameter for the tuyere ; this is three inches in outside diameter, and is six inches high.

The bed is lined with brick and clay. It does not heat through. The bellows are blown up by means of two half circles with straps from a board running across the bottom, all of which will be better under-

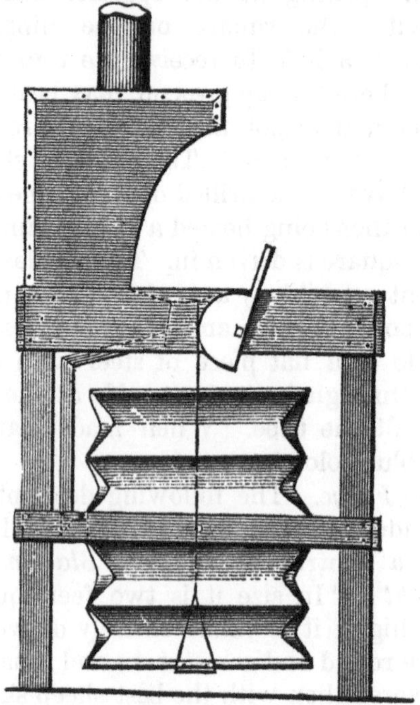

FIGURE 16.

stood by reference to the sketch. In addition to protecting the bed by brick and clay, the tuyere is set through a piece of sheet iron doubled and properly secured in place. The hood which surmounts the forge may be made out of old sheet iron, and will be found sufficient for the purpose. The connection between the tuyere and bellows is a tin pipe."

Vise Appendages.—The best vise for general use is one made by C. Parker, Meriden, Conn., and is termed a "swivel" vise. To the bench is attached a round plate of iron, and on this plate the vise turns to right or left as may be desired. It is held in position by screwing up a nut by means of a handle underneath the bench.

FIGURE 17.

The jaws are of steel, and a small projection back of the jaws, formed like a small anvil, is very convenient for bending work or to lay work upon for cutting, working with prick punch, etc. The width of jaws of No. 22, the size that is most convenient, is three and five-eighths inches, the weight about thirty-five or forty pounds, and the price about eight dollars, or perhaps a little more. This vise is shown in Fig. 17.

As the jaws of the vise where the steel faces come together are cut like a file and tempered, they will necessarily mar or bruise the work. Pieces of brass or copper must be bent so as to be retained in place and at the same time cover the file-like surface of the jaws. Pieces of leather, common belt leather, upon which a little beeswax has been spread, may be placed between the jaws, and by forcing them together with the screw the leather will be retained in place. In holding barrels, stocks, and for stocking a fixture made like the cut, Fig. 18, is best. Two

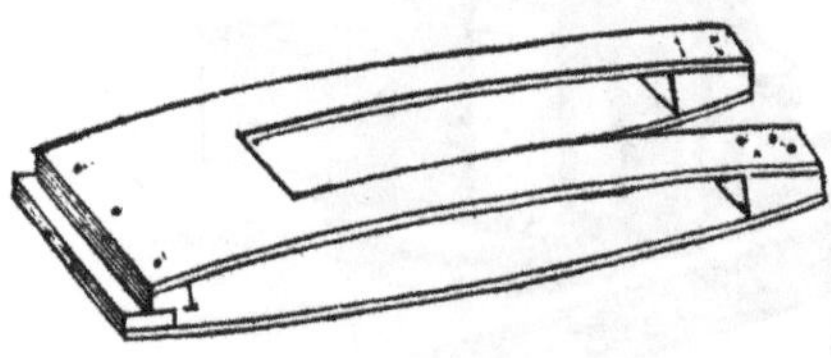

FIGURE 18.

pieces of thin board, or even two pieces of a wide barrel stave may make it. The opening is for the purpose of "straddling" the square box of the vise that encloses the screw. Nail a piece of wood about an inch and a half thick across the bottom part, before the opening is made, and also nail a thin piece across the top of the pieces, being careful to sink the nail heads to as to not mar the work. The top ends of the fixture must come even with the top of the vise jaws.

For holding screws without damaging the heads use a pair of false jaws made of cast brass, like those shown in Fig. 19. The heads being held in the indentations formed along the upper edges of the fixture. For holding rods or small square pieces with-

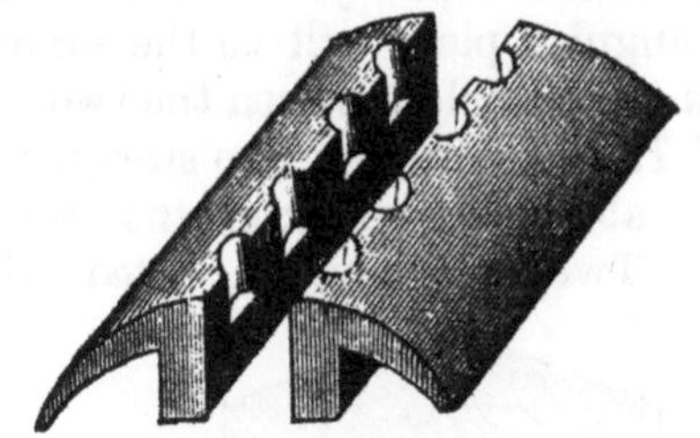

FIGURE 19.

out injury a similar pair of false jaws are made which are shown in Fig. 20.

For holding articles that are tapering a fixture is required like that given in Fig. 21. The yoke clasps

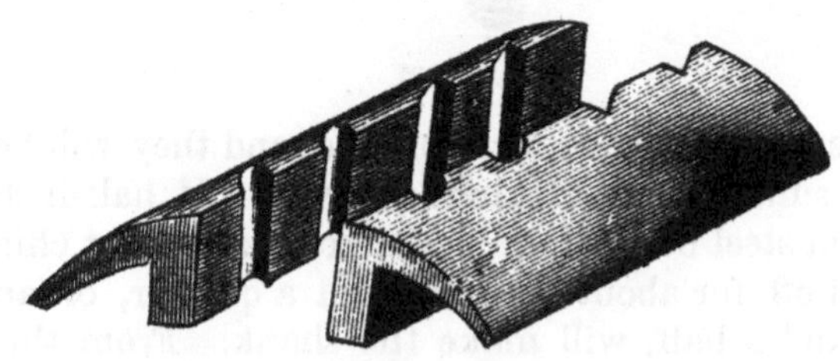

FIGURE 20.

the neck of the vise, and is held in place by a set-screw. The upright pin is received in the yoke by turning on a screw cut for the purpose, and by turning this up or down, the triangular piece at the upper part is made to accommodate itself to the height of the vise. The back angular corner of this piece has a bearing against the jaw of the vise, and the opening made between the other jaw of the vise and the front of this angular piece will be the same as the piece of work that is held between the two.

Shanks of Tools.—The best two sizes for shanks of tools are about seven-sixteenths and about quarter-inch. Two solid chucks, fitted with set-

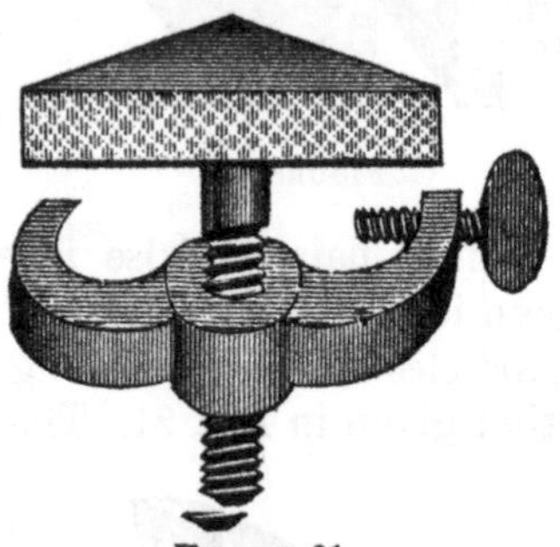

FIGURE 21.

screws, may be made for the lathe, and they will be found sufficient for all kinds of work. If half-inch octagon steel be used for the larger size, a light chip turned off for about an inch and a quarter, or an inch and a half, will make the shank. From this size steel may be made large drills, reamers, countersinks, bullet cherries, etc. The shanks of many other tools may be made to this standard. When a bit stock is fitted to hold this size of shank, the tools may be used either in the lathe or by hand with the bit stock.

Octagon steel, a quarter-inch in diameter, may be used for smaller tools, or round steel rod of this size may be employed. For small drills and tools, taps, etc., it will be found very convenient. No turning is necessary to fit to the solid chuck.

The common cheap bit stock, made from round steel, may be selected, and the square hole filled with a piece of iron and then brazed to make it solid. A hole is then drilled to fit the seven-sixteenths shank. A solid chuck is to be made to fit this, and drilled with a quarter-inch hole to fit the smaller sized shanks. This solid chuck will also fit the chuck for the lathe. If barrel boring tools, quick boring reamers, be made with the larger sized·shank, they can be used both in the lathe and with the bit stock.

CHAPTER IX.

THE WORK BENCH.

Material for the Work Bench.—The first thing to do in fitting up a shop is to put up a work bench. Do not make a rude affair of an unplaned plank and a rough board, but let it be seen that you fitted up your bench for use, and at the same time sought to have it neat and durable. A plank two inches thick is heavy enough, yet in some respects it is light enough; for the front portion of the bench twelve or fourteen inches is a good width. Pine wood makes a very good bench, but as it is soft, it will absorb oil, and in time will become black and dirty. As a remedy for this, give it two or three coats of shellac varnish. The best bench is made from a hard or sugar maple plank that has been well seasoned and has been planed true in a planing machine. Ash wood does very well, so does beech. Oak is not good; it absorbs grease and dirt readily, and if struck much with a hammer will soon show splinters, the fibres of the wood easily separating by the blows. A hard maple plank has one advantage; after being discarded as a bench, it will make good rifle stocks; the years of use will so season it that it will be valuable. For that part of the bench

—that is, back of the two-inch plank—use a board ten or twelve inches wide. Select pine or any other kind that fancy may dictate. Calculate the plank and board so that the width of the bench will be twenty-two or twenty-four inches.

How to Make the Work Bench.—For supports for the bench use 2x4 inch studding, such as carpenters use in house building. Pine, oak or any other material will answer. Plane smooth on all sides. For each support cut three pieces; two of the height of the bench, and one about an inch less than the width, so that when the bench is made the plank in front projects an inch or so in front of the supports. As the short piece on which the bench rests is four inches wide, cut away half of the thickness of the uprights of this width at the upper end, and cut enough in length to receive the short piece, when it is halved together—as is the term used—thus making it four inches thick when put in place. Fasten with nails or screws—the latter being the best fastening. To keep these uprights steady, nail a piece of board about three inches wide, and about twelve inches from the bottom, from front to the rear upright. On these pieces a board or two may be placed, with the other end resting upon a neighboring support, and it forms a convenient shelf upon which to place boxes and other things that will soon accumulate in any shop.

The height of bench from the floor may be about two feet and ten inches and a half. This will be found to be the most convenient height.

Putting the Vise in Place.—In putting the vise in place, fix it on the bench far enough in front so that if a gun stock or barrel were held upright in the jaws it will not touch the bench. If there be a window in front, put it a little to the left of the window. The light will then shine more on the right side of the vise, and consequently it will be more easy to distinguish lines or marks that may be made on work held in the jaws, as it is more convenient to look on the right side of work to see what is being done than on the left. The height of the vise at the top of the jaws should be on a level with the elbow of the person who is to work at it. In no instance try to work with the jaws of the vise higher than the elbows as the workman stands erect before it. The reason is this: as the workman grasps the file handle in the right hand and the point of the file in the left, the arms are in a natural position, and can be thrust forward and brought back in a horizontal line. If the elbows were to be raised from the natural position the horizontal forward and back motion could not be made with facility.

Place for Drawer.—A few inches to the right of the vise is the best location for a drawer. This is generally opened or drawn out with the right hand, and when so placed can be readily opened with that hand without stepping to one side.

The Gun Brace.—A gun brace, as shown in Fig. 22, is made from a piece of inch and a half or two inch plank, with its upper edge of a height about an inch less than the height of the vise jaws. It is hinged or pivoted by a single screw passing through the end of the bottom extension, this screw passing into the bench, the brace turning freely upon it. It can be swung around back out of the way, and when needed for use is turned in front, and is ready to support a barrel or gun stock which is held in the vise. This brace is put to the right of the vise, but if another one like it is put in the left side it will be found useful at times.

In cutting out gun-stocks from the plank, many times pieces of just the right form for these braces

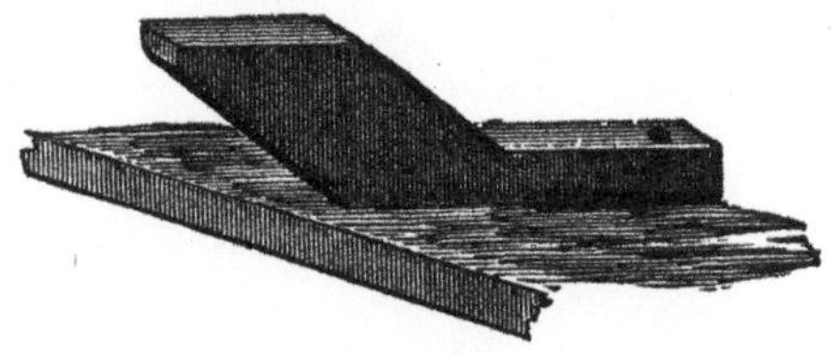

FIGURE 22.

will be found among the "scraps" that will be made. The shape is of little moment so long as they are of the proper height and have an extension through which to put the pivot screw.

To Deaden the Noise of Hammering.—In shops, especially if the work-room be in an upper story, to deaden the noise of hammering, etc., put pieces of rubber under the legs of work benches, the feet of lathes, anvil-block, etc. If rubber cannot be obtained, any woolen texture as felt or thick loose-made cloth may answer the purpose, but not with so good results as the rubber. The anvil may be set in a tub made by cutting off the top of a barrel to the right heigth and filling it nearly full of sand or earth.

CHAPTER X.

ON WORKING IN IRON.

Hand-Forging.—Two rates of heat figure in this operation. If the object is merely a smoothing of the surface of the iron, the "cherry-red heat," so-called, is the rate wanted. The work of smoothing is performed by striking lightly and evenly with the hand-hammer, until the desired condition is secured. The same degree of heat is employed where hammer-hardening the iron is one of the objects to be obtained; in this case the blows with the hammer must be heavier than in the case first named.

If the forging is to extend to a material change in the shape of the iron, the rate of heat must be much higher; it must be increased to what smiths call the "white flame heat." The hammering must be much heavier, of course; if the piece is large a sledge hammer must be brought into requisition. But the gunsmith will seldom have work heavy enough to demand the aid of an assistant with a sledge-hammer.

Welding.—The "welding" or "sparkling heat" is required in this process, which is a higher degree of heat than either named in the forgoing. In securing this heat, the metal is brought nearly to a state of fusion; which condition is made known by its sparkling, and presenting the appearance of being covered with a glaze, or a fresh coat of varnish. So soon as the two pieces of iron to be welded together have both attained to this necessary degree of heat, they are taken from the fire with the utmost dispatch, the scales or dirt which would hinder their incorporation scraped off, placed in contact at the heated point, and hammered until a union has been effected, and no seam or fissure remains visible. If the first effort fails to unite them sufficiently, they must be reheated and rehammered until the desired end is secured.

The fire for welding should be free from sulphur; and the iron, while heating, should be taken out now and then and sprinkled over at the point of greatest heat with powdered glass, or with powdered borax. A small proportion of sand or powdered clay is sometimes mixed with the borax. These applications tend to prevent the iron from running or burning, and they are supposed to assist the adhesion when the two pieces are brought together in the act of welding.

Hardening Iron by Hammering.—Iron may be hardened to the character of a pretty fair spring metal by simply hammering it thoroughly while in a cold state. Many of the cheap spiral springs in use, as those attached to small bells for the purpose of imparting a vibratory motion, are hardened or stiffened in this way. They are first cut from soft sheet-iron and then hammered into the required hardness. Some heat to a cherry red and hammer to and after entire coldness.

Case-Hardening.—The various parts of gun mountings, such as guards, heel plates, etc., and the different parts of locks, such as hammers, tumblers, triggers and plates, as received by the gunsmith from the manufacturer or dealer in such articles, are generally in the rough or partially finished condition. Many gunsmiths, particularly those in the country, where there is more or less a class of cheap work, finish up these parts with a file and a little hand polishing, and when the work is put together hand it over to the customer. Not only tumblers and triggers, but even sears and tubes are finished up in this manner. As these parts are almost always made of soft iron, the result is they soon wear and have to be repaired.

The gunsmith who does good work will thoroughly case-harden the parts when they are fitted and finished, and by so doing will turn out a really good piece of work that will wear as well as hardened steel. Why the majority of the trade do not case-harden their work cannot very well be explained, unless they are ignorant of the process or do not care to be put to the trouble of doing it. It is true it may be made a tedious job or a quick and easy one.

Some gunsmiths, when such work is finished, heat it red hot, smear it with prusiate of potash or cyanide of potassium, and while hot, plunge it into cold water, letting it chill. This produces a superficially hardened surface that is not "skin deep," and as soon as this surface becomes abraded will wear away rapidly.

If the case-hardening of the expert manufacturer be examined, it will be observed that the surface of such work has a fine grayish appearance, and in many places mottled with colored tints that are pleasing and beautiful to the mechanical eye. It will be further observed that the hardening is of such depth that it will wear for a long time. In fact it will wear better than hardened steel. The condition of the material is that of a hardened steel surface stretched over and shrunk upon the iron body of the work. It is stronger than steel, for it has the tenacity of iron for its interior. It has the advantage of steel, inasmuch as it may be bent when cold to a limited degree, and when so hardened will not break as readily as steel. This property of bending is not confined to all articles, as they may case-harden entirely through, and then they will be very brittle and easily broken, but by drawing them to temper after hardening, in the same manner as a tool is drawn to temper, they may be of any hardness desired.

A good way to Case-Harden.—The easiest and perhaps the best way to case-harden gun work is to have a number of short pieces of common gas pipe, such as will be adapted to the size or quantity of the work, and have one end of these pieces securely plugged or closed. One way will be to heat the pipe and close by flattening the end with a hammer on the anvil, but it is a "slouchy" way of doing it. A neater way is to have a gas fitter cut a thread in the pipe and then screw in a plug, such as are used to close ends of gas pipe; if such cannot be obtained, drive in a cast-iron plug and upset the end of the pipe so that it will not readily come out. In these pieces of pipe place the work, packing it well with good, fine bone-dust, such as is used by farmers for fertilizing land. Be careful to so pack that the different pieces of work will not touch each other. Stop the open end of the pipe with a cover, but in such a manner as to be readily opened; place the pipe and its contents in a good fire, letting it remain at a red heat for fifteen minutes or more, dependent upon the thickness of the articles or the depth they should be hardened. Remove from the fire and quickly empty the contents of the pipe into a pail of cold water.

If pieces of gas pipe cannot very well be obtained, thimbles from old carriage hubs may be used instead. Plug up the small end, fit a cover to the large end and use as if it were gas pipe. As these thimbles are made of cast iron they will not bear the rough usage nor the heat that wrought iron will withstand. Common cast malleable iron makes the best receptacles to contain work for case-hardening.

Articles of malleable iron and cast iron are as easily case-hardened as wrought iron. A poor quality of steel is benefited by the operation, as the metal imbibes carbon in which it was before deficient.

Material for Case-Hardening.—For case-hardening, bone-dust is the article most readily obtained and it is clean and neat to use; but it will not produce the mottled tints that charred or burned leather will give. The leather may be prepared by cutting up old shoes or boots, putting them in an old pan and setting the mass on fire. Let it burn until it is a charcoal that will readily crumble in pieces by using a little force. Grind this charcoal to a fine powder by pounding in a mortar or by running it through an old coffee or spice mill. Pack the work with the powder, the same as bone-dust. Bone-black may be used the same as bone-dust, but it is not very satisfactory in its results. It is also dirty to use and to have around a shop. Ivory dust will also answer the same purpose as bone-dust. Gun guards, straps and long pieces of work will become shorter by case-hardening, and it is best not to fit such pieces into the stock until after they are hardened. If it be desired to have a portion of the work left soft and the other parts hardened, securely cover the places to be left soft, with a coating of moist clay, and this will prevent the hardening material from coming in contact, and, consequently, it will have no opportunity to absorb carbon and harden when put in the cold water.

It may also be observed that articles that are case-hardened will not rust so readily as those not so treated.

If the articles be quite thin and there be danger of their cracking by sudden chilling, the water may be warmed a little, or a film of oil may be spread on the water which will tend to prevent a too sudden contraction of the articles while cooling.

If it be desired to have the work present the colors or mottled tints as seen on some kinds of case- ardened gun work, the surface of the work before being put in the receptacles containing the burnt leather, must be nicely polished and then buffed or burnished. The higher the finish the more brilliant will be the colors.

In using prusiate of potash to case-harden, the potash must be finely powdered, the work heated and dipped in, or if the work be large the potash must be spread over it. The work must be hot nough to fuse the potash, and if it become somewhat cold by removing from the fire it must be reheated, removed quickly from the fire and quenched in cold water.

Another way to Case-Harden.—Collect such articles of animal origin as cows' horns, or hoofs of either cows or horses, or leather trimmings from about the shoe-shops, or old cast off boots or shoes, and burn them until sufficiently charred to admit of being easily pounded into a powder. Having finished up the article to be hardened, ready for the final polish, place it in an iron box, and surround it completely on all sides by a packing of the powder. Pour into the box, until the powder is made moist, a saturated solution of common salt in urine. Next close the box and seal it until airtight, with wet and well-worked clay, then put it into the furnace and blow up gradually until heated to a cherry red. Don' run the heat any higher, but hold it at that about five minutes, then take out and plunge at once into the slack-tub.

By this means a piece of soft malleable iron is rendered as hard as hardened steel. Some workmen contend that the salt solution is of no particular importance—that just as good results will come of packing in the animal charcoal alone. The iron box, though very convenient when a good deal of case-hardening is to be done, is not an absolute necessity, If the article, surrounded by the animal charcoal, is incased in a ball of stiff and well-worked clay, and then exposed to the proper heat and slacking, the results will be the same as if heated in an iron box.

Another Formula.—In earlier times, when guns were more in use than either agricultural or mechanical implements, and there was a gunsmith's shop at almost every cross-road, they had a way of case-hardening that was much more simple than either of the foregoing, and yet quite effectual. Scraps of old leather, as cut from old boots or shoes, were tightly wrapped and tied around the piece of iron to be made hard, to the extent of several thicknesses. Around this was placed a layer of sand and salt in equal proportions, to the thickness of half an inch. The sand and salt was dampened with water to make it stick together. A layer of plastic clay, an inch in thickness, was worked around the whole, and the ball, so made, was exposed to heat at about the cherry-red degree, sufficiently long to consume

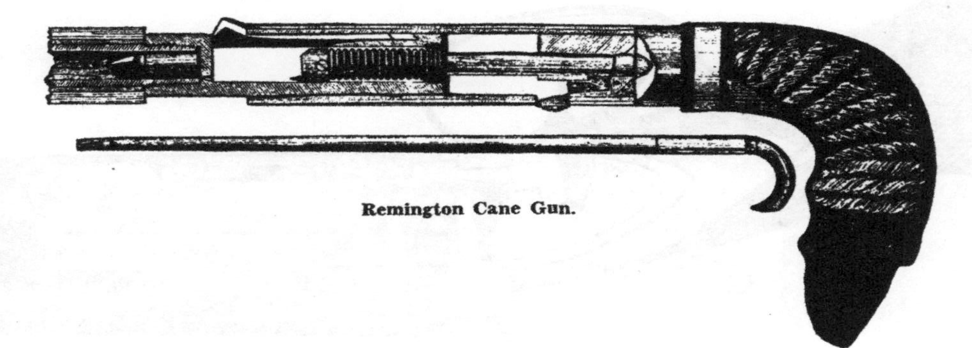

Remington Cane Gun.

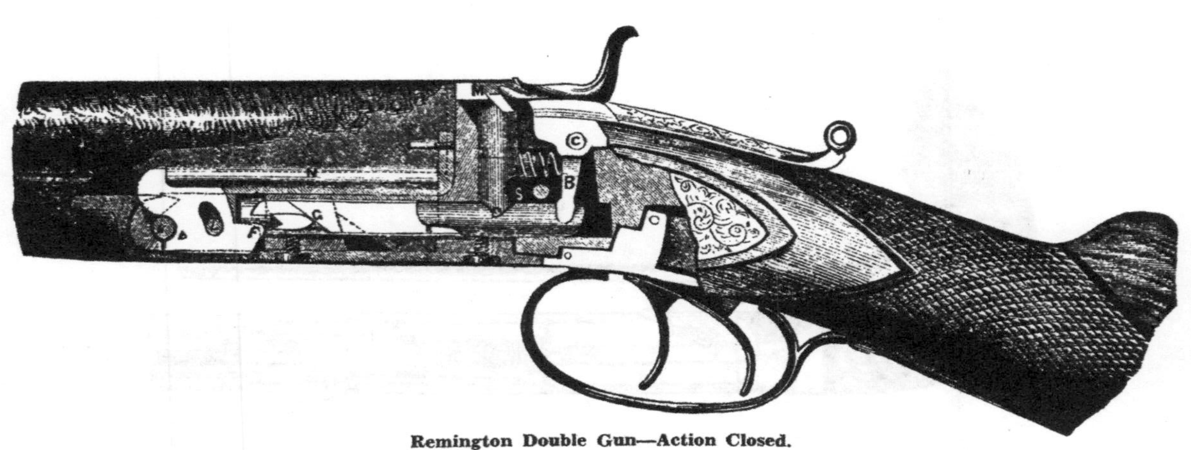

Remington Double Gun—Action Closed.

the leather, when it was dropped suddenly into the slack-tub.

Still Another Formula.—Make a powder of pulverized prussiate of potash, sal-ammoniac and saltpetre in equal parts. Heat the iron to cherry-red and sprinkle thoroughly on all sides with the powder, then immediately plunge into the slack-tub.

Some smiths contend that the pulverized prussiate of potash, used in the same way, is entirely effectual without the other ingredients.

To Chill Cast Iron.—Make a powder by pulverizing together, salt, 2 lbs.; saltpetre, ½ lb.; alum, ½ lb.; ammonia, 4 ozs., and salts of tartar, 4 ozs. Heat the iron to cherry-red, sprinkle thoroughly with the powder and then plunge into cold water.

Another Mode.—Make a solution by dissolving in 10 gallons of soft water, salt, 1 peck; oil vitrol, ½ pint; saltpetre, ½ lb.; prussiate of potash, ¼ lb., and cyanide of potassium, ½ lb. Heat the iron to cherry-red and plunge at once into the cold solution. This makes cast iron hard enough to cut glass, and is the method usually resorted to for hardening the cheap cast-iron glass cutters, now so common on the market.

To Soften Wrought Iron.—Heat the iron with a slow blast to a dark-red, then pour upon the burning coals half a pint of fluoric acid. Keep up the blast gently, without increasing the degree of heat, until all sign of the acid has disappeared, then lay out the iron to cool gradually of itself.

Alloy for Filling Holes in Iron.—Melt together

nine parts lead, two parts antimony and one part bismuth. Pour into the hole while in a moulten state, or drive in while the iron is somewhat hot. This alloy possesses the peculiarity of expanding as it cools, consequently the plug tightens as its temperature falls.

To Harden Iron for Polishing.—Pulverize and dissolve the following-named articles in one quart of boiling water: blue vitrol, 1 ounce; borax, 1 ounce; prussiate of potash, 1 ounce; charcoal, 1 ounce, and common salt, ½ pint. Add to this 1 gallon raw linseed oil. Having finished up the article ready for polishing, heat it to a cherry-red, and plunge into the mixture; a rapid stirring of the mixture should be going on at the time when the plunge is made.

This preparation hardens the iron to such a degree that it takes and retains polish almost equal to the best of steel.

CHAPTER XI.

ON WORKING IN STEEL.

Hand-Forging Steel.—In the main this does not differ materially from the same work in iron. Special care must be exercised to have the fire clear of sulphur, hence charcoal is the best fuel to use. In cases where the use of bituminous coal cannot be avoided, the fire should be blowed up for several minutes before putting in the steel, to drive off the sulphur.

Steel to be forged should not be heated to so high a degree as is employed for iron; for ordinary light work a little above a cherry-red is enough. It does not work well under a high degree of heat; and, to make amends, it can be worked much colder than iron. In fact, it is always best to hammer it with light blows until the red color of the heat has entirely disappeared, as this improves its texture by adding decidedly to the closeness of the grain.

Welding Steel.—The common method employed for welding iron to iron is often resorted to for welding steel to steel, but a great deal more care is necessary to success in the latter than in the former case. There must be much precision so far as relates to the rate of heat, as the margin for variation is extremely small. If the temperature is not high enough there will be no adhesion, of course; and if it attains to only a few degrees above what is actually necessary, the steel either "runs" and is ruined, or is ruined by going into an unworkable condition known as "burnt." It sometimes becomes necessary to weld steel and iron together; this may be effected by the same process as that employed in welding steel to steel. None but workmen of thorough experience would be apt to succeed in either case, on the old plan of proceeding the same as in welding iron to iron.

But steel may be more easily welded than on the old plan by the employment of certain welding compositions. One of them consists of half a pound of saltpetre dissolved in half a pound of oil of vitriol, and afterwards added to two gallons of soft water. Heat the pieces to a cherry-red, then plunge them into this composition; after which proceed to reheat and weld in the usual way. At the welding the strokes of the hammer should be quick and light.

Another composition is made by pulverizing together ten parts of borax and one part of sal-ammoniac. Thoroughly melt the composition so made in an iron pot, then pour out upon some level surface to cool. When cooled grind to a fine powder. Heat the pieces of steel and sprinkle this welding powder over them; then return to the fire, and again heat up, and it is ready to go together under the hammer.

Some smiths claim to weld steel successfully by dusting over the heated pieces a powder composed of clear white sand, 2 lbs., and plaster of Paris, 1 lb.; then reheating and proceeding in the usual way.

In welding steel to iron the foregoing processes are employed the same as if both pieces were steel.

Tempering.—Heat the steel to a bright cherry-red, and plunge it at once into cold water. It will then be as hard as fire and water could make it, and too hard for anything except hardened bearings for machinery, or for some kind of implements necessary to be extremely hard, as tools for cutting glass, and the like. In this condition it is almost as brittle as glass itself, and hence would not stand for most of the uses to which tempered steel is applied. Its great degree of hardness must, therefore, be reduced to the proper standard, depending upon what it is to be used for. This is done by heating and closely observing the resulting colors as they appear upon the metal. If the piece under process is an edge-tool of considerable bulk, only the cutting-edge, and a little back of it, is plunged into the water at the hardening, the rest of the implement being left still hot. It is then held into the light and observed closely, when the different colors, indicating the different degrees of hardness, will be seen moving slowly, one after the other, down towards the edge, driven by the heat still left in the part of the metal not plunged. When the color wanted has reached the edge, the entire piece is plunged into the slack-tub, which stops further action of the heat, and establishes the required degree of hardness exactly where it is desired. But very light articles and implements cannot be tempered in this way, as they will not retain sufficient heat to drive the colors; it will be necessary to reheat them gradually in some way to make the colors move. Very light pieces, as drills and the like, are best tempered in a spirit or alcohol lamp; after having been hardened they should be held in the flame of the lamp a little back of the point or cutting-edge, which will enable the operator to note the movement of the colors. In this case his actions, so far as the colors are concerned, will be governed the same as in the other. Small articles to be tempered alike all over may be placed upon a bit of sheet-iron, after hardening, and the iron held over the fire of the forge, or directly over the flame of the lamp, until the required color has appeared, when they must be quickly plunged into the water. On large articles the colors will be often so strongly marked as to be readily seen on the surface of the metal, rough, just as it came from the hammer, but in small articles they will be somewhat faint; hence it is best to give small articles a slight polish before exposing them to heat for drawing the temper. Nine shades of color will present themselves one after the other as a piece of thoroughly-hardened steel is exposed to gradually-increasing heat. They are:

1. Very faint yellow, appearing at a temperature of 430° Fahrenheit. If slacked at this color, the piece will be very hard, having a temper admirably suited to drills for working in hard metals or hard stone.

2. Pale straw-color—450°. Still very hard, suitable for the faces of hammers and anvils.

3. Full yellow—470°. Shears and scissors.

4. Brown—490°. Gravers and turning-tools for hard metals; also percussion-lock gun tubes.

5. Brown, with purple spots—510°. Wood-working tools and most of the steel parts in a gun-lock with the exception of the springs; also knives of all sorts for cutting wood.

6. Purple—538°. Butcher-knives and other flesh-cutting implements.

7. Dark blue—550°. Tools requiring strong cutting-edges without extreme hardness, as case-knives.

8. Full blue—560°. Chopping-axes.

9. Grayish blue, verging on black—600°. Springs, saws, swords, and the like.

Various other methods of tempering steel are sometimes recommended, as with oils, tallow, lead, mercury and divers solutions; but since the matter-of-fact gunsmith will find use for none of them, it is not deemed proper to encumber this book with anything further on the subject of tempering. It might be well to state, however, that the hardest degree to which steel can be brought is secured by heating the piece to a light yellow and instantly plunging it into cold mercury.

To Restore "Burnt" Steel.—Pulverize together two parts horn or hoof filings; one part sal ammoniac; one part charcoal, and one part common soda. When thoroughly ground together, work in tallow enough to make a kind of wax or paste. Bring the damaged steel to a bright cherry-red heat, and then cover with the paste, leaving it to cool gradually. The process may be repeated several times with profit if considered necessary. While a piece of badly-burnt steel may not be entirely restored by this process, it can be much improved. Entire restoration is scarcely possible.

Annealing Steel.—Heat the steel to a cherry-red in a charcoal fire, the last thing to be done before quitting work at the forge for the day or night; then smother the fire down with a thick layer of ashes or sawdust, leaving the steel in, just as heated. Let so remain until the fire is all out, and the steel entirely cool, which will require several hours. Some smiths use a piece of gas-pipe in which to heat small steel articles for annealing, claiming that it is very advantageous. They put the piece into the pipe and heat to a cherry red, looking in occasionally to ascertain when it has attained to that temperature; then they cover the fire, pipe and all, and leave it to cool as in the other case.

To Blue Steel.—Polish the article to be blued, then place it upon a strip of sheet iron and heat slowly over a forge fire or lamp, until the desired blue color appears. Let cool, and the color will remain permanent.

To Remove Blue Color from Steel.—Immerse for a few minutes in a liquid composed of equal parts muriatic acid and oil of vitriol. Rinse in pure water and rub dry with chamois skin or some kind of soft cloth.

Tempering Knife Blades.—To heat the blades lay them in a clear charcoal fire, with the *cutting edge downwards,* and heat very slowly. It is not particular if the back of the blade, which is *uppermost,* is so very hot or not. Harden in clean luke-warm water. If many blades are to be hardened at once, lay a number in the fire and remove one at a time as they are properly heated. To temper, brighten one side on a grindstone or emery wheel so that the temper color can be seen, and lay the blades in the fire, or on an iron plate heated over the fire, with the backs *down* and the cutting edges *uppermost.* On the plate place wood ashes or fine sand to help keep the blades in proper position, and also facilitate even drawing. When the proper color is seen on the brightened portion of the cutting edge, remove and cool in cold water.

When an extra tough blade is wanted, after it is hardened, handle it so that it will not draw any lower after removing from the fire, and let it cool without putting in water.

Long blades, when they are being drawn, can be straightened, if necessary, by putting them between two pins in the anvil or pins fixed in an iron block and bending between these until straight, wetting the blade with a cloth or sponge saturated with water, when the blade is thus straightened. Surprising as it may seem, when hardened steel is being drawn, it can be bent to quite an extent, and when cooled will remain as bent. File makers straighten files in this manner. Sword blades and blades of butchers' knives undergo the same process of manipulation to be made straight.

The Lead Bath for Tempering.—Among the many secrets of tempering is the employment of the lead bath, which is simply a quantity of molten lead, contained in a suitable receptacle and kept hot over a fire. The uses of this bath are many. For instance, if it be desired to heat an article that is thick in one portion and thin in another, every one who has had experience in such work knows how difficult it is to heat the thick portion without overheating the thin part. If the lead bath be made and kept at a red heat, no matter how thick the article may be, provided sufficient time be given, both the thick and thin parts will be evenly and equally heated, and at the same time get no hotter than the bath in which they are immersed.

For heating thin cutting blades, springs, surgical instruments, softening the tangs of tools, etc., this bath is unequaled.

If a portion of an article be required to be left soft, as the end of a spring that is to be bent or riveted, the entire may be tempered, and the end to be soft may be safely drawn in the lead bath to the lowest point that steel can be annealed without disturbing in the least the temper of the part not plunged in the bath. Springs, or articles made of spring brass, may be treated in the same manner. One great advantage in using the lead bath is that there is no risk of breakage or shrinkage of the metal at the water line, as is often the case when tempered by the method of heating and chilling in cold water.

As lead slowly oxidizes at a red heat, two methods may be used to prevent it. One is to cover the surface of the lead with a layer of fine charcoal or even wood ashes. Another and a better plan, when the work will admit of its use, is to float on the top of the lead a thin iron plate, fitting the vessel in which the lead is contained, but having a hole in the centre or on one side, as most convenient, and large enough to readily admit the articles to be tempered or softened.

Test for Good Steel.—Break the bar of steel and observe the grain, which in good steel should be fine and present a silvery look, with sometimes an exfoliated or leaf-like appearance. One of the best tests of steel is to make a cold chisel from the bar to be tested, and when carefully tempered (be careful not to overheat), try it upon a piece of wrought iron bar. The blows given will pretty correctly tell its tenacity and capability of holding temper. Remember the temper you gave it, and if it proves tough and serviceable, take this temper as a guide and temper other tools in like manner. Inferior steel is easily broken, and the fracture presents a dull, even appearance, which may very appropriately be termed a lifeless look.

Etching on Steel.—Make an etching solution by pulverizing together sulphate of copper, one ounce; alum, one-quarter ounce, and common salt, one-half teaspoonful. Add one gill strong vinegar and twenty drops nitric acid. Stir till thoroughly dissolved. Polish up the metal to be etched, and then cover its polished surface with a thin coating of bees-wax. This can be accomplished with neatness by simply heating the metal till the wax flows evenly over its surface. Now draw upon the wax, cutting cleanly through to the steel the figure you wish to etch; then cover the figure so prepared with the etching solution, and let stand for a short time, depending upon the depth of cut desired. Finally rinse off with clear water, and then remove the bees-wax. It will be found that the solution has cut into the surface of the steel wherever exposed, leaving untouched all parts covered by the wax.

Very good etching can be done by applying, on the foregoing plan, nitric acid alone. Etching offers a good method of cutting a man's name on his gun or pistol. It works on silver or brass the same.

CHAPTER XII.

ON WORKING IN SILVER, COPPER AND BRASS.

To Forge Silver.—The gunsmith will not have much to do with silver in the work of his trade, though instances may occur now and then when he will be called upon to make or repair mountings or ornaments for gun-stocks formed of this metal, and also foresights, particularly for the old fashioned Kentucky rifle.

In shaping silver under the hammer no heat will be necessary at the hammering—it would do no good. The metal is so malleable that it may be drawn into almost any shape by simply hammering cold. The only trouble liable to come up in this kind of work will be the hardening of the metal under the influence of the hammer; but this trouble may be pretty effectually removed by heating the silver to redness, and then letting it cool gradually of itself. Care must be taken not to heat it too much above the first appearance of red, as it melts quite easily.

To Polish Silver.—File it down to the shape desired, then dress with a fine file; then work over thoroughly with a burnisher. Next buff it off with rotten stone, and if a particularly fine finish is desired buff again with rouge.

Light Plate for Copper or Brass.—Dissolve silver

in nitric acid by the assistance of heat; put some pieces of copper into the solution and immediately the silver will be precipitated. With fifteen or twenty grains of the precipitate thus obtained mix half a drachm of alum and two drachms each of tartar and common salt. Pulverize well together. Having thoroughly cleaned the surface to be plated, rub it well and hard with the mixture, using a bit of chamois skin, until it presents a white appearance. Next polish off with soft leather until bright.

Inferior as this kind of plating would seem, it will wear a long time.

To Clean Silver.—Wash with a little spirits of ammonia reduced in strength by twice its bulk of pure water, then rub dry and bright with soft leather. No kind of polishing powder will be necessary. Some workmen clean silver by first washing it over with diluted muriatic acid, then immediately covering the surface with dry prepared chalk, then brushing off and rubbing clean with a bit of chamois skin. It acts very well, but care must be had to get the acid thoroughly cleaned off else it will have a tendency to soon tarnish the silver.

To Work Copper.—This metal is almost as malleable as silver, and works very well under the hammer in a cold state. Heat adds nothing to its malleabilty, though, as in the case of silver, exposure to a low degree of heat, followed by gradual cooling, softens it somewhat when it has been rendered hard and brittle by long hammering. It polishes very well, but does not long retain its polish and brillancy on account of its disposition to oxidize. Heating increases its oxidation; repeatedly heating and cool ing would soon wear it entirely away.

To Work Brass.—This material is a combination of copper and zinc, and since zinc is not so malleable as copper, it renders the brass less malleable. Nevertheless it forges out pretty well under the hammer, in a cold state, the only condition in which it can be so worked. Hammering increases its hardness with great rapidity, soon converting it into a very fair spring metal. Brass springs are quite common—they are all made by repeatedly hammering or rolling the metal while cold. As in the case of both silver and copper, heating and gradual cooling removes this hardness. This is the plan for softening usually recommended in books on working metals, but no advantage will be found to arise from the gradual cooling in the case of either silver, copper or brass. The custom is to heat the metal to the lowest degree that would show redness and then plunge it directly into cold water.

To Cast Brass.—The gunsmith may occasionally find it necessary to cast something in brass. This he can do without trouble, as brass melts quite easily. The mould should have vents at or near the top to admit the free escape of air as the molten metal runs in to take its place; and it is always best, if possible, to arrange so that the metal will enter the mould near the bottom and rise up in the filling. Without such an arrangement there is danger of air bubbles remaining under the metal and spoiling the casting. The metal should be heated only to a degree high enough to admit of flowing freely and no higher.

To Brass Iron. — Clean and polish the iron thoroughly, being extremely careful not to touch its surface with the fingers at the finishing; then plunge it into molten brass. Take out immediately; a thin coating of brass will be found covering the iron, which may be polished or burnished, giving the article the appearance of solid brass.

To Clean Brass.—To half a pint of soft water add one tablespoonful of oxalic acid. Wash the article with this, then cover with prepared chalk, brush dry and polish with chamois skin, as in cleaning silver. The solution may be bottled and kept on hand for use as wanted.

To Solder Brass.—The processes in soft soldering are the same for all metals, full instructions for which may be found in Chapter XXXIV. Hard soldering (see also Chapter XXXIV) is something different, and in the case of brass it is somewhat different on account of the low degree of temperature at which the metal melts. The solder most commonly used is composed of two parts of common brass and one part of zinc, melted together. Reduce your solder to fine bits by cutting or filing, and then mix with sal-ammoniac and borax, the two latter having been pulverized together in equal parts and moistened with water to form a kind of paste. Carefully clean the pieces to be joined, lay them together, place the soldering compound along the upper edge of the joint, which must be held vertically, and then heat gradually over a charcoal fire until the solder is seen to run down between the pieces. The instant the solder is seen to run remove the work from the fire, tap the work gently with a small hammer to jar the solder into all interstices, and, if the work be so that it can be done, scrape off the superfluous solder and burnt borax with an old file.

CHAPTER XIII.

ON WORKING IN WOOD.

The Woods Most in Use.—Various woods are now employed for making gun stocks, but among them all, the most popular, perhaps, is black walnut. It is deservedly so from the fact that it is light, works easily, takes a superior polish, has a rich dark color, naturally, and when finished up does not incline to "check." So popular is it, indeed, that most of the other woods worked into gun stocks are stained and finished up to imitate walnut.

In some portions of the country hard or sugar maple ("sugar tree") is worked quite extensively by the local gunsmiths. It makes a very nice stock, finishing to good advantage, especially "curled maple," which is really beautiful. Soft maple is also extensively used, stained and finished to imitate either hard maple or walnut.

The common dogwood makes an excellent gun-stock, but it works badly on account of the smallness of the tree rendering it difficult for one to get the pieces sawed out in proper shape at the beginning. Holly also makes a good stock, but presents the same objection as the dogwood. Cherry has few superiors, but it is now becoming a very scarce wood. Sweet gum is getting to be quite extensively used for cheap guns, stained to imitate either walnut or cherry. It has fine grain, and works very well, the chief objection to it being that it is wonderfully inclined to warp.

Wood for Gun Stocks.—The wood for a gun stock should combine strength and lightness, and at the same time it is desirable that it be easy to cut. The fibres of the wood should be close and possess great cohesion and should be little liable to split.

In this country black-walnut is generally selected for shot guns, and either black-walnut or hard maple for rifles. The grain of the wood should be straight at the small of the stock, which is the weakest portion of the work. Between this and the end of the breech it little matters how the grain runs. If there be curls, waves or a hard knot, let it come about midway between the small and the end of the butt. As the wood at this place is simply "rounded" it is easy to work it into shape, as the shape given to it is such that any deviation of the fibres or grain from a straight line can be shown to the best advantage, also at this place there is less demand for strength of wood than at any other part of the gun stock. Around the small it is very necessary that the grain be straight and run in the direction of the shape given and also continue straight until past the place where the locks are set in. A little distance in front of the barrel breech it matters but little how the grain runs, but if the fibres of the wood where the barrel is let in run toward the breech it will be found to be easier to work out for the reception of the barrel. For then as the tools are worked toward the breech they are cutting *with* the fibres or grain and not *against* it. But as the majority of guns are now half-stocked the distance to cut in order to let in a barrel is so small that but little attention need be paid to the grain at this spot.

The best and most serviceable stocks are those made from parts of the tree where large branches join the trunk. In these parts, too, will be found the curled and irregular grain that is so much admired when the stock is so made that these irregularities come in the stock a little in front of the butt plate. When large trees are cut down, it will be observed very often that there are portions of the stump that have a kind of convex form, and extending downward terminate in large roots. If these be dug out or separated from the stump by splitting them, they are almost always of a proper shape, to have the grain run nearly straight in the curves as given to the stock. In black-walnut and hard maple these root portions are very firm of fibre, quite hard and have a splendid grain that finishes up beautifully. Portions of some root pieces have a mottled appearance and are of a different color from the wood as cut from the trunk of the tree; this is especially the case with black-walnut. As these stumps can be had by the trouble of removing them, the gunsmith can very cheaply secure pieces of wood that are very valuable. Oftentimes black-walnut stumps are found floating in the water, and on the banks of western rivers, that are perfectly sound and so darkened by water soaking that they make beautiful stocks.

The dryness and fitness of the wood may be ascertained by the easy crumbling of the shavings and by the dryness of the sawdust. It is necessary that the wood be well seasoned, for if any moisture or sap remains in it, the barrel and portions of the lock that come in contact with the wood, will in a short time be covered with rust.

CHAPTER XIV.

ON GUN STOCKS.

Form of Gun Stocks.—When a customer orders a stock to be made, or has a gun to be re-stocked, the gunsmith will observe the length of his customer's arms, length of neck, his height and general carriage. From these he can gather some data as to the length and form of stock to be made. Give him a gun, and observe his mode of raising it and taking aim, and the manner of his holding his head while aiming, and deductions may be drawn as to what the customer requires.

A tall, long-limbed and long-armed man requires a longer stock than a shorter person, and a straight stock will better answer for a short-necked, high-shouldered man than for a long-necked, low-shouldered person. A straight stock is much more suitable for a short-necked, high-shouldered person than a bent one, and for this reason, that, in fast shooting the point of sight at the end of the gun would come up to the range of the eye before the butt could be placed full against the shoulder, and one consequence would be, when fired, a severe recoil of the gun at every discharge. A stock rather long is much better than one too short, and one rather crooked to one that is too straight. If a gun be not held on a perfect level, but the muzzle higher than the breech, the load will be carried over the object aimed at, supposing that object to be on a level with the eye. Let a customer take a gun, such as would be thought to be best suited to his "build," and request him to close both eyes and raise the gun to a level, as if to shoot thus. Have him hold the gun immovable thus, and then request him to open his eyes, and it is evident if he requires a stock to be made different from the one he has in hand. If the face comes naturally to the breech and the eye has a "fine sight" along the barrel, it is just the pattern of gun stock for him to have. If it be too straight he will shoot over, if too much crooked he will shoot under. In the first instance the muzzle is brought too high by an effort of the face to find a position at the breech, and in the other case it so readily finds a place that no further effort is made, except by practice, to raise the muzzle to the proper level.

A tall, slim person requires a gun with a long, crooked stock, and rather heavier and made fuller behind the small, as this will fill up his want of a full face, and will better permit his eye a command of sight along the middle of the barrels, supposing the gun to be a double one. For a short individual a short, straight stock is required, and it should be made thinner behind the small, so as to easily permit access to the line of sight. If a person be in the habit of firing too low and behind a bird, if the stock be made a little straighter it will prove a remedy for the fault.

That part of the stock where the cheek comes to rest should be full, as it gives more support to the line of fire. The heel of the stock should be in a straight line with the upper rib between the barrels. If a single gun, on a line with the barrel. The length of stock from the centre of front trigger to centre of butt-plate, from thirteen to fifteen and a half inches; a short person requiring the less measurement, while a very tall one might require the longest one.

The cut, Fig. 23, gives a better idea of what the stock should be. Place a rule or straight-edge upon

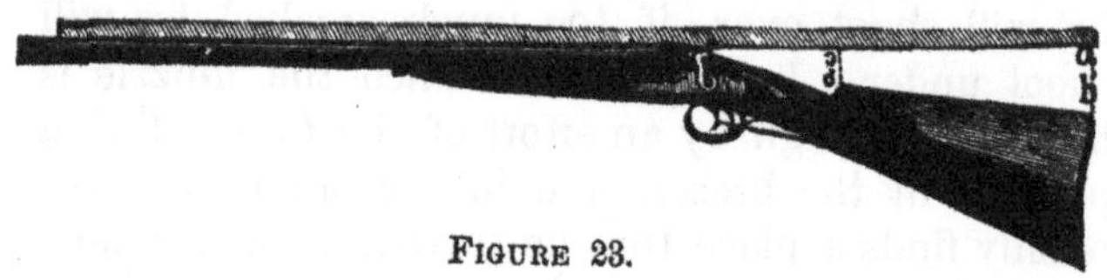

FIGURE 23.

the rib of the gun, and long enough to reach from the sight of the gun over and beyond the butt. Be particular that the straight-edge lies along the rib and touches it at both muzzle and breech. The measurement from *a* to *b* on the butt is what is termed the "drop," and this may be from two and a half to four inches, according to the requirements of the shooter The cheek of the sportsman comes between *c* and *d*, and almost always touches the stock at this place when bending his head forward over the stock of his gun to take the line of sight. This part of the gun should command particular attention.

Another point of considerable importance to observe is, that a due regard be paid to the proper fall of equipoise or centre of gravity of the gun when stocked and ready for use. This centre of gravity should fall at a point about two feet two inches, or perhaps an inch more, from the heel of the butt. In this case the arm is easier to handle and easier to carry. If the breech be too light, lead may be inserted to advantage in the butt, the butt-plate being removed for that purpose.

Dimensions for Single Gun.—The following may be considered very good dimensions for a single gun stock: Whole length of stock, from butt to cap, two feet two inches; length or depth of butt, five and a half inches, with a trifling concave surface; width of stock at butt, two inches; from point of centre of the lock-tumbler to cap, eleven inches; width of stock before the guard, one inch and three-eighths, and made nearly square.

Dimensions for Double Gun.—For a double gun: Length of stock, from butt to cap, two feet one inch; length or depth of butt, five and a half inches, with a slightly concave surface two inches in width; from centre of lock-tumbler to cap, ten and one-quarter inches; width of stock before guard, one inch and three-quarters, and made nearly square.

Laying out Gun Stocks.—Several patterns each, of double and single, and rifle stocks are necessary. These patterns may be made of thin wood or thick straw-board. These patterns ought to be a little larger than the finished stock, and are intended only for a proximate measurement of the stock when to be sawed from the rough wood. Select the wood, lay the pattern upon it, mark around with a pencil or crayon, and then saw out by the lines made.

With a plane, smooth one side of the wood so as to show the grain and the direction in which it runs. This must govern the position of laying the pattern. The weakest portion of the stock is the small, and there it is almost a necessity that the grain should not run across the line of the stock, but with it. If a very little divergence be made, it may not matter, provided the wood be of a hard and close grain. If the grain run across, or at an angle at this weakest spot, a slight blow or accidental fall is liable to cause a breakage which can best be repaired with a new stock. If the wood be in some places mottled, with curled or twisted grain, or has a knot that is hard and sound, let this spot come in the center of the butt, for by its width and thickness no accident is liable to break it, and the rounded form gives opportunity to show off the irregular grain to good advantage. Let the wood where the butt plate is attached be of straight and regular grain if possible. The grain where the locks are let in, and also where the barrel is let in, should be straight and run in the same line as the barrel.

The planks or rough pieces for double gun stocks should be about two and a quarter inches thick before they are reduced. Two inches for a single gun,

Remington—Hepburn's Pat.

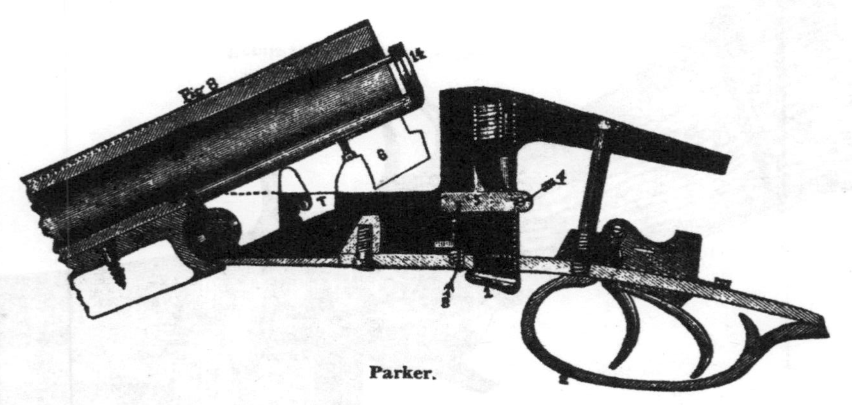

Parker.

and about one and three-quarter inches, or a little thicker, for rifles, depending on their weight and the taste of the customer.

It is best to have a number of stocks roughed out. Maple for rifles and black-walnut for single and double guns. Let them lay in a dry place to thoroughly season, and if they remain in this manner for several years, they are all the better for it. It is claimed that it takes seven years for a plank to season, and even then when sawed into stocks, they will be observed to shrink and change form, and often small cracks will appear.

Unhesitatingly reject all pieces that are unsound, or have any appearance of being brash, or with any signs of decay. Often in laying the patterns upon the wood these places can be readily avoided, and thrown away as the plank is cut up. Draw a straight line where the barrels will come, and cut to this line, but be sure to leave plenty of wood where the breech of the barrels rest, and where the break-off is set in. When the stock is roughed out, this spot will have the appearance of a rise or swell with a sharp curve in front, down on to the line which is just below the centre of the line of the barrels for double guns, and on the centre for single guns and rifles. Except in the case of some who may fancy the old Kentucky rifle, all guns will probably be made with half-stock. It would be hardly advisable to keep only a very limited stock of full length stocks on hand. If such are to be roughed out, pay particular attention to have the grain of the wood as straight as possible the full length where the barrel is to be let in.

How to Stock a Gun.—Stocking a gun is the most difficult portion of the gunsmith's trade. The change from iron work to the manipulation of wood is so great that many workmen refuse to work at both branches of the business. Then again, if the stock be not well done and the parts well fitted, they show a greater per cent. worse than perhaps they really are. The letting in of the barrel and locks should be done with care and nicety, and no apparent openings between wood and metal should be visible. The parts should be closely adherent to the wood, yet easy to be removed and returned to place. Where straight lines of the wood work are required, as along the line of the barrels and other places, let the lines *be straight.* Where the convex lines of the breech and butt occur, let the lines be graceful and of even proportions.

The First Operation.—After receiving the rough formed stock, as roughed out for seasoning, the first thing to do is to plane it to a thickness, and there are two places to measure for this thickness. One is the thickness of the butt, which in double guns may be two inches, and the same width in heavy single guns, and a trifle lighter if it be a light gun. The other place for measurement is across where the locks are to be let in. Observe how the locks are to rest, against the break-off or against the barrels. Note this measurement and add the thickness of the locks. This may be an inch and three-eighths to an inch and a half for single guns, and an inch and five-eighths to an inch and three-quarters for double guns, yet as the formation of the breech and style of locks differ so will these measurements vary from the measurements given. When these measurements are made, and the stock reduced to the proper width, draw a line both on the upper side of the stock as well as the under side, exactly between the breech and lock measurements, and continue this line from the end of the butt to the end of the fore-stock. Cut down to a straight line the stock where the barrels are to be let in, and fit in the break off. Take pains to fit it well, for on the fitting of this in a great measure depends the life of the stock. If the barrels be loose fitted, each recoil of the gun on firing tends to loosen the break-off from the barrels, and the joint soon becomes open and shackling.

When this part is snugly fitted and the strap let in, put in temporary screws to hold it for a season. Cut out the groove for the barrels, keeping in mind all the time that the central line between the barrels must be on the line as drawn on the centre of the stock. If a single gun, this line must pass directly through the axial line of the bore.

Letting in Barrels.—When it is thought that wood enough has been removed to admit the barrels, rub oil on them on the under side where they come in contact with the stock, put the hooks in the break-off, and with the hand press the barrels to place—the oil will show on the wood, on removing them, and then, with gouge or float, remove this portion and again put the barrels in place, observing the oil marks, and reduce the wood again until the barrels lie in their beds evenly and solidly, and the joining at the break-off is in place, square and true. The heel of the stock should come in a straight line with the middle of the rib, and will come so, if observance of the lines first drawn has been made.

Measure for the Stock.—Now measure for the drop of the stock, which is illustrated in Fig. 23. From the line *a* to *b*, which is a continuation of a line along the top of the barrels, may be, for instance about three inches. Cut the stock away on top to this measurement, and fit on the butt plate. To get the length of the breech, measure from the spot where the end of the front trigger will come, and this measurement extended, straight back to the centre of the butt, gives the length. For a person with long arms about fifteen and a half inches is enough; about fourteen and a half for a person with ordinary length of arm, and thirteen and a half or thirteen and three-quarters for a person with short arms.

The Butt.—The depth of the butt for a double or single may be about five and a half inches, but for a light single gun a little less but not very much.

Letting in the Locks.—The locks should now be let in their proper places, and, while so doing, have great care that no more wood be removed than is necessary. See that the lock-plates have all the support possible where they fit into the wood. Cut out enough for full play of the mainspring and searberg spring carefully, do not remove wood where the edges of the lock-plate come, so as to leave open spaces for admission of water, dust or moisture. In letting in the locks the portions of wood to be removed can be ascertained by touching the prominent parts of the lock with oil, or holding the lock over a smoky lamp, so as to have soot adhere, then observe where it touches, on pressing the locks into place. Observe if the cup of the hammer comes squarely on the nipple, and put in the side bolts as they are to remain.

Letting in the Trigger-Plate.—Let the trigger-plate into the stock so that the arm of the sear bears wholly on the thick of the trigger, and not on the outer end. For this reason, if it engages the outer end, on being pulled to disengage the nose of the sear from the tumbler notch, it produces a sort of "twisted leverage" which does not work quick and strong enough to properly disengage the sear without some effort on account of this. If the arm of the sear bears only in part on the thick of the trigger, it works hard and stiff, and the parts soon wear each other. Observe if the arm of the sear be not too short, for it might happen that the trigger will slip off at the end upon a quick pressure being applied, leaving the parts disengaged and the hammer standing at full-cock.

Letting in the Trigger.—The trigger should be so disposed in the plate that a distance of an inch and about three-eighths exist between the right trigger and the front of the trigger guard, and an inch and three-sixteenths or more between the two triggers, and a sufficient space between the rear of the left trigger and the guard behind it to admit of free movement of the trigger. Observe if the triggers do not come too close to each other; if they do they may so rub upon each other that the action of one will compel the other to follow its motion, and the result will be a descent of both hammers at the same time.

Observe if the curves of the two triggers are at sufficient distance from each other so that the left barrel can be fired without the projecting and inner edge of the right or first trigger hurting the finger that pulls the trigger.

Secure Fastenings.—For a secure fastening of the break-off, and, at the same time, to bind the stock together and prevent splitting through where the locks are let in, insert a screw through the tang of the strap and have it received in the front end of the trigger-plate. Have a good thread where the screw goes into the trigger-plate, and have the plate firmly drawn to its bed in the wood. Fit the guard, observing the measurements for space in front and rear of the triggers.

Fitting Bolt-Loops.—To ascertain the position of the loop where the bolt or wire goes through to hold the barrel in place, insert a fine steel needle through the wood until it strikes the hole, and then enlarge around it to accommodate the hole and the loop.

If for a bolt, a slender tool made like a saw will enlarge the hole in the wood, letting the tool follow in the loop and act as a guide to shape the hole. The finishing of the hole in the wood may be done with a bolt float, shown in Fig. 24.

Hints for Finishing.—In finishing up the stock have the part where the cheek rests in firing made pretty full. Make it rather long than short, and

FIGURE 24.

have it more straight than curved. The length of a stock, be it double or single gun, from butt to front end of stock, may be from about two feet to two feet two inches; from the centre of the hammer-screw to front end of the stock, from ten to eleven inches.

Fitting the Break-off.—On good fitting of the break of depends, in a great measure, the lasting quality of the gun. If this be not properly fitted to the hooks of the breech, to the breech itself, and into the stock, the gun is soon "kicked" to pieces by its own recoil. The extension of the break-off that is let into the stock toward the breech is called tang, strap or tail, and these are of two lengths, called the long and the short. These lengths usually correspond with the lengths of breech pins. The smallest diameter of break-off is one inch, and increases by eighths of an inch up to two inches.

To let in Escutcheons, etc.—Do not fit in an escutcheon until that part of the stock is finished or made to form. Then, after the bolt is fitted to its place through the loop, remove the bolt, make the hole in the escutcheon so that the bolt slides easily through it. Hold the escutcheons on the stock in the place they are to occupy and put the bolt through them. Mark around them with the sharp point of a knife and remove them. Cut out the wood of a depth to correspond with the thickness of the escutcheon with a bottoming tool. Put them in place and fasten them. They can now be finished down with a file even with the stock.

It is well to have escutcheons with the ends long enough to admit of small screws being inserted to hold them. They are more permanent than those that are held by a wire-like extension that goes through the wood and is clinched a little. By using the screws the workman can make his own escutcheons. Sheet iron, brass or German silver may be used. The slot can be cut with a punch or drift, and finished with a thin, flat file. The handles of old German silver spoons make very good escutcheons. If too thick, hammer out thinner. Heat them to soften so that they will not crack in hammering.

In putting escutcheons to place where they are to remain, heat them quite warm, smear with gum shellac and, while soft and melted, press into place. If done expertly, a neat job will be the result.

How to Cast Tips on Fore-end of Stock.—Tips

are cast on the fore-end of half-stocked single guns and rifles for the purpose of preventing the stock from splitting, and, at the same time, give it a finished appearance. After the stock is finished to shape and the rod fitted, put the barrel in place, and put a short piece of wood in the rod groove, the same as the rod would be if put there. Let the piece project from the wood four or five inches. It serves a double purpose, preventing the metal from flowing into the hole and making a hole to receive the rod. Now, wind thick, smooth paper—manilla paper is best—around the stock and barrel where the tip is to be cast, confining it with a cord, taking care to have all tight so that no portion of the metal will escape. See that the space between the paper and wood is left large enough, so that the metal can be dressed down a little; little notches may be cut in the wood to have it hold the better.

Fix the gun so as to stand upright, so that the metal will pour evenly. Heat the metal pretty hot and pour carefully into the paper, and pour in more than is wanted for the length of the tip, as the dross will float to the top and can be removed when cold by sawing off a little of the tip. File up and finish to suit the taste.

The best metal for tips is pure block tin, as it remains white. If it be wished to make it a little harder, add a very little antimony, but this is hardly necessary. Old type, when melted, make a very good material for tips when pure tin cannot be obtained. Tin has the advantage of always retaining a clear white color, which when alloyed with lead, it will not do.

Chequering.—To lay out the work preparatory for chequering, take a piece of card—a firm pasteboard, cut it to the shape of the spot to be chequered; mark around it with a lead pencil. If it be the small of a gun stock, place it at the other side from that first marked and mark that place. See that both places are marked alike. Then place the paper on, so that when it is used as a guide the tool will cut a groove where the line was drawn. Cut outlines in the same manner, the paper serving as a guide for the tool. After one groove is cut, this is a guide for grooving the space inclosed by the outlines.

To finish the cuts or grooves, fold a short piece of fine sand-paper and run the folded edge along the cuts. Be careful not to cut down too much with the sand-paper. A fine-cut, three-square file can be used to finish up the grooves made by the chequering-tool. Be careful to select a file that has very sharp corners. If one of the flat surfaces of the file be ground smooth, the teeth on the corners will be found to be very sharp, and will answer first-rate for finishing. The same may be used for finishing the shading or outside lines around the chequered surface.

Coloring Gun Stocks.—Gun stocks are colored with linseed oil in which alkanet root has been placed. The oil will then be of a bright red color. The oil may be applied cold or warm, as most convenient. After the application let the stock stand for a day or two until the wood has absorbed all the oil possible. Four ounces of the alkanet root to half a pint of the oil are sufficient. Unboiled or raw linseed oil is generally used. It may take five or six days to color, after the root is put in. It may be put on the work four or five times, with a bit of sponge or a rag.

To Stain a Maple Stock.—Mix an ounce and a half of nitric acid with about equal quantity of iron turnings or filings. Wait until all the gas evolved has evaporated, and then dip a rag in the liquid and wash the portions of the stock to be colored. When this is dry, wet with the oil and alkanet root.

Another Method.—A stock may be oiled and then passed over a brisk flame, as that made from dry shavings, until the oil is scorched off, and then lightly rubbed down with fine sand-paper and then finished in the usual way.

To Color a Maple Stock Brown.—Dissolve a few grains of sulphate of manganese in water; wet the stock and hold over the flame of an alcohol lamp so as to scorch it. By heating some parts more than others the color can be variegated. Oil with raw linseed oil, and polish with a piece of hard wood. The oil and polishing will develop the color, which may be dull at first.

To Color a Reddish Brown.—Brush the wood with dilute nitric acid, and when dry apply the following with a brush: Dragon's-blood, four ounces; common soda, one ounce; alcohol, three pints. Repeat if not dark enough.

To Color a Black.—Boil half a pound of logwood chips in two quarts of water; add one ounce of pearlash, and wash the work with it while hot. Then, when dry, go over the work with the following: Boil half a pound of logwood in two quarts of water; add half an ounce of verdigris and green copperas, in which has been put half a pound of rusty steel or iron filings.

Rosewood Stain.—Boil half a pint of logwood in three pints of water till the mixture is very dark red; add salts of tartar, one-half ounce, while boiling hot; and while still in this condition apply to the wood, repeating the application two or three times, as the previous application becomes dry. Rub over with a soft cloth when the last application has dried, and set away for a day or so. In the meantime boil one pound of logwood in four quarts of water until of a deep color, then add one pint of vinegar, heat hot and apply to the wood already stained, with a suitable brush, streaking on in imitation of rosewood. When thoroughly dry rub off all loose matter with a soft cloth, and varnish.

Black-Walnut Stain.—Put together gum asphaltum, one pound, and turpentine, half a gallon. Dissolve by gentle heating, taking care not to heat so as to ignite the turpentine. Rub over the wood, and when dry, if not sufficiently dark, repeat the operation. Having the shade to suit, polish down by rubbing hard with a woollen cloth, followed with a bit of soft wood, then varnish. A stain, not quite so good, but cheaper and more simple, is burnt umber, such as can be bought at any paint shop, ground in oil, thinned with a little turpentine. It should be put on very thick, and then rubbed off to the proper shade with a woollen cloth. Dry and varnish.

Mahogany Stain.—It is not often that guns are stocked in mahogany, but the gunsmith ought to know how to stain in imitation of that wood, should occasion happen to call for it. Put together, water, one half gallon; madder, four ounces; and fustic, two ounces. Boil. Lay on the wood with a brush while hot; and while yet damp, but not wet, rub off with a woollen cloth; then, when dry, go over with a second coat in streaks to imitate the grain of mahogany. Rub off all loose matter when dry, and varnish.

Cherry Stain.—Put two ounces of annatto in half a gallon of rain water. Boil until the annatto is dissolved, then add half an ounce of potash This preparation is intended for wood of a light color. It may be bottled and kept for use when wanted. Nothing to do in the application but rub over the wood, let dry, and then varnish.

Oil Finish for Gun Stocks.—Mix common Spanish whiting with some kind of coloring material until it is exactly the shade of the wood you desire to finish. For instance, if it is walnut to be finished. the coloring agent will be dry burnt umber. Having the whiting ready, give the wood, which has been well finished up with fine sand paper, a coat of raw linseed oil, then sprinkle the whiting mixture over it, and with a woollen cloth rub thoroughly and hard. This forces the colored whiting into all the pores of the wood. Lastly, rub down heavily with a piece of soft white pine, and then set away to dry. It may be left in this condition, or it may be varnished, when dry, if thought desirable.

Varnishing and Finishing.—After the stock is shaped and sand-papered so that the surface is smooth and free from any marks of the rasp and scratches of sand-paper wipe it over with a cloth a little moist with water, this will raise the grain of the wood a little, when dry, sand-paper it off smooth. With a small brush, such as is used by painters and called a sash brush, apply the varnish. Shellac varnish is the kind generally used by gunsmiths. It will dry in a little time, but ought to stand about twenty-four hours before being rubbed down. This is done with fine sand-paper the same as finishing the stock, the object being to fill the pores of the wood as much as possible. It may require two, three or even four coats of the varnish to do this, each one after it is thoroughly dried, being sand-papered down to the wood.

The last coat of varnish is laid on with a flat varnish brush made of soft fine hair; see that the varnish be free from dirt or specks and not too thick; put it on evenly and quickly. See that it does not run down so as to show in streaks. When this coat is thoroughly dry, rub it down smooth with powdered pumice stone applied with a rag wet with water. Take care not to cut through the varnish so as to show the wood underneath, as the pumice powder cuts very fast. When the surface is made smooth and even, wash off all traces of the pumice powder with a wet cloth, and wipe it dry. Now go over it with powdered rotten-stone applied with a rag moistened with oil. Rub until the varnished surface shows a finish or a glassy appearance, then wipe off all trace of rotten stone and oil. If a little flour be dusted over, it will better remove the oil traces that may remain; with the hand rub the sur-

FIGURE 25.

face until it presents a gloss. The hand must be soft to do this and must be free from dirt.

The Varnish for Gun Stocks.—Some workmen use copal varnish because it is cheap and convenient, but it is objectionable on account of its softness and its disposition to crack when exposed to the sun. There are a number of special varnishes recommended to the gunsmith, but for general use perhaps good coach varnish, will answer in many cases. It should be made quite thin with turpentine, and be put on lightly.

Varnish Can.—A very good form of varnish can is shown in Fig. 25. The essentials are to have a cover with a stem to receive the handles of the brushes, and a bridge crossing the can a little distance down from the top. The cover never sticks, no varnish collects around the sides, and it is always clean and tidy. The can is round and made of tin. The cover shuts over the outside at the top. In wiping the brush across the bridge, be careful not to get any upon the outside of the can where the cover comes in contact. The size of can may be made according to the needs of the mechanic, but the stem of the cover must be wide enough as well as long enough to receive the brush handles.

CHAPTER XV.

ON GUN BARRELS.

Long and Short Barrels.—A long barrel may be preferable for several reasons: 1st. A longer distance between the sights is given and the back sight can be put farther from the eye, so that finer sighting is possible; 2d. A long barrel is steadier in off-hand shooting; 3d. It permits a slower burning powder to be used, so that the charge starts more slowly and yet allows the full strength of the powder to be used before it leaves the barrel, getting a high initial velocity with but little recoil.

The short barrel has an advantage over the long one inasmuch as it can be handled with greater quickness and the sight can be brought to bear more readily, especially if the game be moving. If the barrel be long enough to give the charge the full benefit of the propelling power of the powder it may be deemed all sufficient. Yet, as to this, tastes and experience may so differ as to raise many conflicting opinions.

Except in some localities, as in case of districts where the old-fashioned Kentucky rifle is used, long barrels have been pretty much abandoned. A few years ago it was not uncommon to find barrels three and even four feet long, now the lengths will range from twenty-six to thirty-two inches. The length of the old Government musket barrel was originally forty inches, but has been lessened about seven inches. With the long barrels, a coarse, slower burning powder may be used and get a good result, but as a general thing cut off the barrel to a convenient length for off-hand shooting and moving game, use a finer-grained powder, which will be quicker burning and just as good results are obtained.

A gun having barrels over thirty inches in length, must needs be made with heavy barrels, and is very fatiguing to carry in an all day hunt. A gun of this kind, to be safe and well-proportioned, ought to weigh nine or ten pounds.

If fine and quick-burning powder be used in a long barrel, the powder is flashed into propelling gas, instantaneously, and beyond a certain length of barrel has no further expansive power, and the result is a friction of the charge in escaping, that affects the shot and consequently the pattern on the target. If slow burning powder be employed in a short barrel, the whole of the powder cannot be so instantly flashed into the propelling gas and some portion of it is, as a result, driven unconsumed from the muzzle of the gun.

This fact can be very readily ascertained by firing a gun over a bed of clean snow or over a spread of white cloth. The unconsumed grains can be readily seen on the white ground. If a less charge be used in order to consume all the powder, less velocity will be given to the projected charge,

Fig 7

Parker.

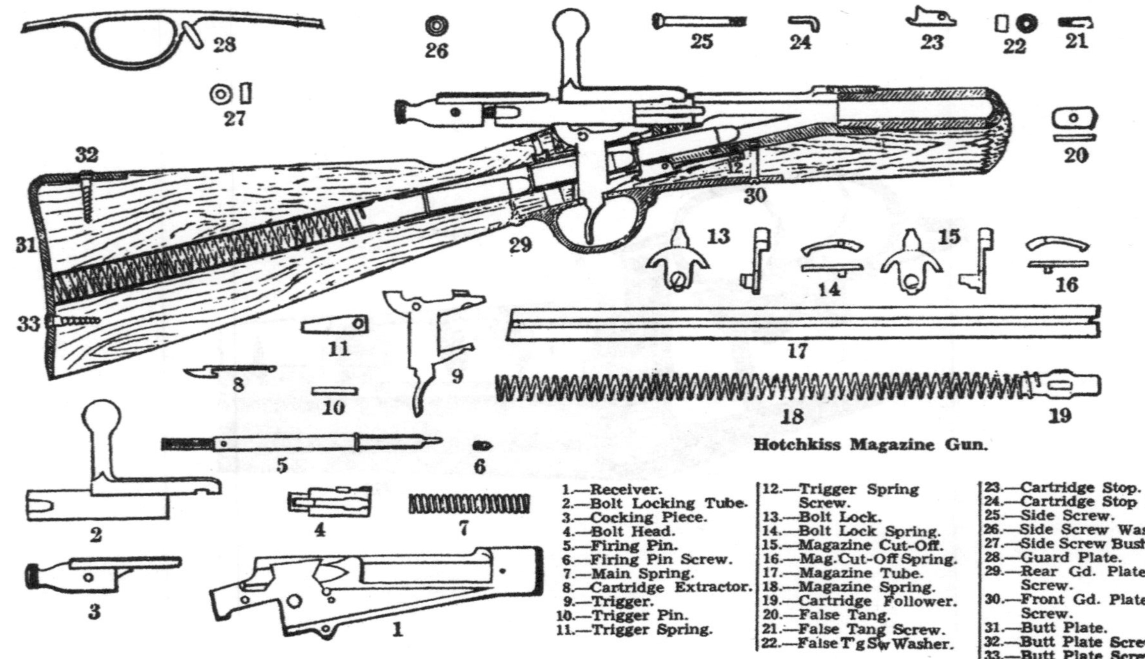
1.—Receiver.
2.—Bolt Locking Tube.
3.—Cocking Piece.
4.—Bolt Head.
5.—Firing Pin.
6.—Firing Pin Screw.
7.—Main Spring.
8.—Cartridge Extractor.
9.—Trigger.
10.—Trigger Pin.
11.—Trigger Spring.
12.—Trigger Spring Screw.
13.—Bolt Lock.
14.—Bolt Lock Spring.
15.—Magazine Cut-Off.
16.—Mag. Cut-Off Spring.
17.—Magazine Tube.
18.—Magazine Spring.
19.—Cartridge Follower.
20.—False Tang.
21.—False Tang Screw.
22.—False T'g S'w Washer.
23.—Cartridge Stop.
24.—Cartridge Stop Pin.
25.—Side Screw.
26.—Side Screw Washer.
27.—Side Screw Bushing.
28.—Guard Plate.
29.—Rear Gd. Plate Screw.
30.—Front Gd. Plate Screw.
31.—Butt Plate.
32.—Butt Plate Screw.
33.—Butt Plate Screw.

Hotchkiss Magazine Gun.

and weak shooting and a poor, scattering effect on the target is the consequence.

Proof of Barrels.—In consequence of the bursting of guns of an inferior quality, all barrels of English manufacture that are intended for home use, and also those designed for exportation, except a certain class of arms, are required by law to be proved and stamped with the proof-mark and also what is termed a view mark, which is a stamp or impress of the inspection after the barrels were grooved. There are two of these proofs called, respectively, the London and the Birmingham proof. In 1855, an Act was passed by the English Parliament, called, "The Gun Barrel Proof Act," which enacted that all barrels should be proved, first, in the rough, and was called the provisional proof, and afterward when the barrels were put together, breeched and percussioned they were proved again, and this was called the definitive proof.

The arms to be proved are to be divided into classes, and the first class comprises single-barrelled military arms of smooth bore, and they are not qualified for proof until they are fitted and complete to be set up or assembled. The second class comprises double-barrelled military arms of smooth bore and rifled arms of every description, whether of one or more barrels, and constructed of plain or twisted iron. The fourth class comprises double-barrelled guns for firing small shot, and these are subject to the two proofs, provisional and definitive. For provisional proof, if of plain metal, the barrels are to be bored and ground to size, the vent hole drilled of a size not exceeding one-sixteenth of an inch diameter, and a vent enlarged to one-tenth disqualified it for proof. Notches in the plugs, instead of drilled vents, also disqualified them. If the arms are of twisted metal, they are to be fine bored and struck up, with proving plugs attached, and vents drilled the same as in plain barrels.

For definitive proof the barrels, either plain or twisted, must be finished ready for assembling, with break-offs and locks fitted. The top and bottom ribs have to be rough struck up, pipes, loops and stoppers on, and the proper breeches in. The same finished condition is required for rifles, but, in addition, the barrels must be rifled. The third class comprises single-barrelled shot guns, and for proving they are to be finished ready for assembling, with breeches in; and all barrels, with lumps for percussioning, are to be proved through the nipple hole. The fifth class comprises revolving and breech-loading arms of every description and system, and for revolving arms are to have the cylinders with the revolving action attached and complete. The barrels for breech-loaders are subject to provisional proof, according to the class to which they belong, and to definitive proof, when the breech-loading action is attached and complete.

Barrels made by the United States Government, or barrels made for the Government, are subject to severe proofs. At the armory at Springfield, the barrels submitted for proof are loaded, first, with a

500-grain slug and 280 grains of powder, and afterward with a slug of the same weight and 250 grains of powder. An inspection of the barrel is made after each firing, and other inspections after rifling, browning, etc.

Probably the most severe proof of barrels was made with the Turkish Peabody-Martini rifles as made for the Turkish Government by the Providence Tool Co. The barrels were first proved for strength, and were loaded with 205 grains of powder and 715 grains of lead. The regular cartridge for service contains only 85 grains of powder and 480 grains of lead.

Proof Marks on Gun Barrels.—The marks applicable to the definitive proof are the proof and view

FIGURE 26.

marks of the two English companies, viz.: the London and the Birmingham. The provisional proof marks consist of, for the London company, the letters G. P., interlaced in a cypher surmounted by a lion rampant, and for the Birmingham company the letters B. P., interlaced in a cypher surmounted by a crown. The London marks are shown in Fig. 26, and the Birmingham in Fig. 27.

The method of affixing the proof marks in arms of the first and third classes, the definitive proof mark and view mark is impressed at the breech end of the barrel, and, if the barrel be designed for a patent breech, the view mark is also impressed upon the breech. In arms of the second, fourth and fifth classes, the proof mark is impressed at the breech end of the barrel; the definitive proof and view marks are impressed upon the barrel above the provisional proof marks. If the barrel be made

FIGURE 27.

with patent breech or with revolving cylinders or chambers, the view mark is impressed upon the breech or upon the cylinders or chambers, as the case may be.

On all barrels the gauge size of the barrel is struck both at the provisional and at the definitive proof. These gauge marks are readily recognized, as shown in the cuts of the proof marks.

Barrels stamped with London marks are not always made in London, for some gunmakers send their barrels to London to be proved, because guns so marked find a readier sale. Barrels with foreign proof marks are exempted, except in case of being marked as of English manufacture. Old muzzle-loaders, if of English manufacture, intended for conversion into other styles of guns, must be subjected to both provisional and definitive proof.

It is said to be a fact that the proof marks of both companies are forged and imitated, both in England

and in Germany, and many cheap guns so stamped are exported to this country. A cheap gun, with the stamps mentioned, may be looked upon with suspicion as to its really having been in the official proof-houses.

The proof marks employed by the inspectors in the U. S. Government armories, and placed on all arms inspected by them, even if made in private armories, are V for viewed, and P for proved, together with the initial letters of the inspector's name, and are found stamped on each barrel. On many guns of the old model arms will be found, in addition to these marks, the head of an eagle. This is the mark that indicated that the barrels were made at the armory at Harper's Ferry, when those works were in operation.

Gauge of Gun Barrels.—Guns are gauged by numbers, and these numbers were originally designed to express the number of round balls to the pound that would fit the bore of the barrel. Thus a ten gauge, a ball of which ten made a pound, would fit the bore, etc. Ten and twelve bores are generally used by sportsmen, especially those who use breech-loaders. The twelve, perhaps, is the one most employed.

The following list shows the sizes of various gauges, the values of the numbers being those adopted by the English proof companies. The diameters of bores being expressed in decimal thousands of an inch :

Number of Gauge.	Diameter of bore in inches.	Number of Gauge.	Diameter of bore in inches.
1	1.669	19	.626
2	1.325	20	.615
3	1.157	21	.605
4	1.052	22	.596
5	.976	23	.587
6	.919	24	.579
7	.873	25	.571
8	.835	26	.563
9	.803	27	.556
10	.775	28	.550
11	.751	29	.543
12	.729	30	.537
13	.710	31	.531
14	.693	32	.526
15	.677	33	.520
16	.662	34	.515
17	.650	35	.510
18	.637	36	.506

Muzzle-loaders are of almost every variety of gauge, while breech-loaders are made of a limited number of sizes. The sizes of this class of guns are 8, 10, 12, 14, 16 and 20, and are limited to these sizes, there being no intermediate sizes. The 10 and 12 bore are mostly in use, the 12 being in especial demand. The calibre or bore of military guns during the Revolution was 75 hundredths of an inch, and has been reduced by successive stages until now it is but 45 hundredths. Down to 1856 the calibre of the Springfield musket was 58 hundredths. In 1856 it was changed to 50 hundredths or one-half inch; and again, in 1873, it was changed to the present calibre of 45 hundredths.

Bursting of Barrels.—Bursting of barrels may result from three causes: Poor quality of iron of which the gun is made; an excess of charge; or some obstruction in the barrel so as to form an air space between the charge and the obstruction. Of poor quality barrels, and excess of charge it is needless to make mention. The instances of bursting from obstructions forming the air space or chamber may be mentioned in military guns, firing the charge but neglecting to remove the wooden tompion from the muzzle of the gun. In sporting guns snow may accidentally get into the muzzle or a lump of dirt may "somehow" get in so as to fill the bore, and when the gun is fired, it will probably, yes, most certainly be blown off or blown open where the obstruction exists; the muzzle of a gun being thrust into water for a couple of inches or more will have like effect. The gas formed by burning the powder finds no outlet of escape, and the whole expansive force concentrates itself on the weakest portion of the barrel, and as a result it is forced apart. In good guns the portion toward the muzzle is the thinnest, and obstructions are generally at or above this place, and it is in this proximity where most guns are burst. If within three, four or five inches from the muzzle, the portion so destroyed can be sawed off, the barrels squared up and it will not always seriously affect the shooting of the gun.

In loading a gun be careful that there be no air space left between the charge and the ball or shot cartridge. In double guns, frequent firing the right barrel, which is the one fired the most, the recoil will often cause the ball or shot charge in the left barrel to be thrown forward from the powder, and when it is fired may either strain or burst the barrel. Even if there be a small air space between the powder and the ball or shot cartridge it will affect the shooting. Every one using double guns should accustom himself to the use alternately of both barrels, not only for safety but for good shooting. A barrel is often said to be a poor shooter, when its bad qualities may be wholly ascribed to the air space produced above the powder by the recoil occasioned by firing the other barrel.

To Prevent Gun Barrels from Rusting.—Heat the barrel to about the temperature of boiling water, no higher, and then cover it with a good coating of copal varnish. Let it stand at same temperature about half an hour, then rub off the varnish while still hot with a soft cloth. In this process the varnish will enter the pores of the metal sufficiently to prevent rusting, but will not show on the surface after having been carefully rubbed off as directed. A polished surface like that of a finished gun barrel, is not much liable to rust, and, indeed, seldom begins to rust, the rust starting in the pores of the metal and finally working outward. This being the case it will readily be seen that sheltering the pores by filling them with some kind of substance impervious to moisture cannot do otherwise than act as a splendid preventive.

Protection from Rust.—It sometimes happens that

finished up articles in steel or iron must be laid away for a considerable length of time, in which case it is desirable to employ some means for protecting them from the effects of rust. One of the most common things is to either grease them or wrap them in a greasy rag. This may answer in many cases, but it is not nearly so good as to paint them over with a mixture of white lead and tallow in equal parts, the white lead to be such as has been ground in oil for the painter's use. In this simple mixture will be found an effectual protection; and as the tallow will prevent drying, it may be entirely removed at pleasure by rubbing with a little kerosene or turpentine.

Where it is desirable to protect an article that must be handled a great deal, as gun-barrels on sale in a store, for instance, a very good plan is to heat the article sufficiently hot to readily melt beeswax brought in contact with it, then rub it thoroughly with the wax. Let it stand until the wax is about ready to harden, then rub off with a coarse woolen cloth. The wax remaining on the metal will not show, but there will be enough left to protect it from rust.

CHAPTER XVI.

ON WORK ON GUN BARRELS.

Boring Gun Barrels.—The tool used for this purpose consists of a rod a little longer than the barrel to be bored, with a cutter head at one end. This cutter is about one-half or three-quarters of an inch long, and of a diameter a little larger than the bore that is to be enlarged. It can be made to be pulled through the barrel or to be pushed through when cutting. In the armories where many guns of the same calibre are made, a portion of the shank, next to the cutter, is made of the bore of the barrel, and the cutter made of the size the bore is to be enlarged. The portion that fills the bore acts as a guide, so that the cutter is forced to follow after it, and the enlarged bore is in the same line as the boring previously made. The cutting edges of the tool are, of course, next to the enlarged portion. As the tool is pulled through the barrel, the cuttings are left behind it as it advances ; oil is to be supplied while cutting, and care must be exercised not to let it get clogged with cuttings, as a tearing of the surface of the barrel would be the result.

When the tool is made to be pushed through while cutting, the cutting edges of the tool is on the end, and it operates like a reamer. This cutting end should be bevelled off so as to follow the bore to be enlarged.

How to make Cutters for Boring.—One way to make these cutters is like a many-fluted reamer, with five, seven, or more cutters. The odd numbers will operate better than even ones. If made with too many cutting edges, there will not be clearance enough for the chips, and clogging will be the result. Then again, the cutters must not be too long, or there will be too much friction, and the barrel will become very hot in working. Also, if the friction is too great, the barrel may be bent and sprung in consequence.

One form of cutter is made like the cherry to make an elongated bullet, or like the cherry of a Minie bullet. They may also be made in form of an egg. A common twist drill welded to a steel rod has been used for small bores. A small fluted reamer welded to a rod will do where the enlarging is quite small. When the tool is to be pulled through the cutter may be made like a short twist drill not over an inch long, with the cutting edges next the rod, and not on the end, as these drills are generally made.

Quick-Boring Gun Barrels.—The way to bore gun barrels by hand is this: Make a steel rod with a square bit about six or eight inches long on one end, and a little less in diagonal diameter than the bore of the barrel. The whole rod should be a little longer, say a foot or so, than the barrel to be bored. Harden and temper the bit end. See that it is true and perfectly straight when ground. The grinding should be done by drawing the bit across the face of the grindstone, and this will leave the sides of the bit a little hollowing, and the edges quite sharp. Pack up one side with a thin strip of soft pine until it will just enter the breech end of the barrel. By means of a strong bit stock, or a handle affixed like an auger, turn it around, at the same time forcing it toward the muzzle, until it has cut its way through the entire length of the barrel. While the cutting is going on keep the interior of the barrel plentifully supplied with good oil. Now, as the bit will be a very little smaller than the bore of the barrel, remove it and take off the little strip of wood and place between it and the bit a strip of writing paper of the length and width of the side of the bit where the wood was placed ; then insert the bit again at the breech and bore through to the muzzle. Repeat the operation again by inserting a second slip of paper, and so proceed, using plenty of oil, until the bore or calibre of the barrel is sufficiently enlarged.

Proving the Size during Boring.—A method of proving the size of the interior of the barrel and at the same time test its being perfectly of the same size throughout, is to cast an ingot of lead about an inch long in the muzzle, and with a rod forcing it through.

If the work be well done the interior of the barrel will present a bright mirror like appearance, and will need no further finishing.

Draw-Boring.—Draw-boring is done with a rod

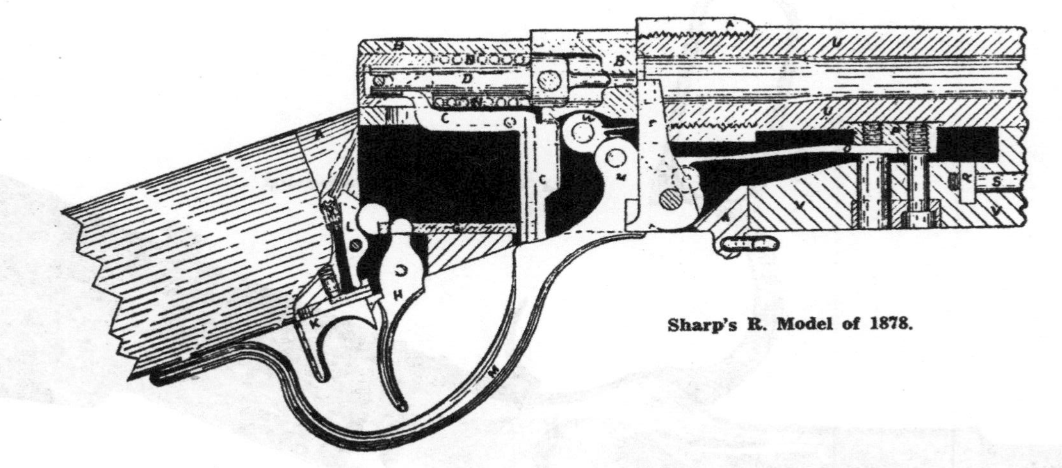

Sharp's R. Model of 1878.

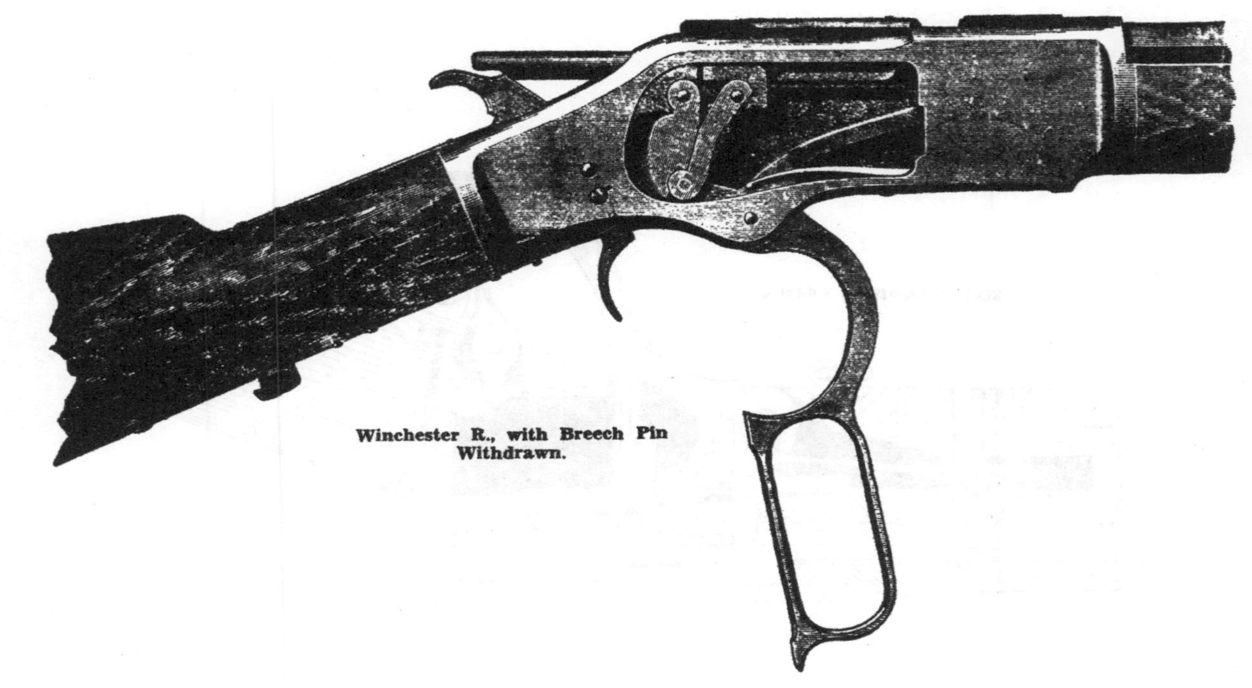

Winchester R., with Breech Pin Withdrawn.

that nearly fills the bore of the gun, and at one end of this rod is fitted a tool made like a short piece of file, but with the teeth made a great deal coarser and larger. This tool may be about an inch long, and of a round form on the cutting side, to fit the curvature of the bore. This tool is put on the end of the rod and worked back and forth, also turning it around, so as to present the cutter to all sides of the bore in which it is to operate. When it will cut no more the cutter is removed from its seat, a slip of paper put under it, and it is put in place and the operation repeated, and so continued until the bore of the gun is sufficiently enlarged.

Pieces of thin files, broken to length and with the ends ground to fit the rod, have been used for draw-boring, but the best and most effective tool is a bit of steel filed up to shape and properly fitted. One half of the cutting teeth should point forward and the other half backward, so that the cutter will remove some of the metal as it works in either direction, forward or back. If the cutter be an inch long, about three or four teeth may point one way, and as many the reverse direction.

In using these tools, keep them well oiled, to prevent tearing into the metal.

Choke-Boring.—The method of making a choke-bore is similar to quick-boring, except the cutting end of the rod does not go quite through the barrel, being withdrawn and again inserted with a slip of paper placed between the slip of wood and the cutter. This is worked not quite so far as the previous boring, being withdrawn and another slip of paper placed between the wood and the cutter, and this is worked in as far as desired. Care must be taken that the choke be gradual and even. A finish can be given by folding a piece of fine emery cloth or emery paper around a rod, and by turning this in the barrel, equalize any unevenness that may occur.

To enlarge the interior of a barrel, boring it choked at both breech and muzzle, push the rod to the distance from the breech the enlarging is to commence, and then commence boring, leaving off where the muzzle choke is to commence.

If the bore of a barrel is made to taper from muzzle to breech, it will scatter. If made to taper too much from breech to muzzle, it will compress the shot, and by so doing mangle or deface them so that they will "shoot wild," while at the same time the effect on the gun will be to spring the barrel, and, if it be thin at the muzzle, as generally made, there is danger of enlargement of the bore at this portion of it.

Choke-Dressing a Gun Barrel.—A very slight variation in the size of the bore of a gun-barrel at one of its ends often has a marked effection its shooting. In case where a shotgun is disposed to "scatter" too much, the remedy lies in enlarging the bore at the breech. Choke-boring would be the means resorted to where such an operation was convenient; but where not, choke-dressing may be made to answer a very good purpose. This consists in dressing out the breech with fine emery paper or cloth, wrapped upon a round wooden rod. A little oil should be used in finishing the dressing, which need not extend above half the length from the breech to the muzzle. No particular attention need be given as to the slope, as the size of the bore, under this operation, is sure to be left largest at the breech.

Barrels most Suitable for Choke-Boring.—Laminated steel barrels are the most suitable for choke-bore guns, being harder and more tenacious than Damascus, and, therefore, resist the repeated strain of heavy charges better; they will be found to be more durable, and lead less than barrels of softer material. Barrels of plain steel, or decarbonized steel, so called, should never be used for choke-bore guns, as they are unsafe for guns with light muzzles. Decarbonized steel is most suitable for rifles, where great strength of metal is employed. The finest pattern in Damascus is not always desirable, as the excessive twisting necessary to make the fine pattern often weakens the fibre of the metal.

Freeing Gun Barrels.—It is often desired to free a barrel at the muzzle, or at both breech and muzzle; and the amount to be removed is so very little that it is hazardous to insert the boring bit for fear of removing too much. It is easily accomplished in this manner: Select a straight wood rod that does not quite fill the bore of the gun and saw a slit with a fine saw at one end, for about three or four inches, and parallel with the length of the rod. Cut strips of fine emery paper, or emery cloth, the width of which should be the same as the length of the slot, insert one end in the slot and wrap the projecting part around the rod, introduce this end into the barrel and work it up and down, if it be desired to finish the barrel that way, or turn it around by means of a bit stock or lathe if the finish is to be thus done.

Many gunsmiths cast soft lead at the end of a rod, using the muzzle of the gun as a size mould, and after removing from the barrel, apply oil and fine emery, and with this work the inside of the barrel.

Another Method.—There is another plan. Make a rod of soft pine wood that almost fills the bore and make a small hole, say about one-eighth of an inch diameter at the point where the saw kerf is to termi-

FIGURE 28.

nate. Cover this portion of the rod with good glue, made thin, and then roll it in the emery, the same as making an emery wheel or a buff-stick. When dry use it in the same way as the other forms of rod. When desired to increase the size, which will be necessary, a thin wedge can be inserted in the saw-kerf and pressed deeper in as the bore increases, or near as the rod diminishes its size. By wrapping the rod with fine twine where the hole is made there will be no danger of splitting the rod when the wedge is pushed in. The same form of wedge can be used in the rod first described, and at the same time the wedge will help keep the emery cloth or paper in place. The cut, Fig. 28, shows the rod as ready to receive the coating of emery.

Finishing Muzzles of Gun-Barrels.—To shorten a barrel, the general custom is to cut it off with a three-square file, by filing a groove around it, or else saw it off with a hack-saw; the latter method being preferable, as by sawing completely through the barrel the piece is removed with no temptation to sever it by bending, as is often the case when cutting off with a file.

After the piece is removed use a tool like the one shown in Fig. 29, to square up the end. This tool

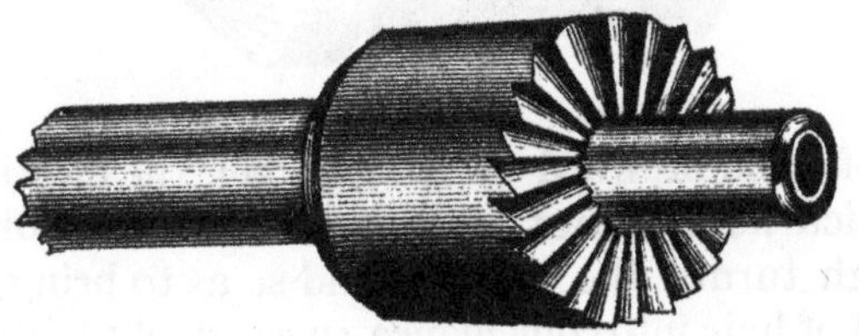

FIGURE 29.

has a cutting part an inch in diameter and about an inch long. It is turned smaller back of the cutting portion, to make it lighter or better to handle. A hole, three-eighths of an inch diameter, is made centrally in the cutting end, and in this hole are inserted iron or brass plugs made to fit, and the other end of a size to fit the bore of different guns. After the barrel is squared up, bevel the inner edge of the muzzle with the tool, Fig. 30, which is nothing more than a common "rose-head," and is made with similarly formed cutting teeth. About sixteen teeth are sufficient for these tools. The rose head tool has the cutting end about an inch diameter and nearly the same length, one-half the length being taken up by the pointed cutting end.

Old Method of Straightening Barrels.—The old-time method of straightening a gun-barrel was by means of a fine thread of black silk or a hair, which was passed through the bore of the barrel. This line was drawn tight by being stretched from two

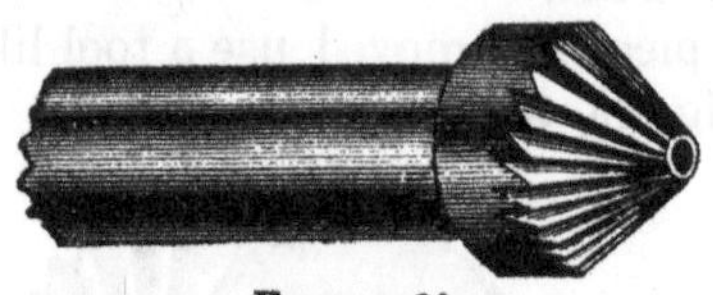

FIGURE 30.

ends of a rod of wood or spring steel, the elasticity of which kept it taut, and the workman looking through turned the barrel round so as to bring the thread of hair into coincidence successively with every portion of the inner surface. If there existed any concavity in any part of this surface, the thread would show it by the distance which would there appear between the thread itself and its reflection in the metal.

The New Method.—There is another process of straightening barrels which was explained by a writer in a scientific paper a few years ago, which is termed "straightening by the shade," and by this method barrels can be straightened with a greater degree of precision than by any other known process. The principle is something like this: If we examine a plane mirror for the purpose of ascertaining whether its reflecting surface is a true plane, we cause objects to be reflected from it to the eye at small angles of incidence. If under these circumstances every part of the mirror gives an image true to nature, he pronounces it perfect; for the slightest deviation from a true plane would cause a manifest distortion of the image. In the process of straightening barrels by the shade, crooks in the bore are detected upon the same principle. The internal surface of the barrel is a mirror, and whatever objects are reflected to the eye from any portion of it that lies beyond a certain distance, will be reflected under very small angles of incidence. As the interior surface of the barrel is not a plane mirror, the reflected image will not be true to nature. If the bore be straight, the image will have a normal distortion, which is due to the transverse or cylindrical curvature of the mirror; while if there be longitudinal flexures or crooks, there will be an abnormal distortion of the image, which will reveal the defect.

When the eye looks into a gun barrel the interior surface appears to be spread out into a plane circular disk, as far from the eye as the other end of the barrel. Through the centre of this disk is a circular orifice, and surrounding this at equal distances from it and from each other, respectively, are several well-defined concentric circles, dividing the disk into as many bright concentric rings, each of an apparent breadth, precisely equal to the diameter of the cen-

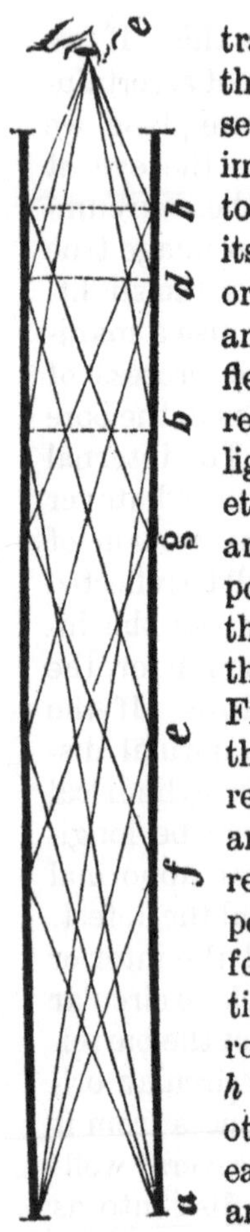

FIGURE 31.

tral orifice which is the other end of the bore as seen by direct vision. The several concentric circles are so many images of the end of the bore reflected to the eye from different points along its length. The first of these circles, or that nearest the central orifice, is an image formed by light once reflected. The second, third, fourth, etc., respectively, are images formed by light reflected two, three, four, times, etc. In order to see how these images are formed, and to find their respective points of location in the bore, consider that a ray of light from each point in the end of the calibre, as shown at *a*, Fig. 31, may pass to same point *b*, on the other side of the bore, and be thence reflected to the eye, thus forming at *b*, an image at the end of the bore, of one reflection. Another ray from the same point may pursue the route *a*, *c*, *d*, *e*, forming an image at *d* of two reflections. Another ray may take the route, *a*, *f*, *g*, *h*, *e*, forming an image at *h* by three reflections, and so on for the other images since in the formation of each of these images, respectively, the angles of incidence and reflection are equal, it follows that the focus, or point of place of the image *b*, formed by one reflection of light, is at one-third of the distance from the eye to the further end of the bore; that formed by two reflections *d*, is one-fifth; that by three reflections is one-seventh, and the succeeding ones, one-ninth, one-eleventh, etc., of the same distance.

Therefore, it will be observed that all these images are located within the third part of the length of the bore nearest to the eye. Consequently there are two-thirds of the entire length of the bore in which none of these images appear. It is to this part of the bore, only that the workman directs his attention, for it is here only that he can cause the "shade" to appear which discloses the crooks in the bore if any exist. When this part is straightened, he inverts the barrel and works from the other end.

The practical application of the process is made in this manner: the workman has a rest, generally consisting of an upright strip of board of convenient height with a V cut in its upper end for convenience in resting the barrel in case of rotating it. Across a window opposite, at almost any distance, say about ten or twelve feet, is nailed horizontally, a strip of board like a common lath, as the horizontal bar of the window sashes where they come together at the middle of the window (provided there be upper and lower sashes) will answer nearly as good a purpose. Now place one end of the barrel in the V of the rest, look into the bore, directing the eye to the lower side of it and to the point just beyond the image *b*; gradually depress the end held in the hand, bringing the direction nearer and nearer to the horizontal strip, or the sash bar as the case may be, and a dark shade is soon seen as shown at *m*, Fig. 32. This is the reflected image of the horizontal strip, or sash bar, the curved part of the outline being the image of the straight-edge. Depress the end more and more and the shade lengthens to *n*, *o*, *p*, etc. If the bore be perfectly straight, the shade will always maintain a true and symmetrical parabolic form, growing more and more pointed at its apex, until it reaches the further end of the bore. But if there be even the slightest flexure or crook in the bore the parabolic figure of the shade will be distorted. If a distortion be discovered, the barrel is slowly revolved about its axis as it is retained in the rest; at the same time slightly elevating and depressing the end held in the hands, until the shade assumes a form in which the two sides near the apex are equally drawn in toward each other as shown at *q*. If the crook be considerable the two sides may be drawn quite together, cutting off a portion of the shade of the apex as at *r*.

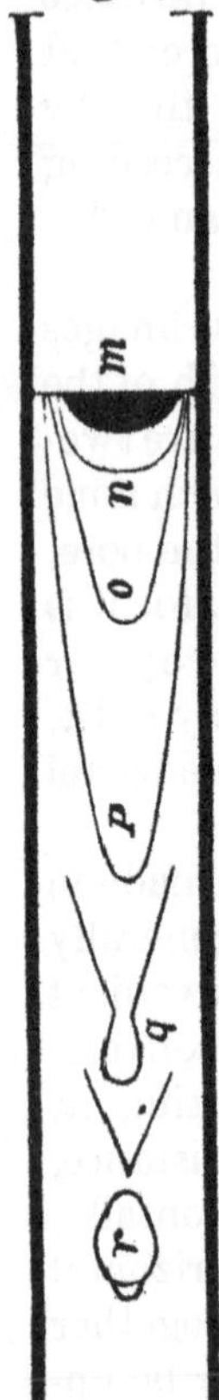

FIGURE 32.

This tells that there is a crook at *q*, and also tells that the bore is concave downward at that point. It will require some experience to tell how far that point is from the eye, but when that is learned, the fore-finger placed upon this point on the under side of the barrel tells where the blow must be given to straighten it as it ought to be.

Another Method.—Another method to ascertain if a barrel be straight, is to insert a slip of card into the muzzle of the gun and then look through the bore to the light. If the slip of card be properly placed the "shade" can readily be seen. The card slip need not be more than one-quarter of an inch in width and in length to just fit the muzzle so that it will be retained in place. It must be placed with the edge of the card toward the eye.

Fitting Barrels Together.—When selecting a pair of gun barrels, preparatory to joining them for the purpose of making a double-barreled gun, it is necessary to ascertain if the barrels be of the same length, and have the same size at breech and muzzle, and also at points between the breech and muzzle. Nearly all shot-gun barrels are ground, or made some smaller at the centre of their length than at other portions. Any one who is not conversant with this may be somewhat surprised on placing a straight-edge along the side of a barrel, a common musket barrel, for instance. Place the straight-edge on the top or bottom side, as the right and left hand sides are flattened, near the breech, and, of course, on these sides the hollowing of the centre is not so readily observed.

As the musket barrel has been mentioned, it may be inferred that two of these barrels are to be joined together. The first step is to cut them off at either end, to make them of the length desired, for as issued from the armories for army use, the barrels are too long to make a gun to be handled with ease and convenience. If they are cut down to the length of thirty or thirty-two inches they will be long enough for sporting purposes. According to the weight of gun desired, cut from either end; cut off the breech if a light gun is wanted, or cut off the muzzle to make a heavy gun.

The first step after cutting off and truing up the ends of the barrels, is to select the two sides to be joined together and file these two sides flat, more at the breech and less at the muzzle, until the smaller diameters at the middle just touch each other, without being so filed.

When you have in this way both barrels flattened as nearly alike as possible and as straight as can be done by testing with a straight-edge, lay both barrels on a level surface, and see that the flattened places touch each other true and evenly. To know if the flattening has been done parallel with the outside flats at the breech (supposing these to be left on the barrels) place a small square on the same surface on which the barrels are laid, letting the upright arm of the square just touch the outside flat. If the square touch the flat alike from top to bottom, then the flats are parallel, but if there be an open space to be seen, then file away the flat to be joined until the square indicates that both inner and outer flats are parallel. Be particular in regard to this, as it is easier to correct the inner flattened surface than to make parallel the outer one.

If the same amount be taken from the breech as from the muzzle, the point of divergence will not be sufficient for accurate shooting. More must be taken from the breech to allow of this divergence to be extended a greater distance. The flattening at the muzzle does not require to be very great, yet must be done to some extent; but, as before remarked, this will depend upon the smallness or size of the middle portions of the barrel.

It is very doubtful if any two gunsmiths will agree as to the inclination of a pair of barrels. Perhaps it would be almost foolishness to insist on any definite or certain inclination, so that the converging lines would come to a point. As an instance, let the point of divergence be two and a half yards, it follows that at forty yards the right barrel, if the gun were rigidly held as if fixed in a vice, would throw its charge about six inches to the left of the mark, and the left barrel, *vice versa*.

Let it be supposed that two barrels are each thirty-two inches in length and one-sixteenth inch thick at the muzzle and three-sixteenths thick at the breech, it requires the difference four-sixteenths be multiplied by the times the length of the barrels are contained in the forty yards, this being forty-five, to ascertain what distance the point of the different lines are from each other. In this case it is eleven and one-quarter inches, or five inches and five-eighths of an inch from the centre or line of sight. It may be remarked that if the point of convergence be forty yards it will be productive of as good results, perhaps, as any other.

Joining Barrels Together.—After the barrels are fitted together so that they are parallel, touching each other their entire length and equally in a vertical line, the next thing in order is to fit the top and bottom ribs. Fit the lower thimble or pipe through which the cross-bolt goes and cut the under rib to fit both above and below it, as this thimble is soldered direct to the barrels, not to the rib. Mark along the sides of the ribs with a sharp scriber, so as to leave a distinct line on the barrels to indicate their location. File bright and smooth the parts of the pipe and ribs where they are to be joined to the barrels and tin with good soft solder. Also tin the barrels where they are to be joined, and where the ribs come in contact. This is easily done by using a clear charcoal fire and heating the barrels and ribs quite slowly. Use muriate of zinc for flux, and apply the solder with a common soldering copper. If the copper be quite heavy and well heated the ribs can be tinned from the heat of the copper, as there is no need of putting these parts in the fire. If the barrels be properly heated and the solder beaten out thin on an anvil, it may be rubbed on the barrels without the aid of the copper. When it melts and flows, wipe off the surplus with a woolen rag which has been slightly moistened with oil.

When the barrels and other parts are nicely tinned, let them cool, and then fasten them in place in the manner they are to remain with binding-wire. Put a rod of iron through the lower thimble, and also through the upper thimbles, if they are to be fastened at this time. The reason of putting in this rod is twofold: it serves to keep the thimbles straight with the barrels, so as to properly receive the ramrod, and at the same time tends to hold the under rib firmly in place.

Before fastening the parts with binding wire, fill the space between the top rib and barrels with small pieces of solder, or what is better, a small rod of solder like a wire, but not large enough to interfere with the rib fitting close to the barrels.

Soldering Barrels Together.—Now begin to carefully heat the work, commencing at the breech, and when sufficiently hot, don't heat too fast nor too hot, apply solder, using the muriate of zinc as a flux, to the joinings of the ribs and barrels. If the solder be hammered quite thin it will be readily melted by the heat of the barrels, and will be "sucked in" until the space between the different pieces is completely filled. Proceed carefully in this way until the entire length of the barrels is gone over. Turn the work often in the fire, so that all portions are evenly heated. At the muzzle fit and insert a small piece to fill the interstice between the barrels and the top rib.

It is necessary that all the space between the top rib and the barrels be completely filled with solder, or rust will form there, which will prove of serious detriment to the barrels, and in time work under the ribs, throwing them from the barrels if even a little torsion or springing of the barrels should ever take place.

During the progress of soldering, see that the parts are kept pressed close together, and that they do not spring away from each other by their expansion during heating. A small iron clamp screw placed at the breech and also one at the muzzle, is very convenient, as by tightening the screw there is less danger of the parts springing apart. When the breech is soldered and somewhat cooled, the clamp there placed can be removed. These clamps, made of malleable iron, can be obtained at the hardware stores.

When the work is soldered and is cool, wash it well with warm water, using a stiff brush to remove dirt and all traces of the acid flux that may remain on the work. With a chisel or scraper remove all superfluous solder and brighten the work with emery cloth or paper of different grades. Begin with the coarser and finishing with the fine or with flour and emery.

Why not Braze Barrels?—It was formerly the practice to braze barrels together, with spelter solder, at the breech or at both breech and muzzle, but good workmen condemn the practice, as heating the barrels to a high heat in order to melt this solder somewhat diminishes the strength of the metal, and as it is also necessary to again clean and brighten the work after brazing, and to perfectly brighten the flats where they lie together is not so easy a matter.

In the life of the gun, it was found to be of no real benefit to thus braze them, as the parts were securely held in place if well soldered with soft solder, and of late years but very few barrels have been thus brazed.

Select solder of good quality, put the work well together, and the barrels will remain firmly and rigidly in place, and will not be separated except by unfair means.

Percussioning.—The term Percussioning is used to designate the operations of drilling, and finishing the cone or nipple seat, tapping, putting in the tube or cone (by some called nipple) and otherwise finishing up the parts bearing relationship to the cone seat.

The first operation, after ascertaining the locality where to drill the hole for the nipple, is to drill this hole. If a double gun the nipples must be inserted as near the centre of the breech as possible to get them and have a direct communication, with no unnecessary angles, in the passage-way of the flame of the cap to the powder in the chamber. From the bottom of the hole drilled for the nipple a small vent, as small as can conveniently be made, must or ought to communicate directly to the powder chamber. The nipple ought to be seated or screwed to the bottom of the hole and the vent be an unbroken continuation of the opening through the nipple. Let there be no chamber or reservoir between the bottom end of the nipple and the bottom of the hole in which it is screwed.

But to return to the drilling. From the axial or central line of the barrel, this hole must be drilled at an angle of forty-five degrees so that the nipple when inserted shall stand at that angle. In the cut Fig. 33, *a* represents the central line of the barrels, *b* a line at right angles to this, and *c* the angle of forty-five degrees. If the workman have no lathe and is necessitated to use a bit-stock or breast drill, a piece of iron can be fitted to lay upon the barrels with one end elevated three or four inches with the end turned

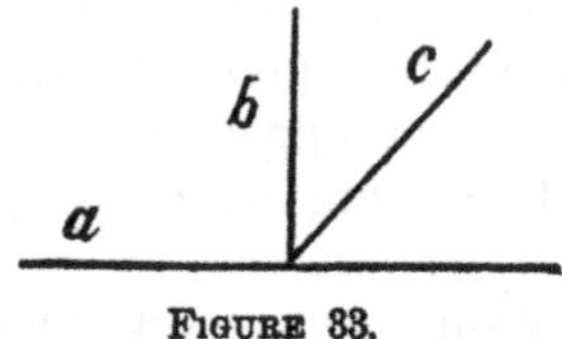

FIGURE 33.

at an angle in a hole drilled in this end to receive the drill, which should fill the hole. By clamping this upon the barrels, inserting the drill in the hole and having a prick mark where the hole is to be made for the nipple, it forms a reliable guide to insure the correctness of the hole, and also to get any number of holes alike. To insure the hole to be tapped or threaded properly the guide can be kept in position and the hole tapped after being cupped to form the seat.

If a lathe be used to drill the hole, a piece of wood or an iron forging can be fitted to the spindle against which the work is held and when made of the proper angle and the barrel confined upon it to drill the hole, no guide is necessary, as the drill being held in the spindle and the spindle running in its bearings operates upon the same principle as the guide clamped upon the barrels. An upright drill can. be fitted with a forging or casting to hold the barrels in the same manner.

The size of hole to be drilled ought to be that of the smaller sized nipples, as in time frequent re-tappings to insert new nipples will enlarge the hole. Perhaps a broken nipple may necessitate drilling or cutting out and the thread may be injured somewhat, so that it may have to be bored out and a new thread made to receive a larger nipple.

After the hole is drilled it is cupped or a seat formed for the shoulders of the nipple to rest upon.

FIGURE 34.

This is done with the tool shown in Fig. 34. The guide is used to get the proper angle of this seat, the same as in drilling. The stem at the end of the cutting portion of the tool, enters and fills the hole drilled, which insures the correct formation of the seat. The tap is held in the guide in the same manner and it follows that the thread has been made at the same angle that the hole was drilled.

Finishing Nipple Seat.—The filing and finishing of the nipple seat is one in which tastes differ or the price of the work may demand. This hint may be given, the seating tool must cut a seat large enough to receive the nipple and in filing keep this seat full size, taking care not to allow the file to take away or reduce any portion of it. A study of this portion of different guns that may come under the observation of the workman is the best guide for forming and shaping these parts. The first effort may be to form a nipple seat from a piece of hard wood shaped like the barrel with its lump, using the drill, the seating tool and even the tap, then finish up with files, as if it were iron, and insert the nipple. Better to correct a fault in a "sham" of wood than spoil a good barrel breech.

The Vent, in Percussion Gun Barrels.—When the old flint-lock was pushed to one side by the introduction of the percussion principle, it was thought by many that there was a difference in shooting and that the flint-lock shot "smoother" than its substitute. In the percussion gun there was thought to be more recoil than in the other form of gun. It was supposed that the hermetically closing of the breech, as the firing took place, was the cause of this, and to remedy the matter a small vent was drilled near the locality of the vent or "touch-hole" of the old-time arm. A few gunsmiths and many users of arms cling to the vent and could "not do without it." Some claim that this vent is of use, as it enables air to circulate through the barrel, after the ignition of the charge. While both these theories are doubted by others, one thing is quite certain, it increases the certainty and also aids the rapid ignition of the charge, as the air contained among the powder and held there in a more or less state of pressure, being so forced and held by the wadding, retards in some measure the entrance of the fire from the percussion cap. The vent allows this confined air to escape, and that is the only real and apparent good that can be accredited to it. In making these vents make them very small, and in no instance let them exceed a thirty-second of an inch. To prevent their being closed by rust or the débris of burnt powder, drill a larger hole, tap a thread in it and screw in a silver wire and then drill the vent through the wire after it has been finished to conform to the shape of the parts adjacent.

The Patent Breech.—The patent breech has been the subject of much discussion and much experimenting, some experts claiming one form to be superior to others, and then again there are those who set the patent breech aside and claim that the old flat-faced breech-pin is as good as any ever yet made. The formation of the base of the breech-loading shell has been called up as evidence in favor of the latter claim. The two forms are called in question, and then the query is made, "Does not the breech-loader shoot better or as well as the patent-breeched muzzle-loader?" But the patent breech is in favor with the mass of those who use the muzzle-loader, and no doubt has its advantages. The attempt has been made to form the interior base of a cartridge for breech-loaders upon the model of the interior of a patent breech, but thus far has not come into very extensive use.

Form of the Chamber or Cup.—While many forms of the chamber or cup of the patent breech are in use, the most simple form, and the one easiest to make, is that of an inverted elliptical cone. This form may be represented by the shape of an acorn if it were cut off even with the top of the cup. The shape is also one that will not weaken the breech nor affect the strength of the thread where it enters the barrel. The tool to shape it is easy to make. Turn a piece of steel the exact shape the "cup" is to be and then make a cutting tool of it by filing a groove on two sides, exactly like a flat drill of the required elliptical form, but with a "bulge" or cheek left on each side, and then file a groove midway in this cheek from point to base, and make it so as to form two cutting edges on each side of the cut first made. Each prominent part must be formed into cutting edges, like the cutting edges of a conical-shaped cherry to cut out bullet moulds. The cut, of bullet cherry, Fig. 71, Chapter XXVII, shows the way to make this tool.

With this form of "cup" there is great solidity of breech, and there need be but little fear of missfire or hang-fire in shooting, if the gun be properly loaded.

CHAPTER XVII.

TOOLS FOR BREECHING GUNS.

Breeching Reamers. — The form of breeching reamers is shown in Fig. 35. The extension is supposed to fill the bore of the gun, and when it does so the tool will make a cut that is straight and true. When this extension does not fill, then slip a brass

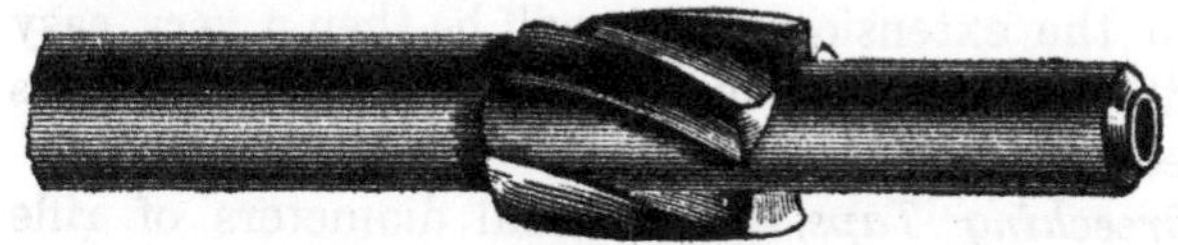

FIGURE 35.

ferrule or a piece of tubing on it, or it may be even wrapped with a piece of card or strong paper, as mentioned in case of taps that have extensions smaller than the bore of the gun.

The size of these reamers must be to suit the taps; that is they must be of a size corresponding to the tap if the thread were removed. The length of the extension may be about an inch, and the cutting portion of a length to correspond to the length of the breech-pins, for when using them where the reamer has entered the barrel until it is flush or even with the length of the cutting part, it is evident that it has penetrated as far as it ought to go.

Be careful to keep the reamer well oiled when using it to ream out a breech.

In making these reamers, turn them to the size and shape, and then file four spiral flutes, equi-distant from each other, with a small round file, but remember to file them "right hand," like a right hand screw thread. About a quarter's turn in the length is sufficient. The end where the cutting is done must be "cut back" between each flute, so as to make a cutting edge, or lip. The flutes serve to carry the chips away from the work, and prevent clogging. Above the end of the cutting portion, the reamer may be turned down to a size a little larger than the extension, and it will be then a very easy matter to nicely cut the flutes with a round file, as directed.

Breeching Taps.—The usual diameters of rifle breech pins are three-eighths, one-half, and five-eighths of an inch ; of shot guns three-quarters and seven-eighths of an inch. The thread of the rifle is generally fourteen to the inch, and the shot gun sixteen to the inch. The breech pins of military arms vary. Some are made with coarse thread and some with fine thread, ranging from ten to eighteen threads per inch. There is no arbitrary rule for breeching guns, and excepting English made guns, almost every conceivable size and thread may be found in guns that are brought in to be repaired. In rifle and shot guns the fourteen and sixteen thread will be found to predominate. In unbreeching guns that have been made by "experts" of some country town, who built the arms "to order," or in overhauling guns that have been repaired at the same kind of establishments, it will not be uncommon to find threads in the barrels that have been cut with a blacksmith's taper tap, and the pin tapered to suit the thread so formed. It will be nothing uncommon to find a breech that is made to one side of the bore, or made with a crooked thread. If tapped with the taper tap, the thread may be found to be ten or twelve to the inch, according as a tap to fit the breech could be found.

Let the workman discard all such ways of breeching guns. Let him procure a set of taps of the sizes and threads as noticed at the beginning of this arti-

FIGURE 36.

cle, and "stick to these sizes." If the thread in a gun be worn, and the pin be loose or leak fire, then ream out the old thread, cut it anew, and put in a new pin.

Breeching taps should be made in pairs, one tapered a little and its mate made straight and with a full thread, so as to cut full at the bottom where the thread terminates. If the first tap be not tapered a little, the thread should be nearly all removed at the end, and gradually increased for five or six threads, when it will be of full size. A stem or projection is made as shown in the cut, Fig. 36, which enters and fills the bore of the gun and so serves to insure a thread straight with the barrel. If the bore be larger than the extension, slip over it a piece of brass tube or a ferrule of some kind, until it fits a little snug in the bore. If but little be wanting to make the fit, a piece of writing paper or a bit of card may be wrapped around it. Old-fashioned

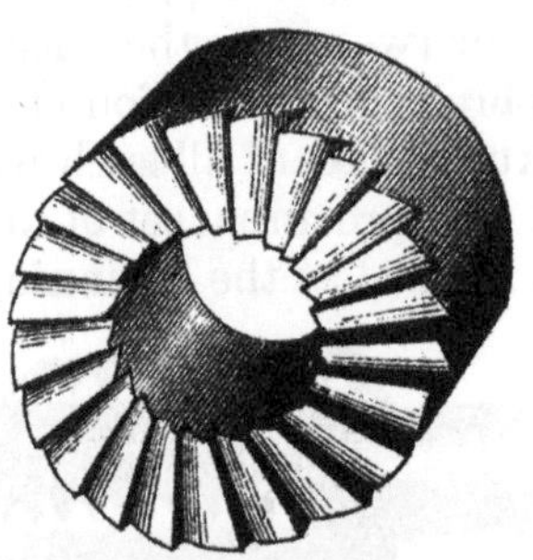

FIGURE 37.

gunsmiths have been known to wind tow around an extension to make a fit.

The diameter of these extensions must be that of the smallest bored gun in which they will be used. The extension of the shot-gun tap may be about half-inch diameter. The length of the extension may be about an inch for rifles and an inch and a quarter for shot guns, the thread about an inch in length. The whole length of rifle taps may be about three and a half inches, for shot-guns about four inches.

Breech Pin Formers.—These tools are made of steel and have holes drilled through them and cutting teeth formed on one end (as shown in Fig. 37). In use it may be held stationary, and the breech-pin turned in the hole until the teeth form it to size and remove enough in length for the screw to be cut on the pin. Eight teeth are enough for the smaller sizes of these tools. If made with more teeth they are consequently finer and shallower and do not operate so well, or cannot be ground to an edge or sharpened with an oil stone if they become dull. The sizes must correspond with the size of the breech taps, or a little less than this size, as the dies used in cutting generally "raise" a thread a little larger than the work. The length of these tools may be about three-fourths of an inch or an inch, as may be best to make them. In use they can be held in a lathe chuck and the pin presented to them while running, or the operation may be reversed, the pin being rotated and the cutter held stationary. If to be used by hand, hold them in a vise or clamp, or make a fixture to hold the pin, using a bit-stock for turning them for cutting.

The advantage of these tools is that the work is done quick, the body of the pin is of the same diameter, and the shoulder where it abuts against the barrel is true with the body; using a file for the work, it is difficult to produce these requirements.

CHAPTER XVIII.

TOOLS FOR CHAMBERING BREECH-LOADING BARRELS.

WHEN chambering barrels for breech-loaders, the utmost care should be observed to make the chamber exactly concentric with the bore, and have it smooth and well finished. Do not trust to a drill or a flat reamer; neither will a half-round or a common fluted reamer answer the purpose. Take, for instance, a bore for a thirty-eight cartridge. Fig.

FIGURE 38.

38 shows the tool for chambering, and Fig. 39 the tool for recessing for the head of the cartridge. The diameter of the tool for chambering is thirteen sixty-fourths. The tool for recessing for the head is seven-sixteenths. The body of the cutting portion is about seven-eighths or an inch long. An extension is formed beyond the cutting part which must exactly fill the bore of the barrel and serves as a guide to insure the cutting part making the chamber in proper relation to the bore.

The neck or recess in front of the cutting part is for a three-fold purpose; it forms a receptacle for the chips or cuttings, which otherwise would clog the tool as soon as the teeth were filled, and would probably result in a rough surface by being forced between the wall of the chamber and the tool back of the teeth; it also serves to produce a better shaped tooth, which is done with a fine cut three-

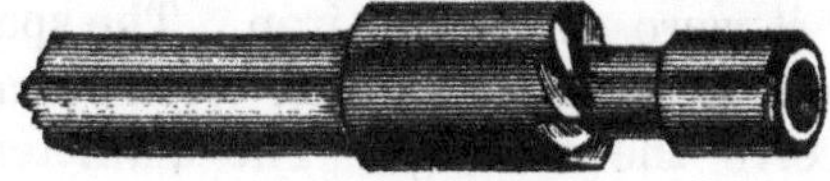

FIGURE 39.

square file, and finally by the teeth being made below the surface of the extension a square cut is produced with no feather edge where the chamber terminates.

The cutting teeth of the chambering tool are made so as to produce a bevel at the end of the chamber, and by this means avoid shaving the ball, as would be the case if it passed over a sharp angle. The recessing tool is made square on the cutting end.

For larger bores than a forty-four, the tools may be advantageously made a little different, as shown

FIGURE 40.

in Fig. 40. The shank of the tool may be made of a cheaper grade of steel and the extension much smaller than the bore of the gun. At *a*, is shown a steel thimble that is turned to the proper size and has teeth cut on the end. This is tempered and is put on over the extension and held by a wire or pin passing through both thimble and extension. At *b* is another thimble, made preferably of brass, that fits the bore. It can then be worked in the barrel with less fear of scratching the barrel, as might be the case if it were of steel or iron. The space left between the brass thimble and the teeth forms a recess to receive the cuttings. The diameter of a twelve gauge chambering tool will be about forty-nine sixty-fourths, and the diameter of the chambering tool will be about twenty-seven thirty-seconds. The length of the cutting thimbles can be about one inch. The brass thimbles about three-quarters of an inch. The cutting thimbles should rest against a shoulder, as at *c*. These thimbles should be fastened, a finish turned on the shanks on which they are to remain, after the shanks are turned. The brass thimbles are held by being driven on the extension, and should be turned up true after being driven in place.

When making these tools, form the cutter for the chamber about one-hundredth of an inch larger than the bore of the cartridge to allow for easy extraction. The brass thimbles ought to be of the size of the interior of the cartridge, which is supposed to be exactly the same as the bore. The tool for recessing the head may be a trifle larger, say about a thirty-second, than the diameter of the cartridge head. If it be made one-sixteenth larger it will not matter. Eight cutting teeth are enough for these tools.

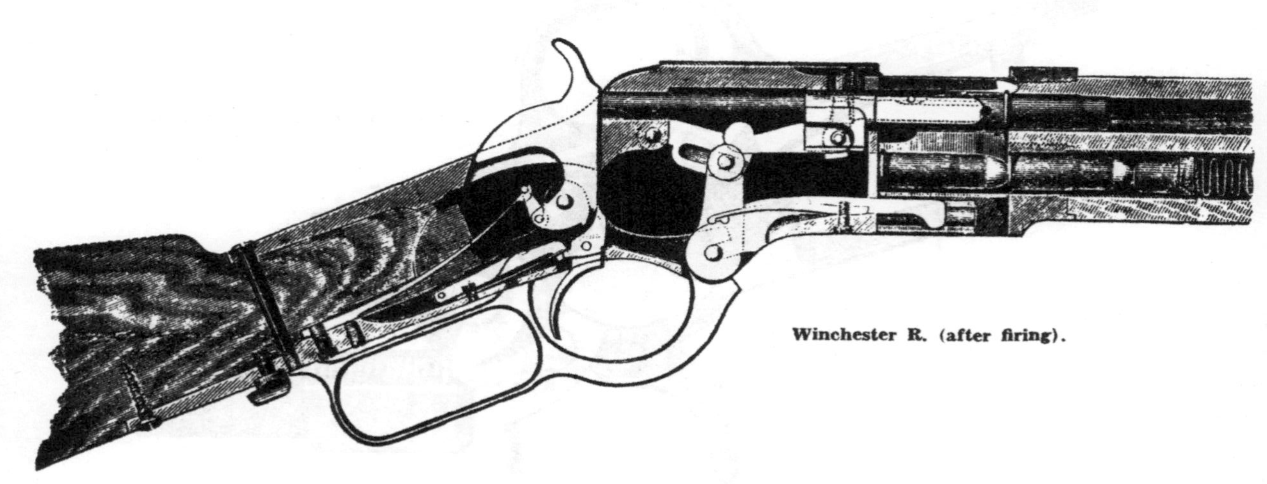

Winchester R. (after firing).

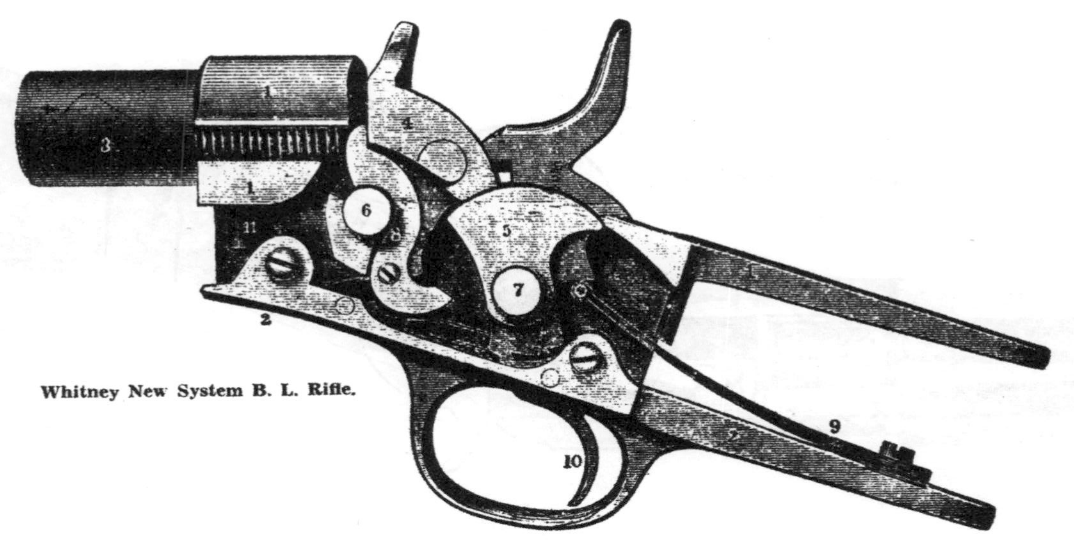

Whitney New System B. L. Rifle.

CHAPTER XIX.

ON GUN RIBS.

How to Straighten a Gun Rib.—Gun ribs, as received from the manufacturer or dealer, are more or less crooked and winding and must be made straight before being fastened to the gun barrel. Sometimes this straightening can be done with the hands alone, by bending and twisting the rib. If there are short crooks, the hammer must be used. Select a hammer that has a flat pene and this pene must be "across" or at right angles to the handle. See that the pene is not too sharp, but smooth and rounded at its edge. Place the rib to be straightened on a piece of hard wood plank, or what is better, get a piece of two-inch plank about a foot wide and long enough to reach from the floor to a height a little above the work-bench, say about the height of the top of the vise. It may be held in an upright position by means of a screw passing through it into the bench, or it can be so held by setting it on the floor and clamping one side between the jaws of the vise. On this hold the rib, lengthwise with the end of the plank, and using the pene of the hammer, strike blows on the inner or curved side of the rib. Do not strike hard enough to dent or bruise the rib so as to show on the opposite side. By a little practice a rib can be made very straight and true.

How to Fit a Rib.—Sometimes one side of a rib is longer than the other. Fit it into a properly shaped groove in a piece of board, clamp it so as to hold firmly and file away the longer side so as to match the narrow one. The clamps can be made of two pieces of wood placed on each side of the part to be filed, holding them and the rib with wood screws, the rib being moved along as a portion is filed.

How to Fit a Rib to an Octagon Barrel.—To fit a rib to an octagon barrel, file the portion where it comes in contact, square across so as to have all the surface possible to touch the barrel. To fit it to a round barrel, file lengthwise with a half-round file, and so file that the outer edges will fit close, leaving the inner edges a little open, or not quite touching the barrel A half-round file for fitting ribs to round barrels should have the tang bent toward the flat side so that when the file handle is put on, it will not interfere with filing.

How to Solder on a Rib.—The inner edges of the rib must be filed bright and smooth, so must that portion where it touches the barrel. Bear in mind that s lder will not adhere, unless the surface is made bright. This being done wet a short length of the rib with soldering acid, warm it to a proper heat in the forge fire, and with a common soldering copper, also properly heated, tin or cover the melted surface with solder. With the acid wet another distance, say about three inches, heat and tin this, and so repeat until the entire length of the rib has been gone over. Be careful to have plenty of solder adhering to the inner sides. Also be very careful not to heat the rib so as to blue or blacken it, for when so done no solder will adhere, and the surface so made must be brightened up again before going any further with the tinning.

The next thing to be done is to draw-file the gun barrel where the rib is to be fastened on, and care must be taken to have the surface bright and clean, or the solder will not adhere. Place the breech end of the barrel in a clean charcoal fire and carefully warm it sufficiently, wet with the acid, and with the soldering copper tin over where it was draw-filed.

Two tests can be applied to learn if the barrel be sufficiently heated. One is that when a drop of acid is put on it will "sizzle" or boil; the other test is to hold it close to the cheek and if a warm "glow" of heat is felt from it, it is hot enough.

When the surface is tinned, and before the barrel is cold enough so as to harden the solder, wipe off the surplus with a rag, and if the rag be slightly oiled, it will operate all the better. The solder used is common soft solder such as used by tinsmiths. Repeat the process of heating and tinning three or four inches at a time, until the entire length of the barrel has been gone over. Then, after it is cool, place the rib in position, confining it in place with binding wire, putting it round both rib and barrel, twisting the ends pretty firmly together. Fasten the rib in this way, at intervals of about six inches, being careful that the rib is held evenly, closely and firmly to the barrel.

Now commence at the breech, heat both barrel and rib carefully, avoiding all smoke and soot, wetting the joint on each side of the rib with the acid, touching the part with solder taken up on the point of the heated soldering copper. The surplus solder on the inner surface of the rib will flow down to the joint, between the rib and the barrel, as it is heated, and by touching the joint with the copper charged with solder, the outer edges of the joint will be completely filled, and both barrel and rib be perfectly united. So continue until the rib is soldered its entire length. When cool remove the binding wires, and wash thoroughly with warm water. This will remove the acid, which would otherwise rust the bright surface. Wipe dry and if the work is to stand for any length of time, oil it lightly by rubbing it over with a rag that is moistened with oil.

The best way to remove the surplus solder at the joints is by means of scrapers. Take an old flat file, about six inches long, grind the teeth clean off on each side for an inch or two at the end, and also grind the end "square." By using this tool in the same way that a chisel is used, it is very effective. A scraper made of an old three-square file with the teeth ground away at the end is also a good tool. Carefully remove all traces of solder or it will show after the barrel has been used a little. If the work is to be browned, the browning will not "take" where the solder remains.

How to Re-solder Ribs.—It often happens that double guns are brought in that have the top rib loosened from the barrels at the breech, and sometimes the soldering of the barrels, also at the breech, has been broken, so that they are quite separated. The cause of this is generally an effort to remove the patent breeches by some one who has not the proper appliances for the work. The barrels being caught in a vise, and a monkey-wrench, or some similar kind of wrench, applied, and as the breeches fit very tight, perhaps being rusted somewhat, considerable force is applied, and the torsion or twisting so occasioned starts and separates the parts as described.

To re-unite these parts, remove the breeches, carefully raise the rib as far as can be done without bending it, and hold it thus in place by inserting a slip of wood so as to retain it. Use a slim-pointed scraper and scrape bright and clean the surface of the rib, and both barrels, where the rib comes in contact. Tin the parts with a heavy soldering copper, but do not put them in the fire to heat them ; rely solely on the heat of the copper, taking time to do the work. When nicely tinned, put the rib in place, confining it with binding wire, and finish the soldering in the forge fire, the same as when putting on new ribs.

Before putting the rib in place, fill the space between the rib and barrels pretty full of solder, cut in strips, like pieces of wire. If necessary, use the copper to assist the soldering, as they are being worked in the fire.

A scraper for such work may be made of a small

three-square file, say about four inches long; grind the sides so as to remove the teeth, and sharpen to a point.

As a precaution against starting the rib from the barrel by heating, put pieces of binding wire tightly around, both above and below, twisting them tightly. With this security there will be no harm done even if the solder be melted between rib and barrel, in proximity to the thimble.

Height of Ribs.—The only way to ascertain the proper height of a gun rib, when put on the barrels, is to take the length of the barrels, and from this length make the calculation, as different lengths require some difference in height of rib. It is to be supposed that forty yards is the distance from the shooter to the object fired at, and at this distance a heavy charge of shot will drop about twelve inches. As the sights on shot guns are fixed, it is necessary that the rib be so elevated as to compensate for this dropping of twelve inches. Of course a lighter charge of shot will not drop so much as the heavy one, but the calculation may be based on the heavy charge.

To ascertain the elevation at the breech, take the thickness of the breech and muzzle and multiply the difference by as many times as the length of the barrels is contained in the forty yards. This gives the elevation of the barrels without the rib, and the difference must be made out by elevating the rib. Many shooters complain that when their barrels have been shortened the shooting is not the same, and they lay this fault to the barrels being cut shorter, when it is often due to the difference of elevation from that they were accustomed to use. Suppose a pair of barrels were to be shortened, say, four inches, at the same elevation there will be more lengths in the forty yards, hence a difference in the sighting and consequently in the shooting.

The calculation for the elevation of ribs is the same as that given for fitting barrels together, and the same principles there given will apply to this subject.

CHAPTER XX.

ON THIMBLES.

How to Make Thimbles.—What is called a thimble by gunsmiths is the short tube, soldered, or otherwise attached to the gun barrel, which retains the ramrod in place when not in use. To make these thimbles, form them on a piece of steel about a foot long, turned tapering; the large end being about nine-sixteenths, and the small end about five-sixteenths of an inch in diameter. This will answer for about all sizes of wooden rods as they are purchased. These rods are generally, the largest of them, about five-eighths of an inch diameter at the large end and about three-eighths at the small end.

The thimbles may be made of brass, iron, or German silver, according to taste, but iron is generally preferred. Take common sheet or Russia iron, the same as used for making stove-pipe. The best thickness is about twenty-two or twenty-three, by the English gauge. For convenience, get the sheet cut in strips from an inch to an inch and a-half in width—the tinsmith's squaring shears being a ready means to cut up the sheet into strips. Generally make the upper thimble about an inch and a half long, and the lower or middle thimbles, be these one or two, a little narrower, say, about an inch. For permanency and looks a long thimble is preferable. Cut off pieces from the strips of sheet-iron, just long enough to go around the ramrod, then roll them up like a tube by bending them around a tapered steel rod, using a small hard wood mallet for the purpose, holding them in the vise to assist in the operation.

For rifle rods, which are not tapered, the thimbles may be rolled up on a straight piece of steel, a trifle larger than the rod, so that the rod will slide easily within when put in place. Take pains in forming them, so that the fold or joint will come evenly and squarely together.

How to Put Thimbles on Barrels.—File bright and tin the thimbles where they are to be joined to the rib. Observe if the thimbles fit the rod properly by putting the rod in them and then inserting the rod in place in the gun stock. Mark the place on the rib or barrel where the thimbles are to be fastened, and remove both rod and thimbles from the gun. If to be attached to a rib, file a spot the length of the thimbles where it was marked, and file it of a depth equal to the thickness of the metal of which the thimble is made. Too deep filing may cut through the rib, and too little filing will leave the thimble projecting above the rib, so that the rod will hit or rub as it is being pushed down in place. Also let the joint of the thimble come in the centre of the rib when it is soldered in place. Tin the places filed, by heating the barrel carefully over the forge fire, using the soldering acid as for tinning the thimbles. A common tinner's soldering copper is best to apply the solder.

When the barrel is cool enough to handle put the thimbles on the rod, and the rod in place as it is intended to be when finished. Confine the thimbles to the barrel with pieces of binding wire, using two pieces to a thimble, one at each end. By putting the rod into the thimbles and confining them thus, there is no danger of their being "askew" after being fastened, and by putting on two wires there is less danger of their moving while being soldered to the barrel.

Make a clear fire in the forge, using charcoal if it can be obtained, heat the barrel very carefully until small pieces of solder will be melted when placed on the inside of the thimble. Have the soldering copper heated, and by using it and applying the acid an even amount of the solder can be applied to the joint outside the thimble where it joins the barrel. When all are soldered let the barrel cool, remove the binding wires and wash with warm water to remove the acid flux, which would rust the work. A stiff brush is best to wash with. Scrape off the superfluous solder, rub the thimbles bright with emery-cloth, or let them remain the black color, as may be desired.

CHAPTER XXI.

ON RIFLING OF GUNS.

Importance of Rifling.—In a rifle the grooving is of the utmost importance; for velocity without accuracy is useless. To determine the best kind of groove has been, accordingly, the object of the most laborious investigations. The ball requires an initial rotary motion sufficient to keep it "spinning" up to its range, and is found to gain in accuracy by increasing this rotary speed; but if the pitch of the grooves be too great, the ball will refuse to follow them; but being driven across them, "strips"—that is, the lead in the grooves is torn off, and the ball goes on without rotation. The English gunsmiths avoided the dilemma by giving the requisite pitch and making the grooves very deep, and even by having wings or lugs cast on the ball to keep it in the grooves—expedients which increase the friction in the barrel and the resistance of the air enormously.

The American gun-makers solved the problem by adopting the "gaining twist," in which the grooves start from the breech nearly parallel to the axis of the barrel, and gradually increase the spiral, until, at the muzzle, it has the pitch of one revolution in three to four; the pitch being greater as the bore is less. This gives, as a result, safety from stripping, and a rapid revolution at the exit, with comparatively little friction and shallow groove-marks on the ball, accomplishing what is demanded of a rifled barrel, to a degree that no other combination of groove and form of missile ever has. There is no way of rifling so secure as that in which the walls of the grooves are parts of radii of the bore. They should be numerous, that the hold of the lands, or the projection left between the grooves, may divide the friction and resistance as much as possible, and so permit the grooves to be as shallow as may be. Fig. 41 represents grooves cut in this way,

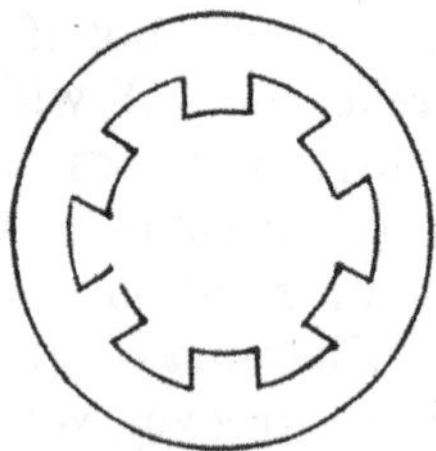

FIGURE 41.

but exaggerated to show more clearly their character. In the Kentucky rifle this law is followed, except that for convenience in rifling, the grooves are made of the same width at the bottom and top, as shown in Fig. 42, which is, for the grooves of the depth of which they are generally made, practically the same, the depth in the cut being two or three times that generally used.

U. S. Rifling Machines.—The rifling machines

in use by the U. S. Government at the Springfield Armory for cutting their grooved rifles may thus be described: The barrel is placed in a horizontal position in an iron frame, and held there very firmly. The grooves are made by three short steel cutters placed within three mortices, made to receive them, near the end of a steel tube which is moved through the bore of the barrel by slow rotary and progressive motion. The cutters are narrow pieces of steel having upon one side three angular shaped teeth about one-sixteenth of an inch

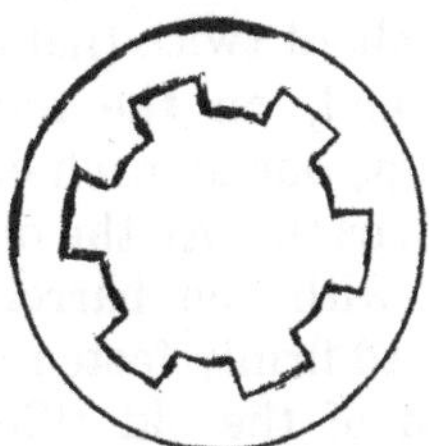

FIGURE 42.

in height, and of the width of the groove, ground to a very sharp edge at the top. It is these which produce the rifling. The three cutters, when inserted in the tube, form upon their inner surface a small opening which decreases toward the inner end. Into this is inserted a tapered steel rod, and is so controlled by a connecting cog-wheel that this rod is pushed, at every revolution, a little further into the tapered opening formed by the inner edges of the three cutters. The effect of this is to increase the pressure of the cutters upon the inner surface of the barrel, and thus gradually, at each stroke of the machine, deepen the cuts as produced by the rifling. The rod makes about twelve revolutions in a minute and it occupies about thirty minutes to rifle a barrel.

Old-Fashioned Rifling Machine.—But the gun-maker who builds rifles to order, and perhaps then but a single one at a time, uses quite a different apparatus for rifling, although the principle involved is the very same. Many of the old gunsmiths made their own rifling machines. The simplest form was a common joist, two inches thick and six inches wide. The length about twice that of any barrel to be rifled. At one end, on the narrow side, was fixed in two bearings, one at each end so as to turn freely, an old rifle barrel. At the other end of the timber, in a line with the barrel was fixed two standards in which to firmly fasten the barrel to be rifled. At the end of the old rifle barrel, and on the end nearest to the end of the timber was fixed a circular plate of iron, like a wheel which was made with divisions on its circumference, and had a catch which was fastened to the wood, and when the end of this catch engaged one of the divisions it would firmly hold the barrel in place. When this plate was turned the barrel also turned. Inside of this barrel was placed a rod of iron, around which was cast some soft metal, as babbit metal or old type metal, or even lead. This was done by putting the rod in the barrel and then pouring in the metal when melted. A handle, similar to an auger handle was fixed transversely to one end, but in such a manner as to turn around freely on the rod. As the rod was pushed back and forth the soft metal followed the rifling grooves, and this caused a turn, first in one direction and then in another. By the rod being loose on the handle the hands were held in the same position.

The rifling rod was attached to the opposite end of the rod in the old barrel and carried a cutter let into a narrow groove made in the extreme end of the rifling rod. Very often these rods were made of wood like a straignt ramrod. It is evident if a barrel be placed in the clamps and the rifling rod bearing a suitable cutter be entered in the bore of the barrel and the rod thurst forward by pushing it with the handle, that a faint spiral like cut will be the result. When the cutter had done its work, or done all that it would cut, the plate was turned one division, rotating the old barrel with the rifling rod just that amount, the barrel to be rifled, of course, not being turned at all. Another cutting was done like the first one, then another, and so on until the complete circle of the divisions had been made, and a certain number of faint rifles made in the fixed barrel. The cutter was then removed from its slot, a slip of writing paper placed in the bottom of the slot and the cutter put in place and a repetition of the same operation gone over again, and then repeated until the rifling was of the desired depth. Oil was supplied to the centres while going back and forth in their work.

Gain Twist Rifling Machine.—What is called a gain twist was made with a slightly different apparatus. What is termed a "lead" was fixed so as to revolve in standards, and at the same time be capable of being thrust forward and pulled back to its starting place. This lead carried at one end the rifling rod. At the opposite end the handle for operating it, was fixed. The lead was several inches in diameter and the holes in the standards that supported it of like diameter. One make of lead had a groove cut spiralling in its surface and exactly the same as the rifling to be made. In one of the standards a stud was fixed that entered the groove and compelled it to turn according as the groove was made. The barrel to be rifled was fixed so as to turn as needed to make the different rifles or grooves. Another make of lead had a rib made of a strip of hard wood that was bent around the rod and was held in place by screws. This rib was the counterpart of the rifling and was received in a mortice cut for it in one of the standards, the management of the rifling rod being the same in all cases.

Re-rifling.—One method of re-rifling is to make a rod with a mortice in one end to receive a rifling cutter or "saw" as some term them, and fix at the other end a handle like an auger handle, but so fixed that the rod will turn around freely no matter how the handle may be held. This rod is inserted in the barrel to be re-rifled and the cutter forced through one of the rifles, which must be deep enough to force it to follow its direction when pushed forward and pulled back until it would cut no more, it would be placed in another rifle and so continued until the circuit of the rifling is made. A slip of paper is then put under the cutter and a repetition of the process made and continued until the rifles are cut as deep as desired.

If it be feared that the rifles, opposite to those where the cutter is at work, will be injured by its bearing upon them, a dove-tailed groove is made across the rod opposite where the cutter is placed, and in this is fitted a slip of wood that is cut to fit the curvature of the base of the barrel. If a bit of half-round file or a cutter be made to be inserted in place of the slip of wood, the lands can be finished at the same time that the grooves are being cut deeper.

When barrels are so worn that the rifles have not depth enough to hold the tool described for re-rifling, another process must be resorted to. Make a rod of hard wood about six or seven inches long and so as to slide easily through the barrel. In one end of this fix the cutter. Around the other end cast lead or other soft metal so as to fill the rifles. It is evident if this short rod be forced through the barrel by means of a longer one, that it must turn with the rifling, being so forced to do by the soft metal engaging the several rifles. The operation of working being the same as previously described.

CHAPTER XXII.

ON GUN LOCKS.

Quality of Locks.—It is impossible to judge the quality of a gun lock by a mere examination, for if the metal be not the very best and the workmanship be also good, some portions, as a spring, may grow weak and in an unguarded moment give way. If the mainspring be not thoroughly tempered it may break the first time it be used on a frosty morning. It is well to see if the attachment of the stirrup or swivel be well made and fitted, as this controls the movements and play of the mainspring. The fitting of the sear spring on the sear is important. If too much cramped, it may give way; if not enough cramped, then it may grow weak and there will not be that sharp, clear click that the admirer of a good lock likes to hear.

On the hanging of the swivel or stirrup depends the smoothness of play of the mainspring. On the placing of the hole for the sear-pin depends the sweetness of the sear operating on the tumbler. On the pitching of the sear depends the cutting of the notches of the tumbler, and on the formation of the first notch depends the liability of the lock catching at half-cock when the trigger is made to be easily pulled from the full cock notch. On the formation of the half-cock notch depends the safety of carrying the arm at half-cock.

The Back Action Lock.—There are various forms of gun locks, and each form has its admirers. The back action shown in Fig. 43 admits of the arm being put together more strongly and securely than any other plan. Other advantages claimed for it

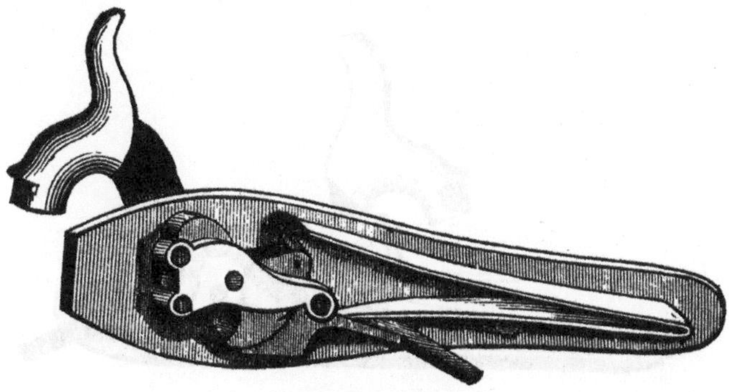

FIGURE 43.

are that the mainspring can be made longer and will therefore be less liable to break, and by such length has a smoother working motion to the hammer. As the lock plate is almost entirely surrounded by the wood of the stock, there is less liability of wet getting into the interior, and this may especially be the case as the hand, in carrying the gun, covers some portion of the lock.

The Bar Lock.—This lock, Fig. 44, is so called from a bar formed at the breech end of the barrel, and to this bar the lock is fitted. The great advantage of this lock is that it admits of the stock to be so shaped that the grasp of the hand naturally tightens as the gun is raised to the shoulder. The objection raised by some to this lock is that it is more pervious to wet than the back action lock.

This lock possesses the advantage of having an arm of the tumbler so made that by the swivel or

FIGURE 44.

stirrup being hung upon that when the lock is at full cock the weight of the spring force is lessened by the arm acting as a lever to bring the moving force in the immediate vicinity of the axis on which the tumbler turns, and when the spring is bringing the hammer down on the nipple, increasing that force by divergence. It is sometimes called the Full Bar Lock.

Side Action Lock.—In Fig. 45 is shown another form of lock, commonly called a side action. The mechanism and arrangement is similar to the full bar, but it has a shoulder that fits up to the barrel.

If the gun be fitted with a plug or cylinder a suitable half round recess is cut in this shoulder to receive the plug.

The Wesley Bar.—The Wesley bar shown in Fig. 46 differs from the common bar lock by being of different shape at the fore end, and this end does not fit up to the barrel like the bar lock. By the wood

FIGURE 45.

almost surrounding the plate, the interior is pretty well protected from wet. It has the same merit of the stock being so shaped as to tighten in the hand when raised to take sight. This lock has one objection, the wood between the lock-plate and barrel has to be cut so thin that the recoil of the gun is very apt to break and splinter it.

The Central Lock.—There is a grade of guns made with locks enclosed in the breech, or a continuation of the breech, in the same manner as common revolvers and other pistol locks are made. A view of this lock is given in Fig. 47. The principle is much the same as the back action lock when the hammer is placed on one side as in the back action lock. One side of the frame has the same office as the lock plate, and the other side supports the tumbler and other parts the same as the bridle. The formation of the tumbler is such that no sear is necessary, the trigger bearing directly against it;

FIGURE 46.

the point of the trigger having the same office as the nose of the tumbler, a small spring keeping it to place to catch in the tumbler notches. Generally this form of lock has the hammer placed directly in the central line of the bore of the barrel, and when so placed the lower end of the hammer has the same office as the tumbler and is shaped and has notches cut as in a side lock tumbler. As this form of lock has few parts, and has a long feather-like mainspring, it is easy and pleasant to operate.

Cleaning Locks, etc.—While the gunsmith will be called upon to clean and repair various parts of fire-arms, the lock is the part with which he will have considerable to do. And, in most kind of guns, it is the most complicated part, and, consequently, the most difficult part to manage. Not a few gun-owners look upon it as a kind of mystery without the range of ordinary comprehension, hence they carry it to the shop, not only at the slightest indication of "something wrong," but so often as it would seem to need thorough cleaning and oiling. This is all well enough, for the gun as much as anything comes clearly within the application of the rule which admonishes that "a stitch in time saves nine." All of which being the case, one of the earliest things that the gunsmith will be called upon to study will be

FIGURE 47.

How to Take Down a Lock.—Having removed the lock from the gun, set the hammer at full-cock. Apply the hand-vise, or mainspring clamp, if he has one, to the mainspring, having first placed a bit of chamois skin or felt between the jaws of the vise and the spring to prevent bruising or scratching the polished surface of the latter. Turn up the vise gently until the hammer feels loose. Now press upon the sear-spring and let down the hammer. The mainspring is now entirely loose, and may be lifted out with the vise. This ends the complication of the lock; it is now only a plain machine, with parts held into position by screws, which may be removed one at a time until every piece has been taken from the plate.

In taking down a lock the beginner should work slowly and cautiously, thinking in every case before acting. His screwdriver should be pressed well-down in the notch of every screw to prevent damage to the head, and if he apprehends the slightest danger of getting "things mixed," he should lay each screw and its piece in different places upon his bench. Of course, there will be no such necessity after a few locks have been taken down, but such a necessity might exist at the very beginning; at least there is no harm to grow out of taking what is known to be the safe side in every case.

The directions given for taking down, refer to the common lock, while locks of some of the modern guns will be made on plans quite different. But the principle will be the same, and hence there is no reasonable demand for going into further detail. The first object will be to get control of the mainspring so that it can be lifted out with ease. This attained, and all the rest of the work is easy enough.

To Clean and Oil the Lock.—Botches usually wipe the old oil and dirt from the parts with a rag, put on fresh oil, and then put the lock together again. This is a poor way, for a portion of the old gummy oil will be left to combine with the new, thus soon making it about as bad as the old. Every part should be thoroughly cleansed and dried before any new oil is used. First wipe the dirt and old oil off as thoroughly as possible with a piece of cloth or felt, and then rub it over with powdered chalk or Spanish whiting. Next brush off and rub with a stiff brush such as is used by jewelers or watchmakers. This will remove all the old oil, after which the new oil may be applied.

Cases may turn up in which the lock has been long neglected, and the oil and dirt have gummed together so badly as not to admit of wiping off. In such cases the parts should be soaked for a short time in kerosene or in benzine, which is still better. This will dissolve the gum and render it easy of removal.

In oiling, only oil enough should be applied to lubricate the parts—there is much more danger of getting on too much oil than too little. It should be put on with a stubbed camel's hair brush or pencil, as the painters call it, and with extreme lightness. And there is but one kind of oil fit to be used on a lock, the very best "watchmaker's oil" obtainable. Such an oil is comparatively costly, but a single bottle, costing 25 cents, will oil hundreds of locks, hence the cost is really not entitled to consideration, on account of its being so decidedly superior to any other oil in use.

How to Put up a Lock.—In taking down the lock the last thing removed was the sear-spring, perhaps—it is most convenient to make that the last thing. Now, in putting up the lock, that is the first part to claim our attention. Screw the sear-spring into position, then the sear; next put in the tumbler, and then put on the bridle. Having this all right, screw on the hammer and let it down. Then take the mainspring, clamped as it was at the taking down, hook it on to the swivel, and bring it up until the little steady-pin is in its hole in the plate. Now unscrew the vise and the lock is ready for work.

It will be necessary to always handle the mainspring with care. It is the first thing to come off in taking down, and the last to go on in putting up the lock; and the vise or clamp must be turned upon it only just enough to bring it loose, and no more. If more, it may be damaged, possibly broken.

Handling the parts of a lock with chamois skin or paper, is a good idea, while brushing off the chalk and rubbing them clean with the brush, and it is also a good idea not to touch them with the naked fingers afterwards. Few gunsmiths would be inclined to take this precaution, but it is worthy of consideration if one desires to be ranked among the very best and most careful of workmen; as handling with the naked fingers is apt to leave the parts in such a condition as will cause them to eventually rust, slightly at least.

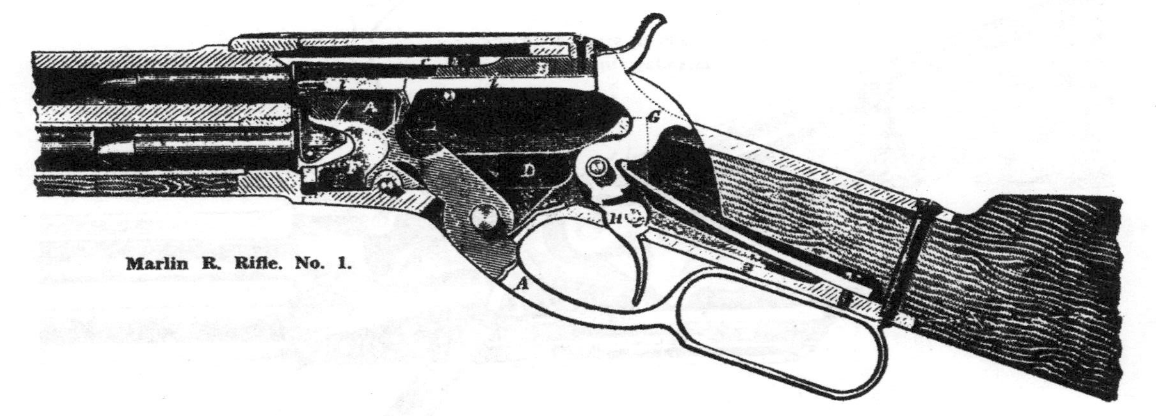

Marlin R. Rifle. No. 1.

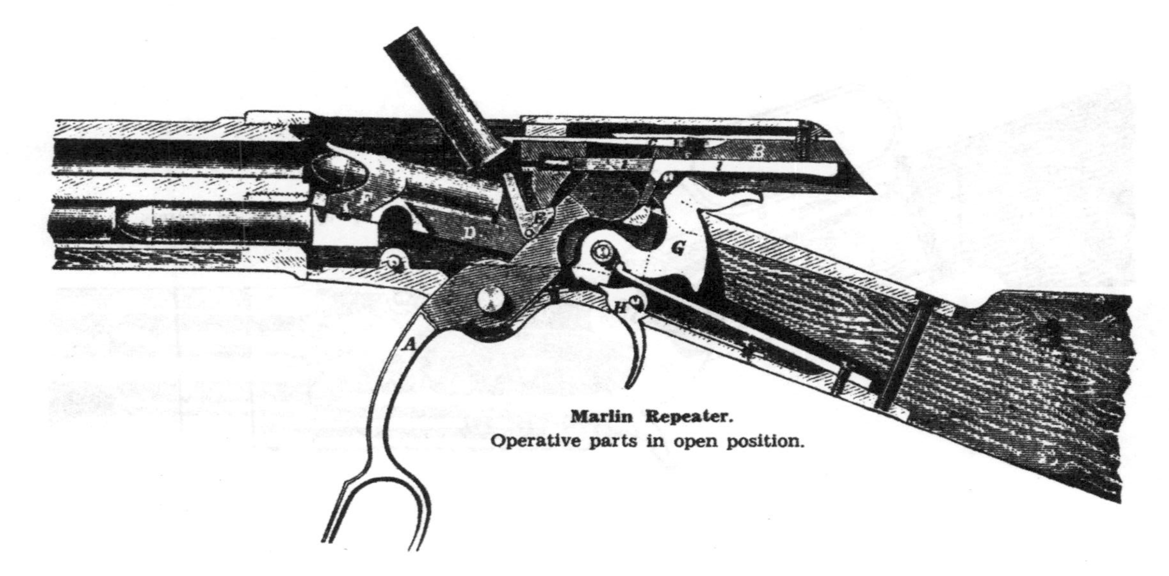

Marlin Repeater.
Operative parts in open position.

CHAPTER XXIII.

ON FITTING GUN HAMMERS.

To Fit a Hammer on a Tumbler.—To file the hole in a gun-hammer so that it will rest firmly and evenly upon the squared end of the tumbler, has tested the skill and patience of nearly every gunsmith. The usual practice is to drill a hole nearly the diameter of the square of the tumbler, then file this hole until it fits the square, and unless skill and patience are brought into requisition, and a nice fit be the result, the hammer soon works loose, then needs refitting. The remedy then generally is, remove the hammer from the tumbler and close the hole a little by cutting around the squared opening. a little distance back from the edge, with a sharp cold chisel, thus throwing some of the metal inward, closing the hole a trifle. The hammer is then put upon the tumbler, and if it be a little tight is driven to place with a hammer. After some usage it becomes loose again, and has to be again refitted.

It is evident that unless what might be called a "perfect fit" be made, that the sudden arrest of the hammer upon the tube or cone, as it descends by force of the mainspring, will cause some slight displacement of metal where the hammer and tumbler come in juxtaposition. A repetition of these sudden arrests increases the displacement, and often there is considerable looseness of the parts.

The Drift for Squaring the Hole.—The remedy for this is very simple, and can be performed with but little labor. After the hole in the hammer is drilled introduce the end of a square drift, and drive it steadily through with blows of a hammer. The drift will cut a clean hole, the exact counterpart of its form, and this hole will need no finishing, if the drift be properly made to insure its correctness as to being smooth and true. Bear in mind that while driving the drift, the work must rest evenly and

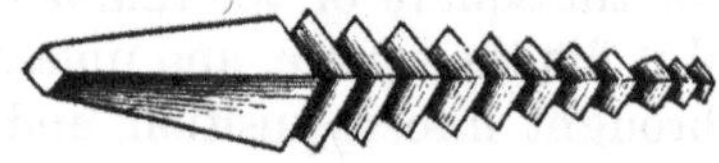

FIGURE 48.

solidly upon some firm support, but in such a way that the tool will easily pass through. The drift is shown in Fig. 48. In construction it is a rod of steel filed or so shaped that its tranverse section is of the precise form that the hole is to be made, and too great care cannot be taken to insure its being as correct as possible. The entering end of the tool should be made round, and almost fill the hole as drilled in the hammer, and it should increase gradually in size until it arrives at the full proportions and then gradually decrease to the upper end, so that it will readily pass through the opening made by the larger portion. On the sides of this tool are cut teeth that extend around it, being continued from side to side after the manner of a screw thread upon a bolt. It will be observed by reference to the cut that the teeth commence on each side of the square and resemble a four-threaded screw, with saw-shaped teeth, made upon a square rod. A file is the most ready tool to cut these teeth. Forge the steel carefully, temper equally, and do not leave too hard. When properly made it will last for an untold amount of work.

The number of cuts or teeth to the inch may be about ten. There must be sufficient depth between the teeth to receive the cuttings, and they must be made strong enough to withstand the hammer blows. In driving use oil on the teeth, and be careful to keep it upright, so as to form a hole that will enable the gun-hammer to stand properly on the tumbler.

If it be feared that there will be a variation of the hole from the "square," turn the drift a quarter turn after the first driving and drive again ; then turn another quarter and drive the third time, and so on of the fourth.

The drift may be made of almost any shape, and will produce holes of irregular form as readily as square ones. Another example is the mortice in the loop attached under gun-barrels, through which the bolt passes, and also the same size mortice or slot in escutcheons, which are let into the stock, through which the same bolt passes. The holes in small solid wrenches to receive square or six-sided nuts can be readily and easily made in the same manner.

A Tool for Fitting Hammers to Gun Locks.—The usual practice in fitting hammers to gun locks is to measure with the dividers the distance from the centre of the tumbler, where it projects beyond the lock-plate, to the centre of the tube or cone, and so get the length of the hammer; then drill the hole in the hammer, square this hole by the rule of "guess," and file until it fits upon the square of the tumbler.

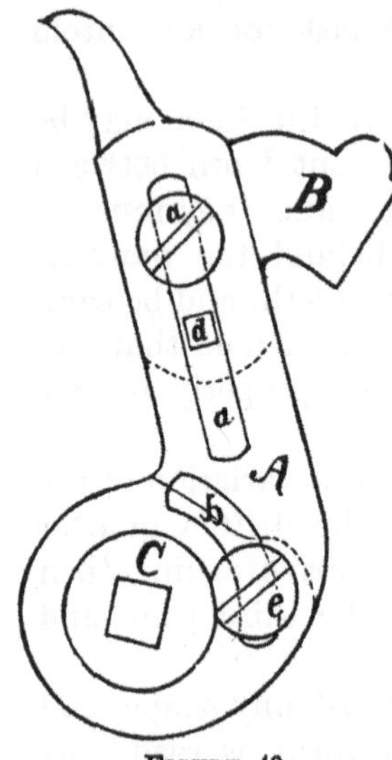

FIGURE 49.

A simple tool can be made by any gunsmith, that will greatly facilitate his operations in fitting hammers. The accompanying cut (Fig. 49) shows this tool in full size. It is made of iron or steel, one-eighth of an inch thick. The body, A, of the tool is one-half inch wide, and has a slot, *a*, three-sixteenths of an inch wide and one inch long. The curved slot, *b*, is the same width, and embraces about one-fourth of a circle. The nose-piece, B, is shaped like the top portion of a hammer, and is held to the body, A, by a screw, *c*, and to insure its moving in a line, and being held properly in the slot, *a*, there is a small stud, *d*, that fills the slot. In the lower curved portion of the body, which is seven-eighths of an inch in diameter, there is a five-eighths hole, which receives the round portion of the piece, C. This piece has an extension, as shown by the dotted lines, and is held to A by a screw, *e*. The square hole in this piece is intended to fit the square of the tumbler of the lock. The thickness of C, at the round part where it enters A, is the thickness of both A and B. There is a shoulder of the thickness of B, and of the size of the body of the tool at the lower end, being of the same diameter, so that the back surfaces of B and C are of the same thickness. The front surface of C is flush with A.

To use the tool, put the square of the lock tumbler in the square hole of C, and put the tumbler screw in place. Loosen the screw, *e*, and turn the piece, C, until the nose of B will rest pretty firmly on the gun-tube; then turn the screw to hold it in place. Loosen the screw, *c*, that holds B in place, and move this piece up or down until the centre of the nose rests squarely on the tube; then confine it in place by turning up the screw, *c*. This is now an exact pattern, giving the length, shape of the hammer, and also a guide to form the square where it fits the tumbler.

It must be observed that the screws and the stud, *d*, ought to fill the slots on the shoulder of the piece, C, a good fit, so that it will turn evenly and properly in the hole of A. The screws may be the same that are used for tumbler screws for army muskets. These screws are hardened, and, as they have large flat heads, they answer for this purpose very well.

The part, C, can be made of two pieces of the same thickness as the other parts. Finish them separately, except the square hole, and then solder or rivet them together. The square hole is best finished up when the two parts are fastened together.

CHAPTER XXIV.

ON NIPPLES OR CONES.

THE terms nipple, cone and tube are applied in rather an indiscriminate manner to that portion of a gun breech on which the copper cap containing the fulminate designed for firing the arm is placed. To be good and serviceable, the nipple should be made of steel, and carefully tempered; but many are made of a low grade of steel, of common iron, and even malleable iron has been used, and case-hardened to render them fit for use.

Forms of Nipples.—There are as many forms of nipples as there are qualities, and they may be di-

FIGURE 50.

FIGURE 51.

FIGURE 52.

vided into classes, as the musket nipple (called "cone" by the armory operatives), the American, English, and German. The German have coarser threads than the American. The English musket nipple has a thread or screw of 18 threads per inch; it has a flat top, and has a hole of one taper, being large at the bottom and smaller at the top. The American musket tube has a screw of 24 threads to the inch, has a vent resembling two inverted cones, meeting with a small opening near the centre. The top of the nipple, consequently, resembles a narrow circular ring. Fig. 50 shows the English nipple, and Fig. 51 the American; Fig. 52 the different forms of vents.

Nipples for Breech-loading Arms.—For breech-loading arms, using loose powder and ball, the nipple is made similar to the American, but the vent is made quite large at the top, and decreases like an inverted cone, and terminates in a small opening a little larger than a common pin. In this nipple the fire from the cap is concentrated and caused to rush with some force through the small aperture, the same as heat is concentrated in a single point by using a blow-pipe for that purpose. The object is to burn through the material of which the cartridge is composed.

Nipples with Flat Tops.—The use of a nipple with a broad, flat top requires a vigorous mainspring, and then quite a volume of the detonating flame escapes outside the nipple and between it and the cap. The small portion that passes down the tube may be so impeded, if the nipple be foul or rusty, as to cause the gun to hang fire, and even to miss fire. Should the mainspring be too weak, the cap will come in contact with the broad surface of the nipple, forcing the priming of the cap from its position, and leaving it unexploded. Often the cap is made to bear the blame, when the fault is due entirely to the formation of the top of the nipple.

The American Musket Nipple.—The American musket nipple has a thin edge and a wide opening at the top, so as to allow the flame to readily enter, the thin edge enabling the cap to be very readily exploded, even with the blow from a weak main spring. In this form of nipple the detonating powder is ignited at the edge, and being forced to enter the wide opening, is compelled to pass down the vent to the powder. If there be any little dirt or obstruction, it is generally forced along with the fire, and the ignition of the powder is certain, and miss-fires are few.

When nipples are made with the small opening of the vent at the bottom, coarse-grain gunpowder can be used, as it is not necessary that the grains need to be admitted to the nipple. This is the case as regards military arms fitted with nipples. The powder is too coarse to be received in the nipple when freed from the cartridge and placed uncovered in the gun breech.

It has been claimed by some that gunpowder can be glazed too smooth to readily take fire, and this is a source of miss-fires. Also that the flame from the detonating powder will form a mass of condensed air around itself, preventing contact with the powder until the heat is expended. This was especially thought to be the fact when there was a volume of air between the powder and the end of the nipple. These two theories are presented for what they may be worth.

Nipples used in Sporting Guns.—Of nipples used in sporting guns there may be found the broad top, the countersunk top, the taper bored, the countersunk taper, the reverse taper, double reversed, etc., etc. They are generally put up with the screw portion made in assorted sizes. The threads also vary, being as coarse as 26 to the inch, and as fine as 32 threads per inch.

Preparing Nipples for Guns.—It is well for the gunsmith to test the nipples with a fine file to ascertain their hardness before inserting them in guns. If too soft, they will be returned on his hands. If there is also a liability of the gun-hammer battering the top where it strikes, which soon is so broad as to cause miss fires. If too hard, they are liable to break short off at the square, and the screw portion left in the gun is difficult to remove. Sometimes so much so that it is necessary to unbreech the gun, remove the patent breech and heat it to soften the portion of broken nipple so that it can be drilled out. In drilling there is a risk of injury to the thread of the nipple seat. The heating necessitates labor to refinish the part and it is to be again case hardened before screwing into the barrel. If found too hard, nipples can be drawn to a better temper by holding the top portion in a pair of pliers in exposing the bottom part to the flame of an alcohol lamp. If they be too soft, enclose in a short piece of gas pipe, pack them well with bone-dust, stop close the ends of the pipe, and heat to a red, letting them remain so for fifteen or twenty minutes and then open the end of the pipe to let the contents fall into water. They can be drawn to temper to suit. They may also be heated hot, rolled in prussiate of potash or cyanide of potassium, again heated, and thrown into water. As cyanide of potassium is a deadly poison, be very careful how it is used and where it is kept. Do not breathe the flames when put on hot iron, and do not let it come in contact with sores or raw places on the hands.

Remedy for Bad Nipples.—In case guns come in to be repaired because they will "not snap a cap," see if a weak mainspring be not one cause, and a nipple with broad top, another. For the latter evil, ream or counter sink it so as to have a thin cup like edge. See also if the cup of the hammer strikes properly on the nipple, and that it be not too much cupped by long usage in striking. In this case, the cup may be filled by drilling in and inserting a bit of iron or steel to fill it and then re-harden.

Pistol Nipples.—Pistol nipples, Colt's for instance, have a different thread from gun nipples. The thread used in Colt's revolver nipples is 40 to the inch. But one size is employed—nipples are sometimes provided with a thin, round washer of copper, which is put on at the shoulder where the thread terminates. This shields that part of the seat where it is placed from rust, and some claim that it acts as a sort of cushion to deaden the blow of the hammer, thus preserving the nipple from breakage.

Plugs for Nipples.—Plugs can be made from a rod of iron of suitable size that is sound and free from flaws. The size of the part that screws into the barrel is about three-eighths of an inch, and the thread is twenty to the inch. This is the size and thread generally used. There may be exceptions that will require a different size and a different thread, but, if possible, let the sizes given govern the work. The end on which the screw is to be cut can be turned in the lathe, cut down with a hollow mill in the method given for making breech pins, or it can even be filed to shape in absence of any other way to make it.

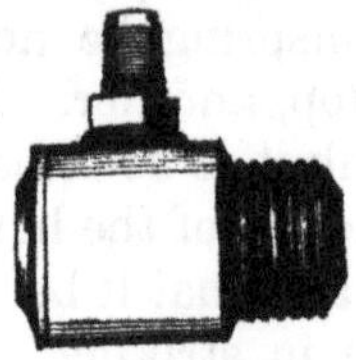

FIGURE 53.

Before cutting the plug to the length where the nipple is to be seated, screw it into the barrel, mark the place for the nipple which can be found by letting down the hammer of the lock, then remove drill and fit the nipple. Cut off all that is not required beyond the nipple and screw into place, the nipple forming a shoulder on which to rest the wrench in screwing it home. The finished plug is shown in Fig. 53.

It is best to remove the barrel from the stock in screwing in the plug. With an improper wrench, it often happens that a nipple will be broken off at the square if it be very hard, and then it is difficult to remove. To obviate all danger of this, make a wrench with a handle at each end, and in the middle have a hole that will fit the plug, and then file an opening so that it will just fit over the nipple. It should fit close to the nipple at the square, and be free so as not to have a bearing at the end of the nipple where the cap is put on.

Plugs are sometimes left bright, but if blued it improves their appearance and there is less tendency to rust. If desired to be very durable, case-harden them. The better polish that can be made on them will make a better blue or case-hardened surface.

Many of the cheap plugs in market are nothing but cast malleable iron. The best material of which to make them is decarbonized steel, or what is known as "soft steel." It comes in smooth round rods and is homogeneous and easy to work. Cold-rolled iron rod makes very good plugs. The diameter may be half-inch or nine-sixteenths, the latter size being most preferable. With a three-eighth size screw the half-inch rod gives a one sixteenth shoulder, which must fit tight to the barrel. If not fitted tight, the gas from the powder when the gun is fired will soon cause a leak which is difficult to remedy. In some localities the name plug is discarded and the term "cylinder" adopted.

CHAPTER XXV.

MAINSPRINGS.

Mainsprings.—Mainsprings are made for right and left side locks, and are known as right and left. Very few gunsmiths make these springs, as they are kept in stock and can be purchased of the dealers at any time. Fig. 54 is called the forward or side-action hook spring; Fig. 55 the forward or side-action swivel, and are used in bar locks.

Fig. 56 is the back-action mainspring, such as used in cheap made locks. These springs are also made

FIGURE 54.

with sear spring combined. Fig. 57 is swivel back-action with sear spring combined.

Sear Springs.—Sear springs are made for right and left hand locks. The side-action or bar-lock springs are shown in Fig. 58, and the back-action lock springs in Fig. 59. In one kind of back-action lock there is used a bent spring similar to the bar-lock spring which is shown in Fig. 60. It will be observed that the lower branch of this spring is longer than that which is used in the bar or side-action locks.

How to Forge Mainsprings.—If the gunsmith desires to forge his own mainsprings he must select a good quality of spring steel, as cast steel is gen-

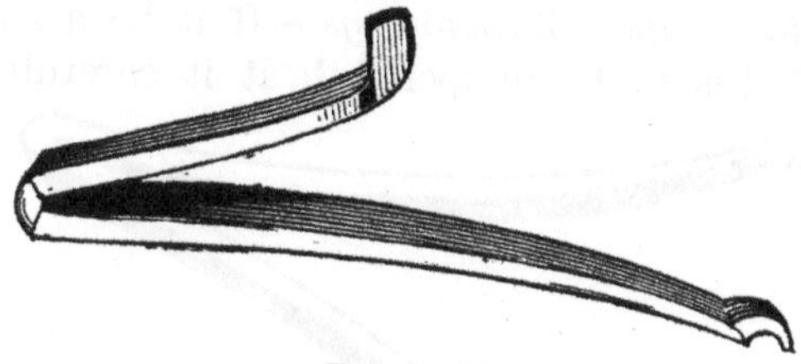

FIGURE 55.

erally too quick or fiery for springs that have as severe a duty to perform as a mainspring. Get the steel of the same thickness as the mainspring and of a width equal to the spring and the pivot that goes through the lock plate.

Draw the spring out carefully over a fire that has been burned enough to free it from sulphur, if bitu-

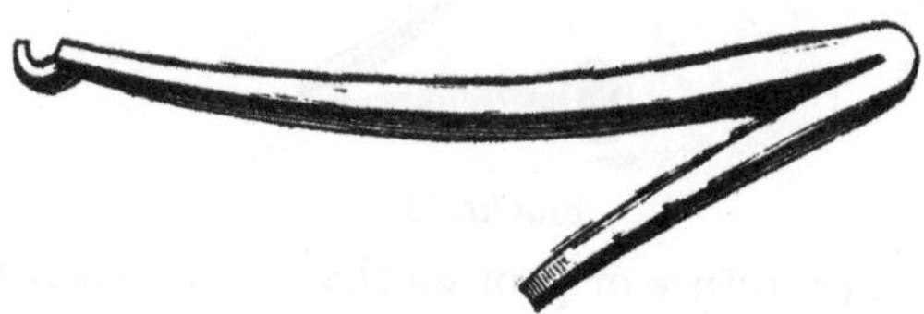

FIGURE 56

minous coal be used, and be very careful not to overheat the metal. Form to shape with any tools or means that may be at hand.

For straight springs, as some kinds of pistol and gun-lock springs, procure steel of the thickness and width of the spring at the widest and thickest end, and draw down to the requisite width and thickness of the smallest end.

How to Temper Mainsprings.—If it be a single spring that is to be tempered, heat it carefully or

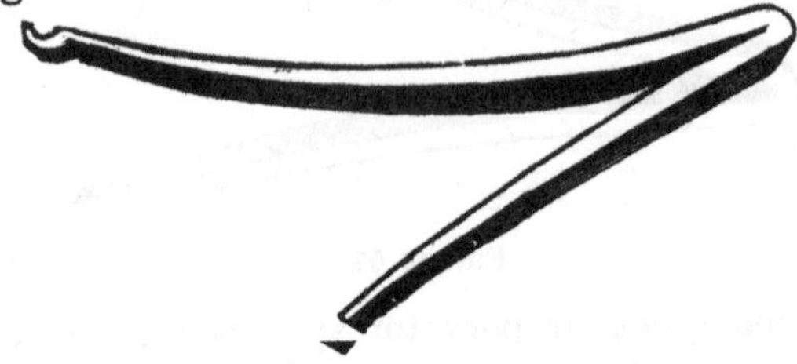

FIGURE 57.

evenly in a fire that is well burned to free it from sulphur, or preferably in a charcoal fire, and when at a light-red heat, harden by plunging it in any animal oil. An iron pan may be used to contain the

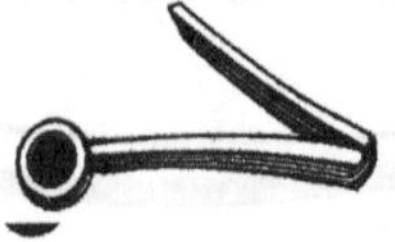

FIGURE 58.

oil, and any refuse or poor oil that may collect may be used. Lard oil is good, but if oil be wanting, use common lard or even tallow. If hard, melt before using.

To temper the spring, remove from the oil, and hold it all dripping with the oil over a clear fire until the oil takes fire and blazes off. It is best to dip it in the oil and blaze off the second time.

If there are a number of springs enclose them in a piece of gas pipe to heat them, and when hot, turn them into the oil. To temper, remove them, put

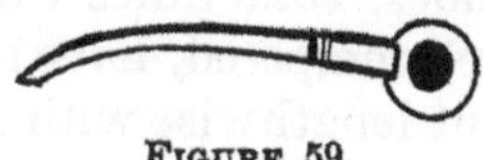

FIGURE 59.

them in an old wrought-iron frying pan, add a little oil, heat the pan over the fire, skaking it in the meantime, until the oil takes fire and blazes off. Let the work cool without putting it in water or oil.

Cheap Mainsprings for Revolvers.—Make springs for cheap revolvers from strips of sheet steel. Cut the springs so that the *length* of the spring will be

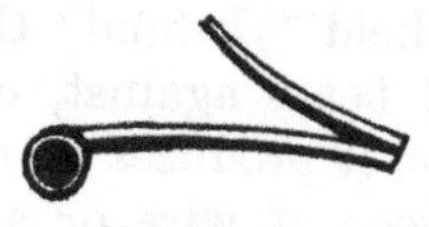

FIGURE 60.

lengthwise of the sheet from which it is cut, or, in other words, the *grain* of the steel must *not* be *across* the spring, but *lengthwise* with it.

When fitted, harden in oil and blaze off in an old sheet-iron pan; an old frying pan being very good for the purpose, and literally *fry* them in the oil. If heavy, blaze two or three times. Agitate well in the pan during the blazing process.

An old saw blade, one that is quite thin, when cut

up in strips will make springs for cheap work. If too hard temper, it cannot very well be used until the temper be drawn to suit. They can be bent into form with a strong pair of pliers. By warming the strips over a fire they can be readily bent into shape. Old table knife blades, sometimes called case-knife blades, that are well tempered, have been employed, the blades being cut lengthwise with a pair of hand shears.

Coiling Wire for Springs, &c.—There are several methods of coiling wire for springs. The most simple is to clamp a rod in the vise and wind the wire around it by hand, but this is a very unsatisfactory method and it is rather difficult to wind the wire evenly. Another method is to revolve a rod in the lathe and let the wire coil upon it as the lathe is turned. To insure equal space between the coils, a piece of metal is held "behind" the wire, and as this piece of metal bears against, or in advance of the coil just made, it produces an even spring. A hook made of a piece of wire or a piece of metal with one end formed into a hook and clasping the rod on which the wire is moved is an excellent way to form an even spring. Two, or even three or more pieces of wire may be wound at one time, and this will insure springs of even space.

Another way in which a spring of even coil can be made, is to hold a bolt that has a good thread, upright in the vise and confine the wire by clamping it to the bolt, then wind the wire, letting it follow the thread of the bolt. When enough is wound, remove and release the spring by "screwing the bolt out of it," the same as if holding a nut fast in the hand and turning the bolt out of it. Springs of almost any coil, but not of "almost any diameter," can be made in this way.

In the absence of a lathe a wire winding tool may be made by bending a rod into the form of a crank and insert the long end through a piece of hard wood, as shown in Fig. 61. This can be held in the vise to use, or fastened by two or three screws to

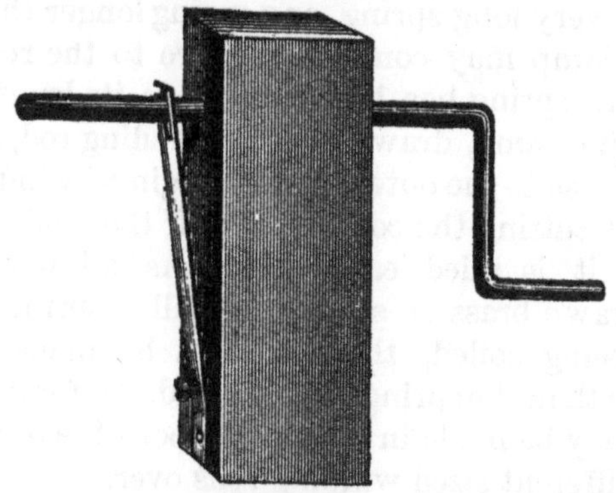

FIGURE 61.

the bench or any convenient place. A slot is made in the end of the part that projects through the wood, and in this slot the end of the wire is placed and is wound *toward* the crank. Of course the spring can be made no longer than this projecting end. To make different sized springs different sized rods must be used, and holes to fit must be made through the piece of wood.

To insure even space between the coils, a strip of thin steel may be fastened by one or two screws at or near the bottom of the piece of wood, and a hole is made near the top of the winding rod to pass through. A space is cut out, as shown in the cut, to admit of the wire being removed. In winding the upper end the steel strip is held away from the wood by its spring, or by a wooden wedge, and the wire must be held close to the wood by the hand or by a piece of wire formed as a sort of staple. To wind a very long spring, or a spring longer than the rod, a clamp may confine the wire to the rod, and when the spring has been wound to its length, remove the clamp, draw back the winding rod, fix the clamp close to the outer end and begin to wind again without cutting the coil, push it off the end of the rod as it is filled each time. As all wire, like hard drawn brass or steel wire, will "spring open" after being coiled, the rod must be made much smaller than the spring to be formed. Different sized holes may be made in the same block of wood to receive different sized winding rods over.

Hooks or eyes on the ends of the rods can be readily made in like manner. When the rod is too large to admit of ready bending to form the crank to turn it with, a crank of cast-iron can be riveted upon it.

If the mechanic wishes to make a tool of this kind, that will be more serviceable and at the same time "look like something," he can procure a casting similar to the movable head of a lathe, and put in the hole where the spindle is placed a similar spindle, but with the end where the wire is to be wound large enough to form a shoulder to keep it in place, and on the other end put a wheel eight or ten inches in diameter, with a handle to turn it with. The end where the shoulder is may be made with a screw to fit the lathe chuck or with a hole to receive the lathe tools, and they can be held there the same as holding them in the lathe chuck. The spindles to wind the wire may be inserted in the hole and held in place by the set screw. The tool may be fastened to the bench by a rod screwed into the base, or held by a nut under the bench.

This tool will be found to be a very ready one with which to work out bullet moulds. The cherry being held the same as a rod. It can also be used to free the muzzle or breech of barrels, using the wooden rods covered with emery, as described in Chapter XVI. It is also useful for reaming holes and can be used for drilling in case of an emergency. As a tool for holding taps to tap the thread in holes it has no equal—the work being held in the left hand and the wheel turned with the right hand.

CHAPTER XXVI.

ON RODS.

How to Make Ramrods.—Ramrods are of two forms, the straight rod used for rifles, and the tapered rod used for shot guns. The wood that is most in use is hickory, which is split and then turned into shape. The other woods used are ebony, redwood, snakewood, rosewood, etc. Rifle rods are generally made of sizes from three-sixteenths inch to half-inch diameter. Shot gun rods from one-half inch to three-quarters inch in diameter. The measurement of the shot gun rods is at the largest diameter.

One way of making rods for rifles is very similar to that in which screws are made. A hollow tool is used with cutting lips, three are enough, and the rod is passed through this tool, the tool being turned very rapidly during the cutting. The operation may be reversed and the wood being rotated while the tool is held in the hand and is passed along as it cuts.

A better kind of tool is made like a wheel about two inches in diameter, and three-quarters of an inch thick. A hole of the size of the rod is made through the diametrical centre, and one side of the circumference is cut away so that a tool partaking of the nature of the gouge and finishing chisel is so held by

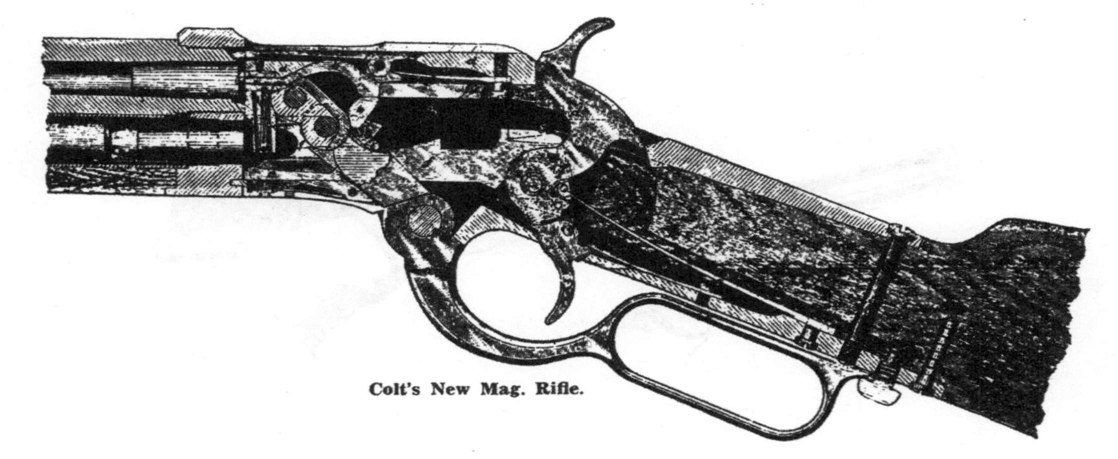

Colt's New Mag. Rifle.

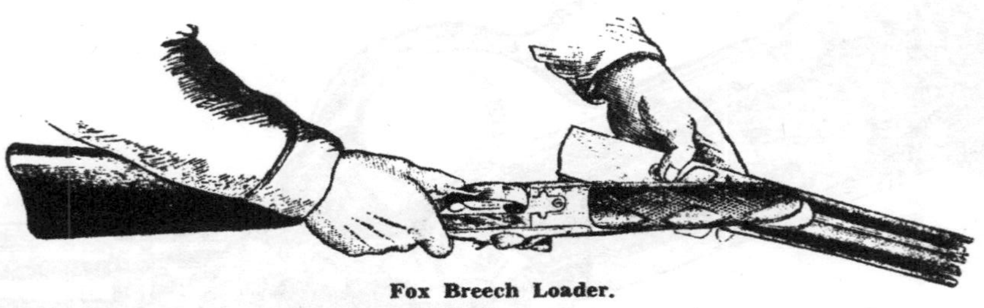

Fox Breech Loader.

a screw, that the gouge portion advances and roughs out the rod, while the chisel shaped part following it shaves the roughness and leaves the work smooth and nice. The hole through the tool must be of the size the rod is to be made, and the cutting tool set so as to allow the work to pass through the hole easily. Only one size rod can be made with this tool, and different sizes must be made for different sized rods; except the cutter which must be of steel, it can be made of cast iron.

To make rods by hand, the wood is split out as straight as can be and then rough shaved into form with a drawing knife. It is then planed square with a carpenter's plane and then the square corners are taken off, leaving the rod of octagon form. A few strokes of the plane will then remove these corners and it will be nearly round. A new file and sandpaper will finish it true and even. After the rod has been planed square, the best way to hold it for removing the corners and make it octagon form is to have a V groove made in a piece of hard wood of the length of the rod in which to lay it. Otherwise, it will be very difficult to hold while using the plane.

Round straight rods can be finished with a tool like a moulding plane, and if this tool be of the proper form, and the work be turned around two or three times during the operation, a good rod can be made very expeditiously.

When wood is cross-grained it cannot be planed very well and must be finished with a file and rasp.

To hold the rod while being worked, get a piece of hard wood about three-quarters of an inch thick and about four inches wide; in one edge have a groove made a quarter inch wide and three-eighths deep. Rest the rod in this groove, holding it at one end with a hand vise so as to turn it while filing, and reduce first with the rasp and then finish with a file. To finish easily with sand-paper, wrap the sand-paper around a piece of wood shaped like a file, and use as if filing.

Pieces of broken window glass may also be used to advantage in reducing rods, and then finish with fine sand-paper.

How to make a Wiping Rod.—Take any straight rod, a ramrod for instance, but be sure that the

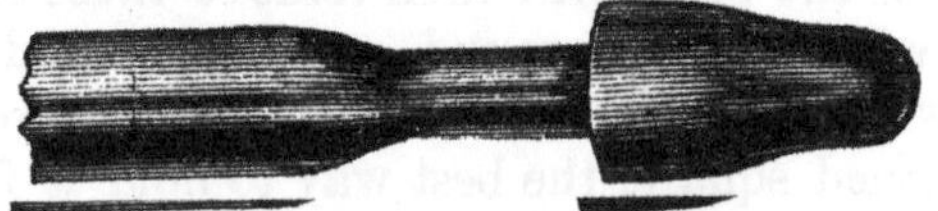

FIGURE 62.

wood be strong and tough, and cut one end like the form shown in Fig. 62. By folding a rag over the end, doubling it so as to fill the bore of the gun, it will be found that it can be used in muzzle-loading guns without pulling off when the rod is being withdrawn. The rounded end prevents the end of the rod being pushed through the cloth, and the deep notch receives the folded sides so that it presents no inequalities to the bore of the gun. The square shoulder prevents its being pulled from place on being withdrawn from the gun.

An iron rod may be made in the same way, but a rod made of good hickory wood has no equal.

A wiping rod may be made of an iron rod having a slot or mortice cut through one end, and through this a rag is drawn. It may be used in breech-loading guns where it can be pushed in at one end and drawn out at the other, but in a muzzle loading gun it cannot well be withdrawn on account of the rag being folded upon itself in attempting to withdraw it.

If a wiping rag be put in a gun and cannot be withdrawn, it may be sometimes relieved so as to be withdrawn by turning a little warm water down the barrel so as to saturate and soften the rag.

Wiping brushes should not be thrust down the bore of a muzzle-loader as they cannot be readily withdrawn, and in instances where they are of larger diameter than the bore, the gun must be unbreeched to have the brush taken out. These brush wipers are very nice for that class of breech-loaders where they can be inserted at one end and withdrawn from the other. In using them in this class of guns, insert at the breech and remove from the muzzle, and then there will be no dirt or debris thrown among the breech mechanism.

CHAPTER XXVII.

ON BULLET MOULDS.

Joints for Bullet Moulds.—Simple as it may seem, the joint of bullet moulds, unless produced by the manufacturer, who has ample tools at his command, is not often well done. The want of the proper knowledge how "to lay out" such a joint may be the excuse for ill-fitting work. Yet it is easy enough, only "know how."

By reference to the cut, Fig. 63, the joint and one side of the body of a bullet mould, it will be observed that the line A is the surface where the two halves abut or come together. The line B is drawn at right angles to this and in the diametrical centre of the round projection that is to form the joint. At the point of intersection of these two lines, or in other words where these two lines cross each other, make an indent with a sharp-pointed prick-punch, and there drill a hole of the size that the rivet is to be made.

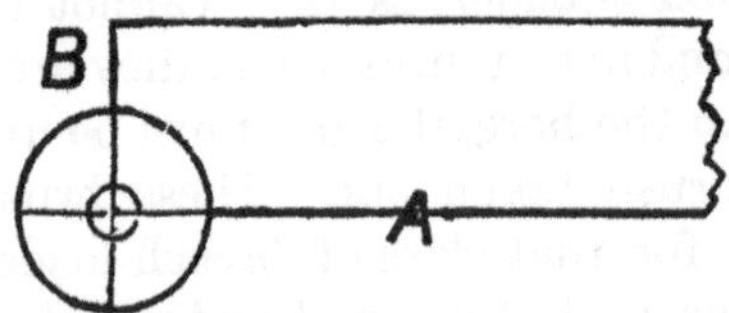

FIGURE 63.

Fig. 64 shows the finished joint ready to receive its mate and be rivetted together. After the hole for the rivet is made, a tool must be used to "sweep" or cut down the surface at C, and also leave a sharp and smooth shoulder as shown at D.

To make this tool, select a piece of steel, centre it in the lathe, and turn one end—say an inch or so—

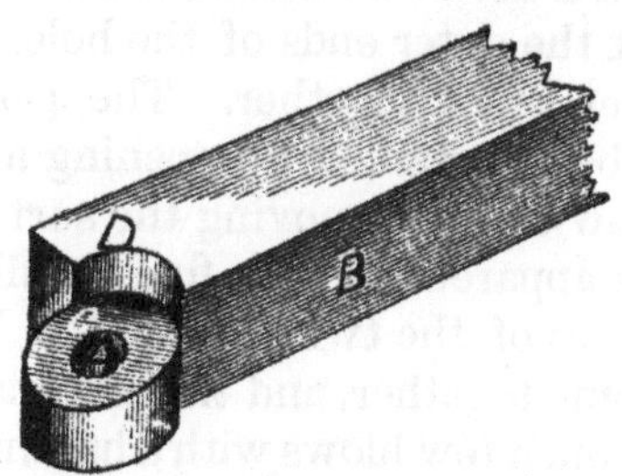

FIGURE 64.

of the same size that the joint is to be. In this end drill a hole lengthwise, but exactly in the centre, of the same size that the rivet is to be. Cut teeth on this end, and temper as any tool for cutting metals. Insert a steel pin in the hole, leaving it

FIGURE 65.

projecting half an inch or more, and the tool is ready for use. The cutting end of the tool is shown in Fig. 65. Of course the other end must be fitted to the lathe chuck or a bit-stock in order to use it.

Insert the projecting end of the pin in the hole A, drilled for the joint, and by means of the lathe or bit-stock, cut down each half of the mould to about half of its thickness. The outer circle or cut of the tool will be a guide to which to file the circle of the joint. If the cutting end of the tool be made a little convex it will form the surface of the joint a little hollowing, and a better fit will be the result.

Countersink the outer ends of the hole, insert the rivet, and rivet them together. The perfection of the joint can be ascertained by opening and closing the mould a few times, removing the surface where the rubbing is apparent, with a fine-cut file.

If the surfaces of the two halves at B, Fig. 64, do not exactly come together, and the material be brass or malleable iron, a few blows with a hammer will insure close contact. It may be necessary to say that the surface at B must first be made true and square, so that the two halves will fit closely, and then "lay out" the joint from this surface.

If there be many bullet moulds to make the circle of, the joints can be made by means of a cutter revolving in the lathe. Make this cutter about two and a half inches in diameter and half an inch thick. Cut teeth in the sides as well as on the circumference. Fit it in a spindle so it will revolve. After the joint is drilled fit it so as to turn on a pin fixed in a piece of iron that is held at one side of the cutter. By feeding the mould up to the cutter the surface or shoulder is cut where the two portions of the joint come in contact when opened. By turning the mould slowly around a portion of the circle is cut, say about one-half. Remove the mould from the pin, invert it, and the remainder of the circle can be cut; the whole "round" and the abutting sur-

FIGURE 66.

faces being produced at two cuts; a little smoothing up with a file being necessary to finish it. This operation and the cutting is shown in Fig. 66.

How to Make a Ball Cherry.—The term "cherry," as applied to the tool used to make the mould for spherical balls or bullets, was no doubt borrowed from the fruit of the same name—in fact the fruit and tool are very similar in form and size. To any one not conversant with the process of producing a sphere in metal it seems a very difficult operation, but nevertheless it is very simple, and only requires a little knowledge and experience to make a cherry to fit any bore of gun. This is the rule governing the operation: A rotating body is passed through a properly-shaped circular aperture in a flat steel die that is held with its upper or cutting in the same plane as the axial line of the body rotating. That's all.

Now, to make application of the rule. Suppose we have a rifle of a certain bore to which is to be fitted a round ball. First, take a piece of steel, we will say about one-quarter of an inch thick, about one inch wide and about six or eight inches long. An old file of good quality, with the temper drawn and the teeth ground away, may answer the purpose. It should be annealed as soft as possible.

FIGURE 67.

With a drill make a hole near one end, but a little less in size than the bullet to be produced. With a taper half-round reamer cut out the hole until that side of it which is to be the upper or cutting edge is exactly the size of the bullet desired.

The advantage of using this taper half-round reamer is the hole is made perfectly round, and at the same time the taper of the reamer gives a bevel to the hole that forms a good, strong and effective cutting edge. With a file cut out a portion of the tool of a V shape, bevelling the edges the same as the hole as shown in Fig. 67. This V may be either cut on the end, a side of the tool, as shown, but in use it is preferred to be cut on the side, as then, if necessary, the hand can find a hold on that end to assist it in operating. When done, temper for use. For the cherry, turn a piece of steel in the lathe to fit a chuck. Half-inch octagon is perhaps the best size of steel from which to make cherries of less diameter than half-inch, and the length about six inches. The end on which the cherry is to be made is roughly fashioned into a ball, leaving the end where the centre supports it to be removed by the lathe tool or by filing.

When fitted so that the rough blank will be held firmly in the chuck, run the lathe at moderate speed,

FIGURE 68.

set the T rest so that the steel die can be held on it about level with the under side of the rotating blank. On the rest lay the die, and press the opening so as to receive the rough sphere, applying oil and not pressing too hard. Let it gradually scrape its way through the circular aperture, the V-shaped opening in the side receiving the stem to which the cherry is attached. In Fig. 68 is shown the finished blank after being passed through the die. If it be preferred the die may be held in the hands and not supported on the T rest. Take care to supply plenty of oil to the work, as this will prevent scratching or tearing the cherry while being formed It is well to make two of these holes, one at each end of the piece of steel, roughing the blank with the first, which is a little larger than the one used to finish the cherry of the exact size. When this tool gets dull grind on the upper or cutting edge, but not too much, as it will enlarge the hole, and the result will be to make a larger cherry.

To form these blanks into cutting tools, a copy can be taken from the cherries as sold to the trade.

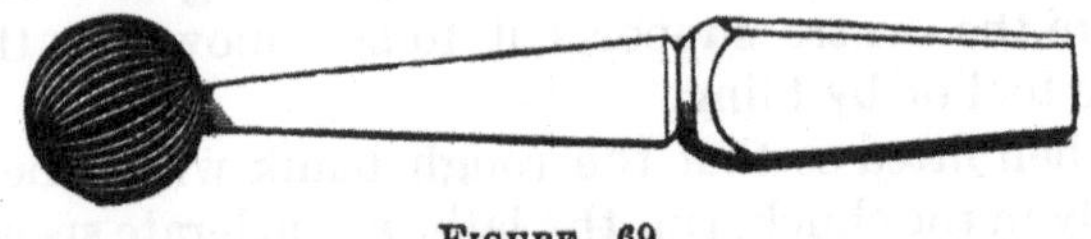

FIGURE 69.

Bear in mind to leave the grooves deep enough to receive the metal cut from the blank mould when in operation.

It will be observed that the cherries as purchased (Fig. 69) do not have their cutting edges terminate in that portion of the mould, but usually on one side. This is done to insure a perfectly spherical form by having a cutting side operating at the bottom of the hole while it is being formed. It is somewhat difficult to make this form of cutting edge, and some patience and care must be exercised or the blank may be spoiled.

Every mechanic knows how nice and rapidly a well-made drill will cut. Suppose this form of cutting edge be applied to the bullet cherry. It is no matter if this cherry be round or of conical form. Fill two cutting edges like a drill on opposite sides of the blank from the shank to the end of the cherry. It is evident that here the two rounded portions that are left on each side of the cutting edges to be removed that the tool is nothing more

FIGURE 70.

nor less than a peculiar shaped drill or reamer that might form an internal sphere. But as this form could not well be applied between the sides of blank bullet moulds, and as the full rounded sides would not permit of these edges cutting, then form the rounded surfaces into similar cutting edges like the two first made, only not so large, making three or

FIGURE 71.

four on each side, according to the size of the cherry. These cuts can very easily be made with a fine cut three-square or half round file. A cherry of this form for a round ball is shown in Fig. 70, and one for a conical ball in Fig. 71.

In using a three-square file, to get a fine cutting edge that will make a sharp V cut, grind away the teeth of one side. This will remove the slightly rounded or blunt edge as usually made on this form of file. By grinding thus, two acute cutting angles can be had from one file. If they get a little dull on the sharp cutting corner, a little grinding will restore the edge and make it sharp again.

Tempering Bullet Cherries.—In tempering the cherry do not leave it too hard, and be careful not to temper too hard above the spherical portion. Leave the shank softer, as it will be less liable to break. It is not necessary to shape the shank so as to exactly conform to the shape of the V opening in the forming tool, for, as the edges of this opening have been bevelled the same as the opening that shapes the cherry, they will act as cutters, and will reduce the shank to conform to the V. It is well to mark the cherries in some conspicuous place on the shank, with their size in hundredths of an inch, the same as cartridges are numbered, and also mark them with the number of round balls to the pound, as was formerly in vogue among gunsmiths. The finished cherries, as purchased from dealers, are so numbered.

Cherries, as purchased, have shanks fitted to be used with a bit-stock, but if the gunsmith fits these tools to be used in a lathe chuck that has a round hole, necessitating a round shank, and also wishes to use them in a bit-stock, he can fill up the square hole in the bit-stock by brazing therein a piece of iron, and then drilling a round hole to fit the tool.

CHAPTER XXVIII.

SCREW-MAKING TOOLS.

THE tools used by the "old time" gunsmith for screw making were few and simple, and are now seldom found except in the shop of some "old veteran" of the trade. Twenty-five or thirty years ago modifications of these tools were used in some of

FIGURE 72.

the armories where Government arms were made, and even now the same principle of these tools is employed but changed in form and adapted to machinery operated by steam or other power.

Fig. 72 shows a tool to be held in the vise by the projection, and the rough form of the screw, or a piece of wire of suitable size is inserted in the hole in the centre of the raised portion, cut with radial teeth, and a screwdriver inserted in a transverse slot in the other end of the rough screw, or bit of rod; it is then rotated by a bit stock until by the pressure applied the teeth cut away the metal and so forms the body of the screw. To form the head of the screw another tool, shown in Fig. 73 having a countersunk hole made in the centre of the diameter of the head but a little deeper, is used. The unenlarged

FIGURE 73.

portion of the hole in the tool corresponding to the body of the screw, which being inserted in the hole is rotated by means of the screwdriver in the bit stock, until the head is shaped in the same manner

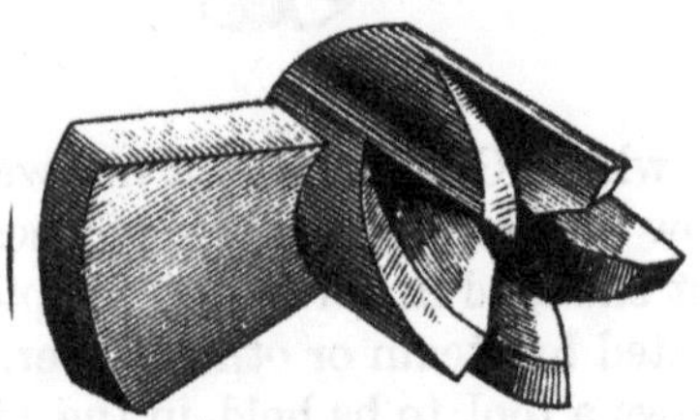

FIGURE 74.

that the body was formed. Of course, different tools had to be made for different sized screws.

In forming the tang screw, which has the head bevelled on the under side, a tool was used like Fig. 74. The rod was turned into a tool in the same manner as for making a flat headed screw; then the body was inserted in the bevelled head-making tool and rotated as for making a flat head. The edges of the bevelled teeth being so formed as to become cutters upon the inner or central edges, and so reduce the screw head to that shape.

For countersinking, to let in the heads of these bevelled forms of screws, a tool is used like the one as shown in Fig. 75—the stem serving as a guide

FIGURE 75.

when inserted in the work, and a slot to admit the screw driver, for turning them, being made in the large end. This tool is made about two inches in length, the head being about half an inch in diameter.

The length of the tools in Figs. 72, 73 and 74, where they are held in the vise, is about an inch and a half or an inch and three-quarters; the width from half an inch to five-eighths, according to size; the thickness one-quarter inch. The round part with the cutting teeth is about three-quarters of an inch in height from the flat portion, and is about the same diameter. The teeth may be in number five, six or eight, as most convenient to make. The tools for bevelled heads are best made with five teeth.

Making Small Taps.—The best manner of making large taps is to turn them to size in a lathe, and then cut the screw by the same means of with a die plate. Small taps cannot very well be so made. A very good way is to get good steel wire—generally sold of all sizes, under the name of Stubs' steel wire—and from this make taps; the thread can be cut by means of a die stock.

When the thread is properly made, there are several ways to form it so as to make it a cutting tool. One method is to file it with four sides, making it a square. In this case it scarcely cuts, but rather "jams" up a thread. Another one is to file it triangular or "three square." This form makes it rather a better form, as regards cutting quality; but as in case of the square form, it will be observed that the inclination of the sides is such that they would not be selected for a cutting tool if such an angle were made as a tool for that purpose. If two flutes or grooves be made of angular form, with a square file, or two hollows be cut with a round file, these flutes running lengthwise with the tool, the edges then present more of the aspect of a cutting tool; but the distance is so great between the flutes that there is great friction, and breakage will result if the hole to be tapped be too small, or too much force be applied. If three or four flutes be made the evil of friction will then be remedied. Be sure to cut the flutes deep enough to receive all cuttings that may be removed or the tap will become clogged, and can with difficulty be turned out, or perhaps may be broken.

Evan's Magazine Rifle.

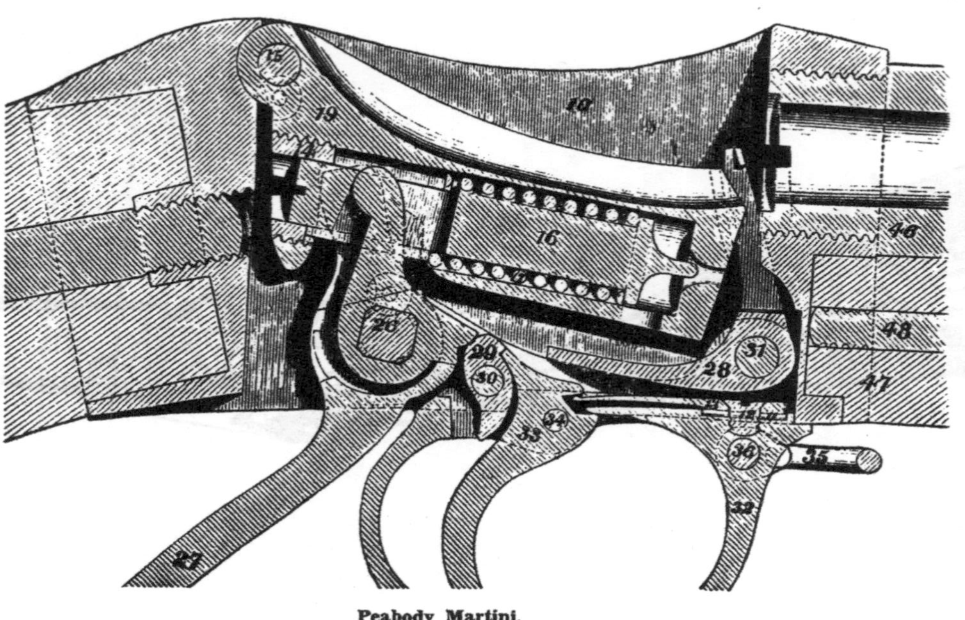

Peabody Martini.

A cheap and good way to finish a tap is, after the thread is made, to file away one-half of its diameter nearly the length of the thread. This will give great clearance and space for the cuttings, and at the same time the cutting edge is very sharp and is strong. It will be found to cut very easily. If a tap of this make becomes dull it can be sharpened by grinding on the flat formed by filing it away. If the tap be too large it can be made smaller by thus grinding.

Large taps work equally well made in this way, but care must be taken in starting them in a hole or the thread may be made crooked.

Reamers, both large and small, straight or taper, can be made in this manner, and are effective as well as cheap to make, and can be kept sharp by grinding them on the flat side.

CHAPTER XXIX.

NOMENCLATURE.

Nomenclature of the Gun Stock.—Fig. 76 shows a gun stock with the locks, plates and other metal

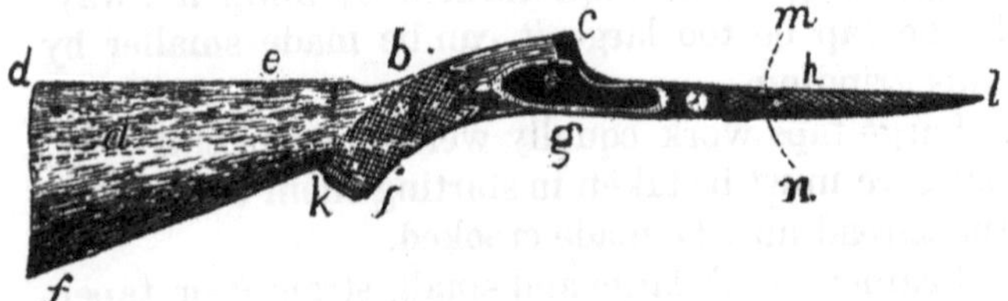

FIGURE 76.

portions removed. *a*, is the butt; *b*, the small or handle; *c*, the head; *d*, the bump; *e*, the comb; *f*,

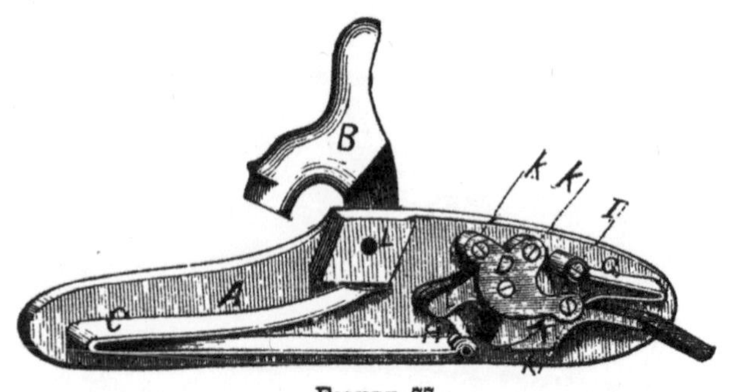

FIGURE 77.

the toe; *g*, lock-bed; *h*, fore-end or fore-arm; *i*, pistol-grip; *k*, cap or end of pistol-grip; *l*, tip of fore-end; *m*, escutcheons; *n*, mortice for bolt; *o*, chequering.

Nomenclature of the Gun Lock.—The number of pieces in a common gun lock, as shown, are thirteen, and are fully illustrated in the cut, Fig. 77. *A*, is the lock-plate; *B*, the hammer;

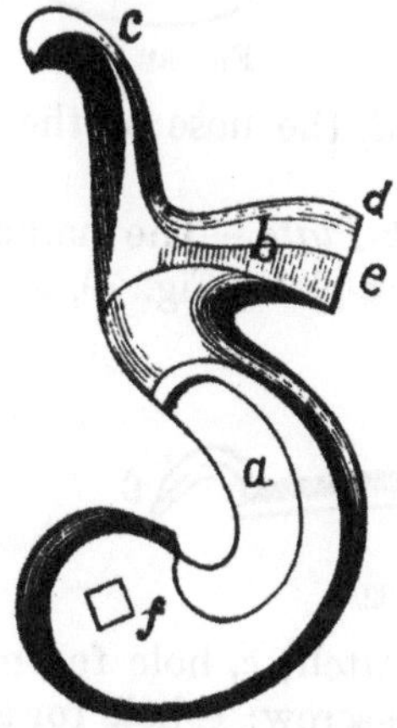

FIGURE 78.

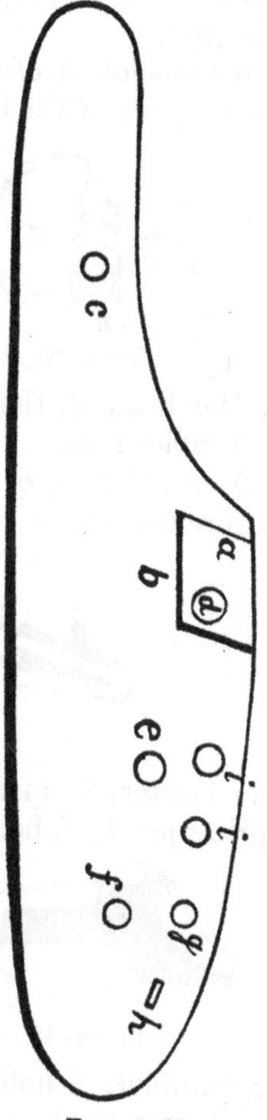

FIGURE 79.

C, mainspring; *D*, the bridle; *E*, the tumbler; *F*, the sear; *G*, the sear-spring; *H*, the swivel or stirrup; *I*, the sear-spring screw; *K*, *K*, *K*, the bridle screws; *L*, hole for side-screw. In some locks there are only two bridle screws. In others a screw holds the mainspring to place instead of a lip catching under the stud.

Nomenclature of the Hammer.—The names of different parts of the hammer, Fig. 78, are: *a*, the body;

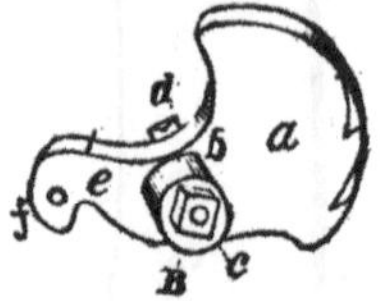

FIGURE 80.

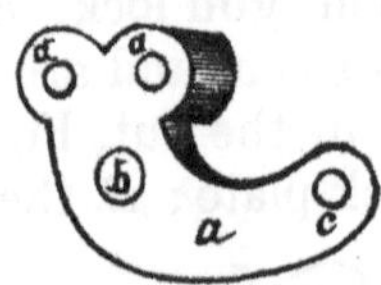

FIGURE 81.

b, the head; *c*, the comb; *d*, the nose; *e*, the cup; *f*, tumbler-hole.

Nomenclature of the Lock-Plate.—The names of different portions of the lock-plate, Fig. 79, are: *a*,

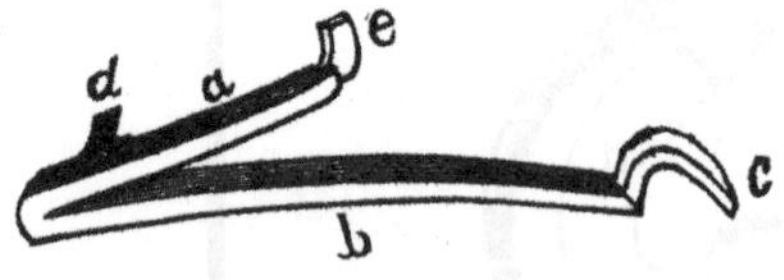

FIGURE 82.

the bolster; *b*, mainspring-catch; *c*, hole for mainspring-pivot; *d*, hole for side-screw; *e*, hole for arbor

FIGURE 83.

FIGURE 84.

of tumbler; *f*, hole for sear-screw; *g*, hole for sear spring-screw; *h*, slot for sear-spring stud; *i*, *i*, holes for bridle screws.

Nomenclature of the Tumbler.—The names of the tumbler, Fig. 80, are: *a*, the body; *b*, arbor; *c*, squares; *d*, pivot; *e*, swivel-arm; *f*, pin-hole, and *g*, the tumbler-screw hole.

Nomenclature of the Bridle.—The bridle, Fig. 81, consists of: *a*, the body; *b*, the eye for tumbler-pivot; *c*, hole for sear-screw; *d*, *d*, holes for bridle screws. Some tumblers have a pin that goes in a hole in the lock-plate, and this pin is called a pivot.

FIG. 85.

Nomenclature of the Mainspring.—The mainspring, Fig. 82, consists of: *a*, the upper branch; *b*, the lower branch; *c*, the hook; *d*, the pivot; *e*, the catch which is sometimes called the tang.

Nomenclature of the Sear.—The sear, Fig. 83, con-

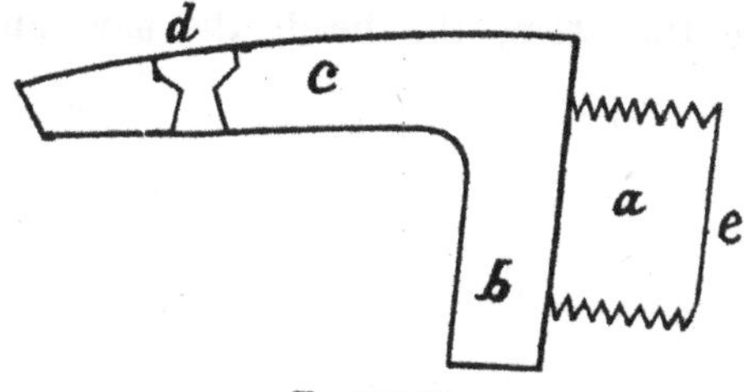

FIGURE 86.

sists of: *a*, the body; *b*, the nose; *c*, the arm; *d*, screw-hole.

Nomenclature of the Sear-Spring.—The sear-spring, Fig. 84, consists of: *a*, the blade; *b*, upper branch; *c*, lower branch; *d*, the stud; *e*, screw-hole.

Nomenclature of the Swivel.—The mainspring-swivel or stirrup, Fig. 85, consists of: *a*, the body; *b*, the axis; and *c*, the tumbler pin hole.

Nomenclature of the Breech-Pin.—Fig. 86 shows full size of musket-barrel breech-pin. *a*, plug wich threads; *b*, tenon; *c*, tang; *d*, tang-screw hole; *e*, face.

In sporting guns the tang is often called the "strap," and is distinguished as long and short. The length varying from two and a half inches as shortest, and five inches as the longest. Sometimes the term "tail" is employed instead of tang or strap. The diameter of the plug is generally one-half, five-eighths, and three-quarters of an inch. The diameter of the pin used in United States muskets and rifles is three-quarters of an inch.

Nomenclature of Screws.—In all the screws, the parts are the stem, the head, the slot and the thread.

CHAPTER XXX.

ON BROWNING.

Object of Browning.—Browning is done for the purpose of subduing the bright color of the barrel from the sight of game; to bring out the fibres of the metal to show their form and beauty, and also to show whether the metal be free from flaws. It does not prevent barrels from rusting, but rust will not attack so readily as if left in a bright condition. The browning is very certain to make all defects appear, except those designedly hidden, and not only defects of materials but the filing and finishing of the barrel, if not well done, will appear in marks in certain lights. A thoroughly well-filed barrel presents, what may be called, a deep liquid appearance.

Preparatory Process.—The process of browning is simple and cheap, and at the same time serves to protect a gun, in some measure, from rust, and also adds to its appearance. The operation consists in producing a very thin uniform film of rust, or oxide, upon the iron and giving a gloss to its surface by rubbing wax over it, or by coating it with some kind of varnish, as shellac varnish.

Preparatory to browning, the barrel having been filed and polished bright, is rubbed with lime to remove all grease. Some gun makers use wet lime or lime water and then rub in dry powdered lime. The vent holes are to be stopped with wax or wooden plugs, and both breech and muzzle are to be plugged with wooden rods which serve as handles to hold the barrel during the operation. The object of plugging is to prevent the mixture from finding its way into the interior of the barrel and the breech and muzzle plugs also serving as handles, prevent the hands from coming in contact with the barrel, which would prevent the stain from "taking," and consequently cause a spot of different color from that on other portions of the work. The solution is generally applied with a sponge or cloth, sponge being preferable, until the surface is equally moistened, and after standing in a warm place, generally about twenty-four hours, it is rubbed off with a stiff brush or a wire card. The state of the atmosphere will have much to do with the action of the browning mixture. It can be easily ascertained when the barrels are dry enough to work, as by applying the card, if dry, the rust will fly off quickly, but if not dry, the rust will adhere firmly and the surface of the barrel will look streaky. Some mixtures will dry in twelve hours or even less, but twenty-four hours will insure their being perfectly dry. The process of wetting and brushing, or "carding," is repeated until the barrel has acquired the desired color. When this stage is reached the barrel is freely washed with hot water, in which a little potash may be mixed. Then wash with clean water and dry thoroughly. A little lime water may be used as a wash to destroy any free acid that may remain in the pores of the metal.

The Processes of Browning.—A browning or rust may be obtained very speedily and well by enclosing the barrels in a chamber and subjecting them to the vapor of muriatic acid. The same end may be obtained by moistening the surface with dilute muriatic or nitric acid. There is another material sometimes used, which is butter or chloride of antimony. It is sometimes called "bronzing or browning salt." In using this substance, a uniform mixture is made with it and olive oil; this is rubbed upon the barrel, which is slightly heated, and is then exposed to the air until the required degree of browning is arrived at. The operation of the antimony is quickened by rubbing on after it, a little aquafortis.

Browning Damascus Barrels.—Damascus barrels are browned by first burnishing the barrels very nicely, then cover with bone oil; pound, or drop, or strew wood ashes all over, then heat in a wire cage filled with charcoal, until the first dark blue is obtained. After the barrels are cold, mix a small quantity of sulphuric acid in water, and with a hard brush apply to the barrel. The acid will remove the color from the steel portion of the barrel, leaving the iron, on account of its greater adhesion, still retaining its blue color. Take care to keep a good color and not extract too much.

Browning Belgian Damascus Barrels.—The characteristic, bright, wavy appearance of Belgian Damascus barrels is generally "eat up," and the process is termed "pickling." The process results in eating away the softer metals from the harder, used in forming the barrel. The preparation used is one pound of blue vitriol dissolved in a gallon of soft water, at the boiling point, and the boiling continued until the quantity is reduced about one-fourth; then let it cool, and pour out into a lead trough. Plug the barrels securely at both breech and muzzle, so that the liquid cannot get into the interior. When the barrels are immersed in the solution, it will act upon the metal in fifteen to twenty minutes. Remove and wash with water, and if not satisfactory, immerse again, until the operation is complete. Pour boiling water over them, and scratch well with a steel brush or card, which will eventually give the beautiful, bright, wavy appearance. Laminated steel barrels may be subjected to this same operation.

Browning Inferior Barrels.—Inferior quality of Birmingham barrels are browned as follows: Dissolve as much muriate of mercury as can be taken up in a glassfull of alcohol. Mix this solution in one pint or more of water. A small quantity of this mixture is poured on a little whitening and laid on the barrel with a sponge, rather lightly. As soon as dry, brush off and lay on a fresh coating. So proceed until the barrel is dark enough, which is generally about two or three days. The effect is to make the softer portions of the metal a beautiful brown, while the harder portions remain quite light. The rusting process is killed by washing in hot

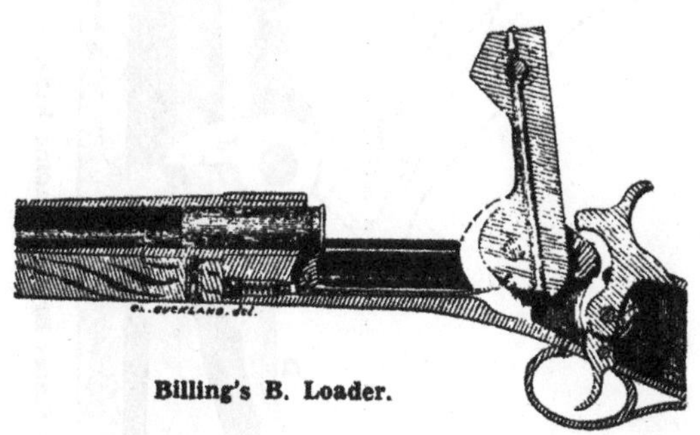

Billing's B. Loader.

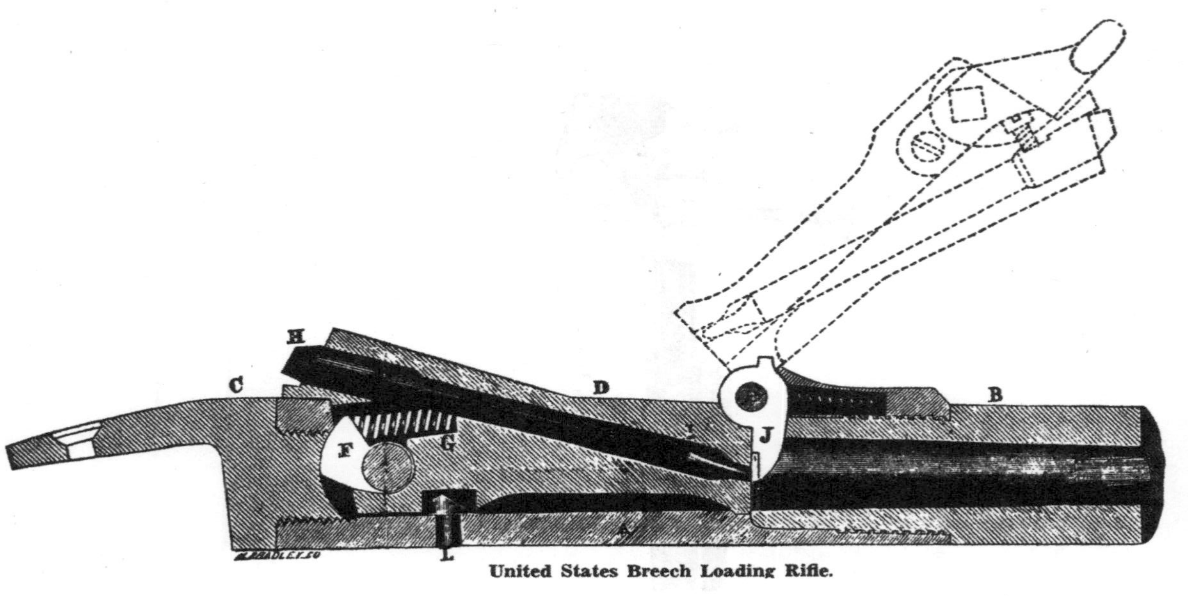

United States Breech Loading Rifle.

water, after which the barrels are suddenly immersed in cold water. This has the effect of heightening the brightness of both colors.

Plain Welded Barrels made to Resemble Twist.—Plain welded barrels are made to resemble twist barrels by wetting a thread or fine cord with dilute acid, and winding it around the barrel so as to make spiral lines, running all along its surface. Wherever the thread touches a slight coating of rust will be formed. The barrel may be treated in this way two or three times, and the spiral windings of the thread will exhibit fine dark lines closely resembling twist barrels. To wind the thread the barrel may be put between the centres of a lathe, and so turned while it winds the thread upon it, being guided by the hand, or the barrel may be supported between centres or put on a rod of wood, which may be turned by a crank or handle.

Barrels may be colored by exposing them to a degree of heat sufficient to produce a blue tinge, and is done to color pistol barrels, but when double gun barrels are soft-soldered together this cannot be done on account of danger of melting the solder. The inner surface of the barrel, which is also so colored, must be polished after the operation.

Smoke Staining.—This method of coloring barrels is as follows: The barrels are washed with a little sulphuric acid, to cause the metal to receive the effects of the gas more readily; it is then washed off, and the barrels rubbed dry. A fire is built with coal possessing as much hydrogen gas and as little sulphur as possible. Burn the coals until they give a clear, white flame, with no black smoke. Pass the barrels through that flame, backward and forward, until the whole are covered with a black, sooty coating. Place them in a damp, cool cellar and let them stand about twenty-four hours, and if the place be sufficiently damp, the iron parts will be covered with a red rust, while the steel portions still retain the sooty coat. Scratch them off with a wire card and rub with a piece of cloth, and wash or polish with water, using on the cloth a little flour of emery. The steel will be found to be of the original bright color, while the iron will be a little darker. Rub dry, and pass the barrels through the flame again. Allow them to stand about twelve hours to rust, and then polish as before. With every smoking the colors will be a little darker. The darkest color to be obtained is a fine purple-black color on the iron ; the steel inclining to a copper color.

The principle of this stain is simply the hydrogen gas contained in the coal acting on the iron, iron being of a softer nature than the steel, which it does not affect, the flame also possessing a quantity of tar, it is imperceptibly embodied by the iron during the action of the oxide, and, when finished, by filling up the spaces created, it becomes decidedly more impervious to damp or wet than any other stain or browning which is composed entirely of oxide of iron.

CHAPTER XXXI.

RECIPES FOR BROWNING GUN BARRELS.

Solution for Browning Gun Barrels.—Make a solution by putting together in a glass vessel, spirits of nitre, three-quarter ounce; tincture of steel, three-quarter ounce; black brimstone, one-quarter ounce; blue vitriol, one-half ounce; corrosive sublimate, one-quarter ounce; nitric acid, one drachm, and copperas, one-quarter ounce. Mix with one and one-half pints of rain water, and bottle for use. Clean the barrel till entirely bright, rubbing it over with finest emery paper, then apply the solution with a clean white cloth. Set away for twenty-four hours. At the end of this time a rust will have formed over the barrel. Go over it with a steel scratch-brush, then rub off all the rust with a woolen cloth. If you find the brown not dark enough, cover again with the solution and set away twenty-four hours longer. Remove the rust exactly as in the first instance, then, the color suiting, wash off with a wet cloth, rub to thorough dryness, and finish by rubbing with linseed oil, to prevent further rusting.

This application browns the barrel beautifully, and in case of twist leaves the markings prominently plain.

The tincture of steel is sometimes not to be obtained at a small drug store, in which case the unmedicated tincture of iron may be made to answer reasonably well.

2. Sulphate of copper, one ounce; sweet spirits of nitre, one ounce; water, one pint. Mix. In a few days it will be ready for use.

3. Tincture muriate of iron, one ounce; nitric ether, one ounce; sulphate of copper, four scruples; rain water, one pint; if the process is to be hurried, add two or three grains of oxymuriate of mercury. Put in lime water to neutralize acid.

4. Spirits of nitre, one pound; alcohol, one pound; corrosive sublimate, one ounce. Mix and cork for use.

5. Tincture of muriate of iron, one ounce; nitric ether, one ounce; sulphate of copper, four scruples; rain water, one pint.

6. Alcohol, one and a half ounce; tincture of steel, one and a half ounce; corrosive sublimate, one and a half ounce; sweet spirits of nitre, one and a half ounce; blue vitriol, one ounce; nitric acid, three-quarters of an ounce. Mix and dissolve in one quart of warm water. Keep in glass bottles.

7. Nitric ether, six ounces; alcohol, one ounce; sulphate of copper (blue vitriol), one and a half ounce; muriated tincture of iron, one and a half ounce; tincture of gum benzoin, one and a half ounce. Dissolve the sulphate of copper in water, add the other ingredients, previously mixed, and then add three pints of boiling water.

8. Spirits of nitre, one pound; alcohol, one pound;

corrosive sublimate, one ounce. Mix in a bottle and keep corked for use.

9. Soft water, one quart; dissolve in it blue vitriol, two ounces; corrosive sublimate, one ounce; and one ounce of spirits of nitre. Put on one coating, and in about an hour a second one, then let the work stand twelve hours. Oil and rub with cloth.

10. One ounce nitric acid; one ounce blue vitriol; dissolve in four ounces rain water, and mix all together in a pint of water. Warm the mixture slightly and apply gently with a sponge.

11. Nitric acid, one-half ounce; sweet spirits of nitre, one-half ounce; alcohol, one ounce; blue vitriol, two ounces; tincture of iron, one ounce; soft water, one quart.

12. Sweet spirits of nitre, one and a half ounce; nitric acid, one ounce; tincture of steel, two ounces; alcohol, one and a half ounce; blue vitriol, one-half ounce. Dissolve the blue vitriol in cold rain water, and add the other ingredients to make one quart.

13. Apply the following fluid by means of a clean white cloth: Spirits of nitre, one pound; alcohol, one pound; corrosive sublimate, one ounce. Mix in a bottle and keep corked for use. Apply one coat and set in a warm, dark place, until a red rust is formed over the whole surface, which will require, in warm weather, from ten to twelve hours; in cold, from fifteen to twenty hours. Then card it down with a gun-maker's card, and rub off with a clean cloth. Repeat the process until the color suits, as each coat gives a darker shade.

Browning Recipes for Twist and Laminated Barrels.—1. Sweet spirits of nitre, one-half ounce; tincture of steel, one-quarter ounce; corrosive sublimate, one-half ounce; aqua fortis, sixty drops; nitrate of silver, four grains; a small lump of chalk and one pint of rain water.

2. Tincture of sesqui-chloride of iron, one-half ounce; corrosive sublimate, one drachm; sulphate of copper, one-half drachm; nitric acid, one drachm to one and a half drachms; alcohol, six drachms; water, eight ounces. Dissolve the corrosive sublimate in the alcohol, then add the solution to the other ingredients and let the whole stand for a month or six weeks, when it will be ready for use.

3. Sweet spirits of nitre, one ounce; tincture of steel, one-half ounce; blue vitriol, one-quarter ounce; nitric acid, six drops; corrosive sublimate, fourteen grains; water, one pint. When the barrels are dark enough, drop a few drops of muriatic acid in water and wash the barrel slightly to brighten the twists.

4. Muriatic tincture of steel, one ounce; alcohol, one ounce; muriate of mercury, one-quarter ounce; strong nitric acid, one-quarter ounce; blue vitriol, one-eighth ounce; water, one quart. Thoroughly mix the ingredients. Let them stand about thirty days before using. Wet the barrels with the mixture, applied with a sponge, about once every two hours. Scratch off with wire card every morning until the barrels are dark enough.

To Blue Gun Barrels.—A very pretty bluish color may be imparted to gun barrels by dressing them off to brightness with fine emery paper, and then rubbing them over quickly with nitric acid. When the desired color has appeared, wash them off with clean water, rub dry with a soft cloth, and then rub with linseed oil to prevent any further action of the acid.

Brown Tint for Iron or Steel.—Dissolve, in four parts water, two parts of crystalized chloride of iron; two parts of chloride of antimony; and one part of gallic acid, and apply the solution with a sponge or cloth to the barrel, letting it dry in a warm place. Repeat the process according to the depth of color desired. Wash with warm water, and dry; then rub over with boiled linseed oil. The metal receives a brown tint and resists moisture. The chloride of antimony should be as little acid as possible.

Transparent Blue for Iron or Steel.—Put together Demar varnish, one quart; fine ground Prussian blue, one-quarter ounce. Polish the metal to brightness, and put on thinly with a varnish brush. A beautiful transparent blue color, but one that will not stand rough usage.

Varnish for Browned Barrels.—1. Dissolve ten parts clear grains of mastic, five parts camphor, fifteen grains sandarac, and five parts elemi, in a sufficient quantity of alcohol. and apply the varnish without heat. The articles treated with this varnish will not only be preserved from rust, but their metallic lustre will not be in the least dimmed by exposure to dampness.

2. Another varnish may be made by using gum shellac, one ounce; gum sandarac, one ounce; Venice

turpentine, one drachm; and ninety-eight per cent. alcohol, one gallon.

3. Another formula consists of shellac, one ounce; dragon's blood, one-quarter of an ounce; alcohol, one quart. A little less dragon's blood may be used if the color be too great.

Finish for Browned Barrels.—There are many ways of finishing barrels after browning. Some gunsmiths warm the barrels and rub them while quite warm with a flannel cloth and finish with a little bees-wax and turpentine. Some polish with a steel burnisher or rub with white wax; others use a wash of thin shellac varnish laid on carefully and evenly with a camel's hair brush. Some finish off with a solution of two ounces of shellac and three drachms of dragon's blood dissolved in two quarts of good alcohol.

To Remove Old Browning.—To remove old browning, plug the vent and muzzle of the barrels; immerse the browned parts, for about one hour, in hot lime water, or strong lye, to remove the varnish or grease; wipe them and put them in vinegar, in a wooden trough, for an hour or less, when the browning may be wiped off with a rag.

CHAPTER XXXII.

MISCELLANEOUS.

Shellac and its Uses.—Gum shellac is the gunsmith's friend. It is the best material from which to make the varnish he uses, and in wood-working, if there be cracks or checks in the material, or in stocking should a little slip of the tool occur while letting in locks or other parts, a little of the gum judiciously applied remedies the defect, and, like charity, "covers a multitude of little sins."

Shellac is often adulterated with resins, and it requires some knowledge of the article to detect this adulteration. It can only be ascertained by experience in handling, or by ocular demonstration with an expert.

To make Shellac Varnish.—To make varnish, put the shellac in a clean vessel and put over it a quantity of good alcohol, enough to about cover it, if it lie somewhat compact in the receptacle; if too thick when made it can be thinned with alcohol. While the gum is dissolving keep it covered from dust and let it stand in a warm place, as in the sun during the summer, or near a warm stove in the winter. Too much warmth will tend to evaporate the alcohol; and for this reason it ought to be somewhat sealed from the air. It may take two or three days to thoroughly dissolve the gum for varnish, according to the temperature in which it is placed, etc.

When the gum is dissolved, thin with alcohol to the proper consistency for easy application with the brush. If it be dirty, or it be desired to have it clear and nice, filter it through good blotting paper. When not using the varnish, keep close covered to prevent evaporation.

How to conceal Bad Places in Wood-work.—If there be cracks in a stock or a bad cut made in stocking, as will sometimes happen where locks and straps are let in, apply a piece of the gum to the place and with a warm iron melt it into the place, so that it will be well filled; also warm the wood in close proximity to be sure of good ahesion. Let it remain until cold and solid, and then finish down the same as the stock is finished down.

Another Method.—Another method of filling bad places in wood-work is to get fine dust, as made with a fine rasp or file, and mix this dust with thin glue, and rub it into the interstices, letting it remain until hard and solid, and then finish same as the adjoining wood. Neither this nor shellac will adhere where there is oil, or where the surface to adhere has been oiled.

Emery Cloth and Emery Paper.—Emery paper is the cheaper, but is not so durable as the cloth. The paper is soon worn out and is torn in using, but the cloth is seldom destroyed, and can be used so long as any abrasive material remains upon it.

There are about six grades, say Nos. 00, 0, 1, 1½,

2 and 3, which may be selected. To use on plain surfaces cut the sheet up in small, convenient pieces, fold a piece around a file and use as if using the file. In using a finer number, be careful to remove all the marks left by using the previous number. If moistened with oil, a fine, soft-appearing, dead finish is obtained. To use in a lathe, run the work with fast speed and hold the cloth to place with the hand, or put it around a file and so hold it. After the pieces are somewhat worn, they can be used to finish with.

In selecting by the numbers remember that 00 is the finest, and is called flour of emery cloth, or paper; 0 is a little coarser, and then follow the different grades in numerical order.

Uses of the Alcoholic Lamp. How to make Small Springs.—An alcohol lamp is almost indispensable to the jobbing gunsmith. Suppose a small bent spring is to be made, a little trigger spring, for instance, such as is used in many kinds of revolvers, it can be easily formed in this manner: Take a bit of old watch-spring, heat it in the lamp until it is blue, then, with the snips or hand-shears, divide it lengthwise to the necessary width; heat in the flame of the lamp, and, with a pair of pliers, bend to the required shape. It is not always necessary to temper these springs, but if it be necessary to do so, heat until red in lamp, using a blow-pipe if the heat be insufficient, harden in oil, and then draw the temper to suit. The whole operation can be done without moving from the bench, and much quicker, and certainly better, than could be done at the forge.

How to make Small Drills.—Then, again, to make small drills of steel wire, use the lamp for heating and tempering. If a small drill be broken, draw the temper in the lamp preparatory to forming it anew. Drills of larger size may be hardened in the forge fire, brightened by grinding or rubbing on a piece of fine emery cloth, and the temper readily drawn in the lamp. The same process may be applied to tempering small screw taps. Small screws can be readily blued in the same manner.

Advantages of the Alcohol Lamp.—The lamp has this advantage over the forge-fire; it draws the temper very evenly, and the temper color can be readily seen, as the flame of alcohol makes no smoke to obscure it. Even for small tempering, when once employed, no gunsmith will think of discontinuing its use.

The Soldering Copper.—The soldering copper for the use of the gunsmith should be about one and a half pounds in weight. The length of the copper should be about four or five inches, of octagon form, with a square pyramidal shaped point. It is fixed to an iron rod about eight inches long, on the end of which is a wooden handle.

How to Heat the Copper.—When heating the copper for use, the best way to ascertain the proper heat is to hold it near the face, and if a bright warm glow is felt, it is hot enough for use. If heated too hot the tinning will be burned off, and it will not work satisfactorily. To replace the tinning, heat it warm enough to just melt the solder, and file the surface to be tinned bright and smooth, then place a little solder and a bit of resin on a piece of sheet-tin, and in this rub the heated copper until the brightened surface has received a coating of the solder, the resin acting as a flux during the operation.

How to Tin the Copper.—Another method to tin a copper is to put the solder and the resin on a brick, heat the copper and rub until it receives the tin coating. The common soldering acid may be used instead of the resin for a flux. During the operation the point of the copper may be dipped in the acid to facilitate the tinning. It will be found that a too free use of the acid, if used as a flux, for general work, will soon destroy the point of the copper. When this is the case file off the roughness and heat the copper quite warm, and draw it out to shape on the anvil, the same as if working a piece of iron. When so shaped, file smooth and re-tin as directed.

To Prevent Gun Barrels from Glimmering.—It sometimes happens that gun-barrels are disposed to throw off a kind of glimmer without any apparent cause, thus seriously interfering with the hunter or sportsman in getting a correct sight. Of course, the gunsmith would remedy the evil by browning the barrel, but the sportsman in the woods could not do this. Had his friend, the gunsmith, known that such a thing was going to happen he would have told him to get a green hazel-nut pod, crush it, and rub the juice over the barrel, which would produce a beautiful non-glimmering brown. If a green hazel-nut pod could not be had, a green wild plum or a green wild crab-apple or a bunch of green wild grapes would answer the same purpose reasonably well. In the absence of these an unripe black-walnut crushed and rubbed over the barrel would stop the glimmering; and early in spring, when no kind of fruits had yet appeared, a young sprout of wild grape-vine crushed and rubbed over the barrel would make a very good substitute. These were the means resorted to by the "hunters of Kentucky" in the long-gone days of backwoods life, when "Old Kentuck" was young.

Repairing Shot-Chargers.—Very often the stud that holds the lever of a shot-charger will become loose or be forced from its position. The best method to repair it is to remove the lever with its spring and the cutters, put the stud back in place, wet the joint on the inside the charger with soldering acid, and, holding it with the stud downwards, put a bit of soft solder upon the joint, and hold it over an alcohol lamp until the solder melts. If well done it will "stay put."

Sometimes the lever spring will not remain in place, but will slip out. To remedy the evil, take a common Berdan cartridge primer, or any other kind will do, only take one that has been used or has had the priming removed, put inside it a drop of soldering acid and a bit of solder, enough to fill it when melted. Hold it over the lamp until the solder fuses. When it has cooled, wet the charger with a touch of the acid just where the bend of the spring comes, and there place the primer with the solder next the wet place. Hold it in position with a bent piece of wire or a strip of steel bent like a loop. Hold over the lamp, with the primer downward, until the solder is melted. Replace the spring, and it will be found that it will remain firmly in its place.

Broken Plunger Nipples.—When plunger nipples are broken or are lost from the gun, and none are at hand to repair the damage, a substitute may be found in a common gun-nipple by filing away a portion of the cone where the cap is placed. It is worth while to save broken nipples, as they are taken from guns with this end in view for their use. They can be annealed or the temper drawn, and they can be kept ready for drilling for the strikers and cutting over to fit the gun in which they are to be inserted. The nipple used in military arms makes a good substitute for a broken plunger nipple, as the thread is nearly the same as that of some pluuger nipples.

How to Remove Rusted Screws, Broken Nipples, etc.—Sometimes it so happens that a screw is so rusted in a lock or other part of a gun, or a rusted nipple refuses to start from its seat, and by repeated trials the sides of the screw-head adjoining the slot are worn away or the squares of the nipple are forced off, and the removal of either screw or nipple an almost impossibility with the hand screw driver or nipple wrench. In such cases have a screw-driver or the nipple wrench fitted to the lathe chuck, and, holding the screw or nipple in place to be thus turned out, move the dead spindle of the lathe so that the work be firmly held in place, with no chance to "give back," then turn the lathe by moving the fly-wheel with the hand, or hold the wheel fast and turn the work, and, as there is no chance for the tool to slip from its place, the screw and nipple is almost sure to be started. If so, it may be readily turned from its place by hand.

Converting Muskets to Sporting Guns.—Very often old muskets are brought to the gunsmith to have the rifling bored out and changed so as to present more of the appearance of a sporting gun. If properly worked over they make a gun not very bad-looking, but very serviceable, as they will stand a great amount of abuse and will bear large charges. For shooting hawks and keeping corn-fields clear of depredators they are "just the thing."

After the rifling is removed, cut off the barrel to 30 or 32 inches in length. Take off the bands and throw them away. Cut off the stock where the top of the lower band comes, solder a rib on under side of the barrel and attach two thimbles to receive a wooden ramrod. Bore out the stock to receive the wooden rod, using the thimbles on the rib as guides in so doing. Fit the rod as in sporting guns. Cast a tip on fore end of stock where the lower band was, using the lower shoulder where the band rested for the shoulder of the tip. Remove the elevating sight by heating, if it be soldered on, and fix muzzle sight by soldering on a bit of brass, or by drilling a hole and putting in a pin and filing to shape.

In boring for the rod the bit may strike the forward lock-screw, and when this be the case float the stock so that the rod will go above the screw. Don't attempt to change the shape of the stock by removing any portion of it, otherwise than stated, for by so doing the shape and symmetry will be lost, and it will show to be a botch job.

To hold the barrel in place a loop for either wire or bolt must be attached to the barrel a little distance back from the fore end, and a wire or bolt put through the stock the same as other guns are made. In place of the wire or bolt a very good plan is to put a short stud on the barrel, and from the under side of the fore end put in a screw with a large head, like a tumbler-screw. In this case it is necessary to drill a hole through the stud to let the ramrod pass through.

Patent Breech, Bursted.—As the right-hand barrel of double muzzle-loading guns is fired more than the other, it sometimes happens that the patent breech of this barrel is destroyed or becomes defective. It can be replaced by taking a piece of good sound iron, cut down one end of it, and cut a thread the same as if making a breech-pin. After being fitted to the barrel cup it for powder-chamber like the one removed, and cut the hook end off to length. Make the nipple seat as given in the article on that subject. File the hook so as to fit the break-off, remove from the gun, and case-harden. A somewhat formidable-looking job to the one who never made one, but very easy and simple when once accomplished.

Broken Tumblers.—It often happens that the tumbler in a lock is broken off where the hammer goes on, and no tumbler is at hand to replace it. A repair may be made by filing away the broken square and filing a groove or slot down the round part where it went through the lock plate. Fit a piece of square iron or steel, of the size of the broken square, or a round piece that will make the square, to the tumbler by filing away one end to fit the slot filed in the round part. Hold it in place with a piece of binding wire twisted around it, and braze it with spelter solder or good soft copper or brass, then finish to fit the hammer.

Another way is to remove the end where it goes into the bridle and then drill a hole through the tumbler of the size of this end or bearing; make the piece to be brazed on with one end to fit this hole and put it through far enough to make the end filed away. When fitted, braze and finish.

When the trigger catch of a tumbler is broken or is worn away, it can be entirely removed by filing and a piece of steel fitted or held by a small rivet and then brazed. After being finished up and fitted to the trigger, the tumbler can be hardened, care being taken not to heat it sufficiently to melt the brazing material.

Describing Lines on Bright Surfaces.—Many gunsmiths find it difficult to make the pattern of work upon iron or steel, especially after the surface is finished. Yet it is necessary to have the outline of the intended form. For instance, if the pattern of a hammer for a revolver or a gun hammer, the sides of which are both flat (in fact the hammers of many breech-loading rifles are made in this manner), be required to be made on a piece of iron or steel that has been faced down, the method is to drill a hole for the screw or pin on which it turns, then fasten the pattern to the work by driving a piece of wire into the hole, and, with a sharp scriber, mark around the pattern, which is then removed and the work filed away to the line. If the hammer be a broken one, then care must be taken to have the pieces held carefully as they were before being broken. If the pieces be somewhat small and difficult to hold properly, warm them over a spirit lamp and smear the sides to be put against the blank, lightly with beeswax, and this will tend to hold them better in place and prevent their slipping.

To obtain a more permanent line and one that will show very distinctly in all its tracings, coat the surface on which the line is to be made with a film of copper. To do this take a lump of sulphate of copper, sometimes called blue vitriol or blue stone, wet it with water and rub over the bright surface of the work. The moisture will dry in a few minutes, leaving a surface or film of pure copper. Put the pattern in place and describe the outline. Upon removing the pattern the line will be found to be clear and showing very distinctly through the coppery surface. Three or four light rubs with the sulphate are sufficient to produce this surface, which is so very thin that it may be easily removed when the work is done with a fine file or by rubbing with a bit of emery paper or emery cloth.

CHAPTER XXXIII.

ON POWDER AND SHOT.

To Select Buck Shot.—The proper way is to put a wad in the muzzle of the gun, about half an inch down, and fit the shot in perfect layers; if this is observed, there will be no necessity to try them in the cartridge case, as they will be sure to fit. Buck-shot cast from a mould with nine to the 1⅛ ounce, will just fit a twelve-bore barrel at the muzzle in a choke bore. If smaller shot is required, choose four to a layer, or five, and avoid the sizes that come between. At forty yards, all these pellets ought to go in a 26-inch circle, and the penetration be equal to a small rifle.

Weighing Powder, etc.—For weighing powder charges for rifles, Apothecaries' scales and the Apothecaries' table of weights and measures are used. The table is:

20 grains, 1 scruple;
3 scruples, 1 drachm;
8 drachms, 1 ounce;
12 ounces, 1 pound.

Powder is bought and sold by Avoirdupois weight, which has 16 ounces to the pound. The table is:

16 drachms, 1 ounce;
16 ounces, 1 pound.

The standard unit of weight of the U. S., is the pound, Troy weight, the table of which is:

24 grains, 1 pennyweight;

20 pennyweights, 1 ounce;

12 ounces, 1 pound.

The grain, ounce, or pound, Troy, and the grain, ounce, and pound, Apothecaries' weight, are precisely the same; but the ounce is differently divided.

The grain weight is the same in both tables. The pound Avoirdupois, like the pound Troy, contains 7,000 grains. The pound Apothecaries, contains 5,760 grains.

One pound of powder, Avoirdupois weight, will load 140 fifty-grain cartridges; 93 seventy-five-grain cartridges; 70 one-hundred-grain cartridges.

A dram Avoirdupois is equal to $27\frac{11}{32}$ grains.

In weighing bullets and powder in grains, Troy weight is used, and $437\frac{1}{2}$ grains are equal to one ounce Avoirdupois. The drachm, Dixon measure, is $27\frac{1}{2}$ grains, Troy or Apothecaries' weight.

COMPARATIVE SIZES OF SHOT.

DESCRIPTION.	SOFT SHOT PELLETS TO OUNCE.							
	Sparks....	Tatham....	Le Roy....	Baltimore ..	Chicago....	St. Louis...	English	Diameter of Shot....
Extra Fine Dust..........	....	84,021	....	....	....	....	....	$\frac{1\frac{1}{2}}{100}$
Fine Dust..........	....	10,784	....	....	....	....	....	$\frac{3}{100}$
Dust..........	5910	4565	....	....	....	....	....	$\frac{4}{100}$
No. 12..........	3316	2326	1778	2232	2400	2820	....	$\frac{5}{100}$
" 11..........	1660	1346	982	1536	1414	1700	....	$\frac{6}{100}$
" 10..........	950	848	822	815	854	1006	1728	$\frac{7}{100}$
" 9..........	615	568	560	600	596	680	984	$\frac{8}{100}$
" 8..........	426	399	375	365	434	490	600	$\frac{9}{100}$
" 7..........	305	291	278	290	323	360	341	$\frac{10}{100}$
" 6..........	245	218	209	190	246	250	280	$\frac{11}{100}$
" 5..........	182	168	166	150	172	190	218	$\frac{12}{100}$
" 4..........	130	132	121	125	146	158	177	$\frac{13}{100}$
" 3..........	118	106	98	90	118	126	135	$\frac{14}{100}$
" 2..........	90	86	82	70	92	95	112	$\frac{15}{100}$
" 1..........	80	71	69	60	75	82	82	$\frac{16}{100}$
" B..........	63	59	58	50	62	68	75	$\frac{17}{100}$
" B.B..........	55	50	49	45	53	55	58	$\frac{18}{100}$
" B.B.B..........	48	42	44	40	46	....	47	$\frac{19}{100}$
" A..........	....	....	....	....	....	50	....	......
" A.A	....	....	....	....	....	40	....	....
" T..........	41	36	38	35	....	....	....	$\frac{20}{100}$
" T.T..........	36	31	32	30	....	....	....	$\frac{21}{100}$
" O..........	....	....	....	....	38	39	....	$\frac{20}{100}$
" O.O..........	....	....	....	....	33	34	....	$\frac{21}{100}$
" O.O.O..........	....	....	....	....	27	28	....	$\frac{22}{100}$
" T.T.T..........	....	....	27	26	....	....	....	$\frac{22}{100}$
" T.T.T.T..........	....	....	24	....	....	....	....	$\frac{23}{100}$
" F..........	22	27	....	....	....	....	....	$\frac{22}{100}$
" F.F..........	....	24	....	....	....	....	....	$\frac{23}{100}$

COMPARATIVE SIZES OF SHOT.

CHILLED SHOT PELLETS TO OUNCE.

Description.	Sparks....	Tatham....	Le Roy....	Baltimore...	Chicago....	St. Louis...	English....	Diameter of Shot....
No. 12	3328	2385	....	....	....	....	....	$\frac{5}{100}$
" 11	1670	1380	....	....	....	....	....	$\frac{6}{100}$
" 10	960	868	....	....	....	....	1700	$\frac{7}{100}$
" 9	618	585	....	....	....	....	1000	$\frac{8}{100}$
" 8	432	409	....	....	....	....	606	$\frac{9}{100}$
" 7	318	299	....	....	....	....	350	$\frac{10}{100}$
" 6	253	223	....	....	....	....	270	$\frac{11}{100}$
" 5	190	172	....	....	....	....	220	$\frac{12}{100}$
" 4	142	136	....	....	....	....	180	$\frac{13}{100}$
" 3	120	109	....	....	....	....	130	$\frac{14}{100}$
" 2	106	88	....	....	....	....	110	$\frac{15}{100}$
" 1	89	73	....	....	....	....	80	$\frac{16}{100}$
" B	....	61	....	....	....	....	....	$\frac{17}{100}$
" B.B	....	52	....	....	....	....	....	$\frac{18}{100}$
" B.B.B	....	43	....	....	....	....	....	$\frac{19}{100}$

COMPARATIVE SIZES OF BALLS.

Description.	Balls to Pound.							
	Sparks	Tatham	Le Roy	Baltimore	Chicago	St. Louis	English	Diameter of Shot
Buck 3	320			312				$\frac{25}{100}$
" 8					320			$\frac{25}{100}$
" 4			300					$\frac{25}{100}$
" 3		288	270					$\frac{25}{100}$ $\frac{28}{100}$
S.S.S.G							272	
S.S.G							240	
Buck 2	212	225	238	250				$\frac{28}{100}$ $\frac{27}{100}$ $\frac{29}{100}$
" 8						234		$\frac{28}{100}$
" 7					212	194		$\frac{29}{100}$
S.G.							176	
Buck 6					165	176		$\frac{31}{100}$ $\frac{29}{100}$
I. C.				174				
Buck 1	165	172	160	182				$\frac{31}{100}$ $\frac{30}{100}$ $\frac{32}{100}$
O				166				
Buck 5						147		$\frac{30}{100}$
O	144	140	145					$\frac{32}{100}$ $\frac{32}{100}$ $\frac{34}{100}$
M.G							136	
C.P	136							$\frac{33}{100}$
Buck 5					136			$\frac{33}{100}$
L. Buck	128							$\frac{34}{100}$
Buck 4						127		$\frac{32}{100}$
O.O			120	120				$\frac{35}{100}$
Buck 4					113			$\frac{34}{100}$
" 8						113		$\frac{34}{100}$
O O	112	113						$\frac{35}{100}$ $\frac{34}{100}$
R. 4	100							$\frac{36}{100}$
O.O.O		100						$\frac{36}{100}$
Buck 3					100			$\frac{36}{100}$
" 2						97		$\frac{36}{100}$
O.O.O				88				
L.G							88	
O.O.O	85		85					$\frac{38}{100}$ $\frac{40}{100}$

[Continued on next page.]

COMPARATIVE SIZES OF BALLS.

Description.	Balls to Pound.							
	Sparks	Tatham	Le Roy	Baltimore	Chicago	St. Louis	English	Diameter of Shot
Balls 38		85						$\frac{38}{100}$
N.P				85				
Buck 1						84		$\frac{38}{100}$
" 2					70			$\frac{40}{100}$
58				58				
R. 2	55							$\frac{44}{100}$
A P				53				
Balls 44		50				48		$\frac{44}{100}$
Buck 1					50			$\frac{44}{100}$
R 1	36							[illegible]/100
32				32				
½ oz						32		$\frac{52}{100}$
M. 18	18							$\frac{63}{100}$
M. 16	16			16				$\frac{65}{100}$

COLT PISTOL SIZES.

Colt 31	Buck 1				Buck 6			
" 36	R. 4	000			Buck 3	Buck 2		
" 44	R. 2	B'lls44			Buck 1	44		

COMPARATIVE SIZES OF GUNPOWDER.

Commencing with the Coarsest Grain of each Quality.

Common Sporting.				Fine Sporting.			
Oriental	Orange.	Hazzard	Dupont.	Oriental	Orange.	Hazzard	Dupont
....	C.......	....	Fg......	Falcon..	......	American..	......
Fg......	Fg......	Fg......	FFg....	No. 1.....	......	No. 1..	......
FFg....	FFg...	FFg...	FFFg..	" 2....	......	" 2..	......
FFFg ..	FFFg ..	FFFg..	......	" 3....	......	" 3..	......
....	....	....	......	....	......	......	......
....	....	....	......	....	......	......	......
....	....	....	......	....	......	......	......
....	....	....	......	....	......	......	E.R..

Fine Ducking.				Best Quality Sporting.			
Oriental	Orange	Hazzard	Dupont.	Oriental	Orange.	Hazzard	Dupont.
Falcon & Wild Fowl.	....	....	....	Di'mond Grain.	Lightning.	Electric.	......
No. 4...	No. 5...	No. 5...	No. 1...	No. 4...	No. 7.	No. 4..	......
" 3...	" 4...	" 4...	" 2...	" 3...	" 6	" 3..	......
" 2..	" 3...	" 3...	" 3...	" 2...	" 5.	" 2...	......
" 1...	" 2...	" 2...	....	" 1...	" 4.	......	......
....	....	....	....	Fg......	......	......	Diamond Grain.
....	....	....	....	FFg....	......	......	
....	....	....	....	FFFg. .	......	......	

Dupont's Eagle Rifle powder is the finest grain of sporting powder made; Oriental Falcon Sporting, No. 3 grain, is the nearest to it in size.

CHAPTER XXXIV.

MISCELLANEOUS RECIPES.

Soft Soldering.—Soft solder, so called, is a composition made by melting together two parts tin and one part lead. If the gunsmith ever has occasion to use it, he will need a soldering fluid, which is made by dropping clippings of zinc into muriatic acid until ebullition has ceased, then adding to the acid its equal in bulk of pure water, although some mechanics do not consider the addition of water as necessary.

Clean thoroughly the parts to be soldered together, then wet them with the soldering fluid. Next place in the joint a thin bit of the soft solder, and expose to heat, the heating agent to be clear of oil. The pieces should be held, pressed between the blades of large tweezers, so that when the solder melts the two parts will come directly together. So soon as the solder melts, the work must be taken from the fire, as the soldering will be complete. A little longer exposure would burn the solder and spoil the work.

Good Soft Solder.—Good soft solder is composed of equal parts of pure tin and good soft lead. The lead from old tea chests is excellent. Plumbers' solder is often made of lead three parts and tin one part.

Soldering Fluid.—A soldering fluid for jewelers' use is made by adding to alcohol all the chloride of zinc it will dissolve.

Brazing.—This consists in uniting iron and other hard-melting metals with a brass solder. Put the parts together as for soft soldering, lay the brass between the pieces or along the upper edge of the joint, if it can be held vertically, and add a goodly supply of pulverized borax to act as a flux. Heat over a charcoal fire till the brass melts and runs down into the joint, then take from the fire and cool. Before beginning the operation of brazing the parts to be put together must be made entirely clean, and then freshly filed to brightness.

To Braze Lugs on Gun Barrels.—When not practicable to fasten the lugs by means of pins or rivets, hold them in place with binding wire. Take a piece of iron, say ¼ inch thick and 2 inches or more in width, and make in it a slot some larger than the lug to be brazed. Lay the barrel on the iron sideways, and pack up the lug so as to lie level, if necessary, also taking care that it is on straight. Pure copper is excellent for all kinds of brazing, when the color of the copper is not objectionable.

Hard Soldering.—See "To Solder Brass," in Chapter XII, which about covers the whole thing, varying only in the composition of the solder for different metals. The brass solder there described acts equally well for soldering copper, but for silver a solder is made composed of two parts silver and one part brass.

Hard Solders.—1. A hard solder that is yellow and easily fusible is made of copper, 4½ parts, and zinc, 5½ parts.

2. To hard solder iron use good tough brass or sheet copper, with borax as a flux.

3. Pure copper, cut in thin strips, with borax as a flux, is excellent for brazing iron or steel.

Alloy for Adhering to Iron or Steel.—Melt together, tin 3 parts, zinc 7½ parts, and copper 39½ parts. Clean the iron or steel, file to brightness and cast the alloy upon it. The iron or steel should be heated up to about the melting temperature of the alloy. This alloy will adhere firmly to the other metal, and as its rate of expansion is about the same as the iron or steel, under all circumstances, it will never come loose. It finishes up nicely and presents a very neat, light yellow appearance. Some gunsmiths use it for brazing purposes on account of its adhesive properties and its ease of fusion. It does not make so strong a joint as brass or copper, and therefore would not give so "honest" a job.

Gun Oil.—A good quality of sperm oil is undoubtedly the best oil to apply to gun work, especially the locks. Any fine animal oil may be used as a substitute. The oil from the fat of the woodchuck or ground-hog is admired by many. Fine quality of sewing-machine oil is very good. It must not be thinned or "cut" with kerosene or benzine, as this reduces its wearing quality. It must not thicken with exposure to the cold.

Vegetable oils are unfit for the locks of guns. Castor oil will gum up and become filthy in the extreme. Olive oil or "sweet oil" has very often been agitated, with common salt, nitric ether, sulphuric acid or hydrochloric acid to keep it from becoming rancid. Application of such oil, in addition to its bad lubricating quality, will rust and spoil work where applied.

If desired to clarify oil, put in a bottle, say a quart of oil, and add about half a pound of fine lead shavings. In a short time the impurities will collect on the lead, when the clarified portion may be poured off. Let the bottle stand in the sun for two or three weeks during the process, and then filter through fine white blotting-paper. If some portion be found to congeal by cold, separate the clear portion from the other, reserving the uncongealed for use during exposure of the gun to cold weather.

Gunsmith's Glue.—Dissolve four ounces of good glue in sixteen ounces of strong acetic acid by exposure to gentle heat. This is not exactly a liquid glue preparation—it is only semi-liquid. It may be kept for any length of time desired, and, when wanted for use, a slight warming up is all the preparation necessary. The gunsmith finds it not only very convenient, in case he should have occasion to use glue about his woodwork, but also very good.

CHAPTER XXXV.

ON JUDGING THE QUALITY OF GUNS.

The Muzzle-Loading Shot-Gun.—In the days when the gun of this character was at its zenith, its quality could be approximately decided upon by a glance at the manufacturer's brand which it bore, but at present that rule cannot be so safely trusted. Many of the houses which built for themselves a fine reputation by the manufacture of fine guns of the muzzle-loading order, have either ceased to exist, or have gone exclusively into the manufacture of breech-loaders, consequently the old brands, though they may still be met with, are not reliable. In truth they are more often dangerous signs than otherwise, in consequence of the fact that unscrupulous manufacturers not unfrequently apply them surreptitiously as an agent to aid in working off their bogus goods. It is, therefore, best to give brands but little consideration in judging the quality of new muzzle-loaders, trusting mainly on personal knowledge as to what a good gun should be, backed up by thorough test in all cases where such a thing is necessary.

The man capable of becoming a good gunsmith will require no special rules for his government in this matter. He will know that a steel gun is preferable to an iron gun, and he will be able to readily distinguish between steel and iron. He will also know that a gun finely finished in every particular, is, undoubtedly, a better gun than one put together in the rough, and his own eyes will quickly tell him as to the finish. Prompted by these considerations, the muzzle loading shot-gun is turned over to the good sense of the gunsmith for adjudgement as to superior or inferior qualities, leaving him to decide upon it, unbiased by any rules that could be given, which is the most rational course to pursue, since, under existing cirumstances it would be impossible to make rules that would be entirely reliable.

The Muzzle-loading Rifle.—In the case of the old-fashioned Kentucky rifle, still on the market in limited numbers, eyesight and test, if necessary, will have to be the main reliance of the gunsmith in judging of quality. The barrel of a first-quality gun of this character is wrought iron, made eight-square, and finely finished. The lock is steel, well put up, and provided with double or set triggers. The stock is either black-walnut or maple highly polished and oil-finished. The bore is given as perfect a degree of finish as iron is capable of taking, and the rifles are deeply-cut and entirely regular all the way through. The sights are made with great care, some of the finest guns having an elevating hind-sight to be changed for long or short range—say, for 500 or 50 yards. In some of the older made guns the foresights are silver, though as a general rule they are made of some kind of white metal compound not so liable to glimmer as silver. The tube-cylinder has a vent screw in the end of it, which may be taken out for the purpose of working in powder in case a ball should have been accidently put down without powder, which accident, without this provision, would be apt to necessitate an unbreeching of the gun. The barrels are of different lengths, ranging from 26 to 40 inches, and the size of bore is equally varied. It is usually estimated by the number of round bullets a pound of lead will cast to fit it, as 200 (smallest bore), 175, 100, and so on down to 50, which is considered the largest bore in common use. The weight of the gun complete usually ranges at from six to twelve pounds.

A steel-barrel rifle made on the Kentucky plan may be met with occasionally, though not often. The steel barrel generally adds about five dollars in cost over that of the iron barrel finished in the same way, and is supposed to be at least that much better on account of less liability to wear and roughen in the bore.

The muzzle-loading rifle of more modern style differs very materially from the old Kentucky rifle in many respects. Mr. Barber, in his "Crack Shot," says of it that so many changes are constantly taking place, and opinions are so diversified, that it is really difficult to state what is the prevailing style; but he is of opinion that a barrel of from thirty to thirty-four inches in length, with a bore from thirty-eight hundredths inch to forty-four hundredths inch will be found to answer best for general purposes. If for sporting purposes exclusively the barrel ought to be a little shorter, perhaps, though he believes the great hunters of the plains use rifles with barrels of from thirty five to forty inches in length, and of a calibre so small as to enable them to make sixty round balls out of one pound of lead.

But, still adopting Barber, it is very difficult to lay down particular rules as to what a muzzle-loading rifle of modern style should be, as marksmen and gunmakers are both whimsical, and each has his set ideas and notions concerning the matter. Some advocate a long barrel, while others maintain that anything beyond thirty-three inches militates against good shooting.

There are many prominent establishments engaged in the manufacture of modern muzzle-loading rifles, some of them carrying splendid reputations, hence in this case a good deal of reliance can be placed upon brands. For instance, should a rifle be seen marked to Wesson, it is a guarantee of a good gun, for the reputation of the manufacturer is worth too much to admit of risking its tarnish by putting upon the market goods bearing his brand that are not fully up to all that is claimed for them.

And now that reference has been made incidentally to Wesson, a description may as well be made of some of the peculiarities of his muzzle-loading rifle as presenting a fair sample of a first-class gun of this order. And to do this under the best of authority, reference is made to Mr. Chapman's book on the Rifle, which is generally accepted as a standard work.

Referring to the Wesson muzzle-loading rifle, Mr. Chapman says that the barrel is made of cast steel, not highly carbonized, but thoroughly annealed in an air-tight oven. The length of the barrel is two feet eight inches when the loading muzzle is off. Outside, the barrel tapers a little from breech to muzzle, the difference in diameter being one fourth of an inch. The barrel is not furnished with a rib, except it be that the short tube at the breech can be called a rib, the peculiarity of stocking doing away with the necessity for a regular rib. The gun has a patent breech, which is made of iron case-hardened. It is joined to the break-off by the old-fashioned hook, with the addition of a half-lap joint, secured by a square-headed screw. Such a mode of fastening the barrel destroys the necessity for wood forward of the breech, and gives a peculiarly elegant and striking appearance to the arm. The loading-muzzle is put on by means of four steel wire pins about one-eighth of an inch in diameter and three-eighths long, and the holes for these pins are located as near the outside as possible.

The grooves of this rifle are cut with a twist, which turns the bullet once in three feet six inches. There are six grooves, and the spaces between them are left entirely square to the interior surface, presenting a kind of dove-tail appearance. The grooves are not quite so wide as the spaces between them. The breech is furnished with a vent or breathing nipple, about the diameter of a common pin, and bushed with platinum. The lock has back-action, furnished with a single set. The stock is of black walnut, made as straight as possible. It is furnished with a patch box, and also a small box to contain a wiper, which can be attached to the end of the ramrod. A globe sight is fixed into the stock, just behind the break-off, while a bead sight holds position at the muzzle-end of the barrel. The weight of the gun complete is ten pounds.

Of course it will be clearly understood that this description is not offered as of the best muzzle-loading rifle made, but simply because it happened to be convenient to make. There are, doubtless, other guns equally as good, and a preference of one over the other, in all probability, would have to be born of circumstances, as something peculiar in the tastes or requirements of the person by whom the gun was to be used, or in the particular line of use to which it was to be applied.

The Breech-loading Shot Gun.—Gloan tells us that, in judging the quality of a breech-loader, there are other things to be taken into consideration besides the mere shooting of the gun. First among these is its safety relative to the person using it. There is more machinery and complication about it than there is about the muzzle-loader, and to that extent, if not made upon sound principles, and perfectly well made, it is more dangerous, to say nothing of being less durable.

But the principle must be a prime consideration, for, if a gun, no matter how well made, is constructed with a working movement which presents great strain and great friction, it must speedily wear out. Even the best breech-loader, with the soundest known action, must wear out sooner than would an arm of less complication, because some peculiar strain and friction cannot possibly be avoided; hence the great importance of passing judgment entirely favorable upon only the best.

The first thing to decide upon, then, is the principle upon which the gun works. No special rules can be given to govern in the formation of this decision other than that simplicity is always worthy of favorable consideration—the greater the simplicity the better, provided it works to the full accomplishment of all the ends desired. Next to simplicity may be ranked durability, and next to this may come in good shooting and safety. These last two considerations are put as third and fourth, when many persons would be inclined to rank them as second and first. Why this is done is because many of the most common guns are safe enough, so far as that is concerned, while not a few of them shoot very well for a while.

Some most excellent shooting has been done with extremely common guns, working upon a principle so complicated and so imperfect as to render it impossible for them to remain in order beyond a comparatively short length of time.

The English manufacturers, of good reputation, take great pains with their breech-loading shotguns; hence, until within a very few years, English guns were considered entirely superior to those of

American make, but now it is acknowledged, even by the English people, that in America we put up, at least, some guns that have no superiors. This last named fact has somewhat destroyed the weight of English brands with persons who are looking for a gun of the very best quality. But the advance on the part of American gunmakers is not the only thing that has worked against the reputation of English guns for being eminently the best. The gun-making business of Belgium has seriously injured the general good name of English guns, just as the watch-making business of Switzerland has injured the good name of English watches. For instance, Liege, in Belgium, is almost literally a city of gunmakers. It is estimated that there are now more small fire-arms made in Liege than in all the rest of the world put together, though Leige gets credit for comparatively few of them. The different parts are manufactured there, and shipped to other countries as gunmakers' materials, where they are put together and branded with the name of a maker who really played no part whatever in the making. In Liege each manfacturing house is devoted to the manufacture of but a single part, knowing nothing whatever of the other parts manufactured at other establishments. As a result the gun made of Liege materials is simply a patchwork, and hence could not possibly be so reliable as a gun whose every part is made in the same establishment, and under the eye of the same general superintendent. England has gone largely into the putting up of these patchwork guns, simply for the reason that she can buy the Liege materials much cheaper than she can make them at home. This cheapness is due to the inferior materials used by the Liege manufacturers, and to the extremely low rate of wages in Belgium. It is asserted, upon good authority, that the English "manufacturer" can get his finished materials from Liege, paying regular Government duty, and put together what would appear to be a fair quality of double-barrel breech-loading shot-gun, at the cost of about seven dollars. And he does it, giving the gun to the market under his own brand, or surreptitiously under that of some other house known to be more reliable than his own. As a consequence, English reputation is sadly injured as regards the business of making the best guns, and gunsmiths can no longer trust to English brands as a sure guarantee of first-class quality. Of course there are some English manufacturers whom it will always do to trust, provided one knows to a certainty that the gun is really genuine.

If that patchwork game is played in this country at all it is on a small scale as yet, and is confined to the cheapest guns. A gun from any of our prominent houses is quite sure to be as represented; and, until the gunsmith becomes so familiar with all the requirements of a good gun, the maker's price may be taken as a pretty safe rule by which to judge of quality. Each manufacturing house is apt to have its guns graded, and priced accordingly—the higher the price asked the better the gun in every case, for it is as much the desire of the prominent manufacturer to make a good name as it is to make a good gun.

Of course this rule can only be considered entirely safe in case where the scale of prices has been obtained directly from headquarters. Passing through half a dozen or so of middle houses might work important changes from the original price list.

Where none of these rules can be brought to bear it is but natural that the inexperienced gunsmith should turn to his MANUAL for aid in forming judgment upon the quality of the gun. A few general ideas may not be out of place.

All the movements of the action should be smooth, and all the joints should fit to perfection. The locks should have due consideration. When the hammer is drawn back it should come with less and less resistance as it rises, and *vise versa* when the hammer is let down, exerting its greatest power immediately on reaching the nipple or firing-pin. But this increase and decrease of power should be extremely gradual, and not great. Throughout the movement there should be a steadiness and freeness, or, as Gloan says, an oiliness, which when once realized, can never afterwards be mistaken. And when by a regular pressure upon the trigger the hammer is expertly raised and lowered in rapid succession, the locks should emit a clear ringing sound at the whole and half-cock with the resonance and regularity of beats in music. When once heard, this, too, can never afterwards be mistaken. The locks which perform to perfection under the tests mentioned are technically said to "speak well."

Turning from the lock to the lever, the latter should close with such ease as not to require any particular exertion of the wrist, and when closed it should hold with such a degree of firmness as to place safety, while discharging the gun, entirely beyond question. The wedges of the action should be fully and squarely set in the lump.

If a pin gun the pin should fit in the hole with nicety. If too tight, the barrels might not close, or the pin might be held back to such an extent that the cap would not be exploded. If too loose an unnecessary escape of gas at the discharge would be unavoidable, to the discomfort of the gunner and the weakening of the shot.

If a central fire the plungers should strike the centre of the cap unvaringly. The hammer should come upon the plunger with a blow--not a mere push.

The countersink of the chambers, and the length and breadth of the action bed, should be closely observed. The countersink should be cut clean and deep enough to take the rim of the cartridge without leaving the slightest projection—else the gun will not shut perfectly. But if, on the contrary, the countersink be too deep the cartridge comes back on the breech before the charge makes its exit, which increases the recoil and renders accuracy less certain.

The central fire strikers should not be too short, an imperfection which might cause the discharge of the gun while closing it. On the other hand, they should not be too long, as that would interfere with the free motion of the gun. In the case of a pin gun the pin should invariably stand in exact line with the hammer, otherwise the blow would be apt to bend it, and the chances for exploding the cap would be less certain.

There should be no crevices between the wood and iron. If any such crevice exists between the stock and the false breech it is likely that the wood was green when put up, which would settle it that the gun was not the work of a responsible maker, for no such person would work imperfectly-seasoned wood.

The extractor of the central fire should never be permitted to escape the closest scrutiny. It should work without the slightest hitch, and its arms should enclose about one-half of the cartridge rim. The countersink should fit the rim precisely, in order that there may be no slipping.

The Breech-Loading Rifle.—Most of the rules suggested as aids in forming judgment upon the quality of the breech-loading shot gun, can be trusted as bearing with equal force in case of the breech-loading rifle. The makers of breech-loading rifles in the United States have won for themselves a noble reputation throughout the world; and, to be perfectly plain, there are very few unreliable manufacturers to be met with among them. As a consequence, there is not much risk to run in passing judgment upon a breech-loading rifle of American make. The first thing to decide upon is the principle, if there is a preference in this direction. Such decision brings up the gun of some particular maker, after which the road is easy enough—the price set upon the grade of gun by the maker, may always be accepted as a clear indication of its quality.

In referring thus to American rifles the idea is not advanced that good guns are not made in other countries—such a position would be going wide of the truth. There are *some* gunmakers in England who turn out the finest rifles that the world has yet seen, and the most costly. They are models of perfection in every particular, but when the best shooting is ascertained it is discovered that they have not proven themselves superior in that respect, to the more substantial (generally speaking), but less finely finished and less expensive guns of the American makers. It is this matter of a really good rifle at comparatively low figures that has given the American product such an enviable reputation throughout the world.

Then there is another reason for favorable mention of American rifles in cases where the quality of the gun is to be judged—there are fewer chances for meeting with counterfeits on American guns than there are on guns of foreign make. Here the gunmaker is so deeply concerned in his own good name that it would be very unsafe to attempt running a "bogus" upon him—he would trace it to the "last ditch." Not so in case of the English maker—having no direct interests thrown all over this country like a network, as have the American makers, he would, in all probability, never hear of the bogus gun branded to him and sold on his good reputation for many times more than it was really worth.

In case where there are no means of getting at the quality of a rifle from the grade affixed and tests made by a responsible manufacturer, the gunsmith will of course be forced to fall back upon his own resources. What these are we need not state. The gun must be subjected to a most critical examination in every part, in obedience to rules laid down for examining breech-loading shot guns, after which its shooting qualities must be thoroughly tested. To no botch at the business can be trusted the shooting test, if it be wished to decide whether or not a certain rifle can be recommended as being of first-class quality—the work must be performed at the hands of an expert, and it must be continued until is secured unmistakable proof as to how the gun shoots. When a man buys a good rifle he does it in the expectation of becoming the owner of a gun qualified to shoot well, and, no matter how perfect it might be in all other respects, the slightest deficiency in this particular would be sure to rouse a high degree of uncompromising dissatisfaction.

CHAPTER XXXVI.

ON USING THE RIFLE.

The Old Kentucky Rifle.—The old backwoods hunters who used the long Kentucky rifle, had really but a very imperfect idea of its capabilities. The gun was provided with a hind and a fore-sight, the latter a "bead" located near the muzzle and rising but little above the common level of the surface of the barrel, and the former a small vertical plate set in the barrel a short distance in advance of the lock, and containing in the centre of its upper edge a fine slit through which to look at the "bead" in the act of taking aim. The hind-sight stood further above the barrel than the fore-sight, but why it so stood was something about which the owner seldom concerned himself. Of course the gunsmith knew it was for the purpose of setting the "aim" below the starting line of the bullet, in order that the natural curve in its flight might be accommodated, but this was usually a secret of the gunsmiths which nobody cared to possess. The sight was immovable, could neither be raised nor lowered, consequently the gun could not be adapted to circumstances of long or short range. The elevation of the sight usually crossed the line of vision and that of the flight of the bullet at about one hundred yards distance, hence the shooting at shorter range was apt to be a little too high and too low at longer range. At two hundred yards it was merely accidental, though the bullet struck with a degree of force apparently unabated at that distance. If the hunter killed his game at two hundred yards, he did it by aiming a few feet too high for a "sight" at one hundred yards, consequently he never shot at that distance so long as there was a prospect of being able to creep nearer. And yet, with the right kind of elevated sight the gun would have been equally as effectual at two hundred yards as at one hundred; in truth it would have been good for four and perhaps six hundred yards, but the old hunter had not so much as a dream of any such thing, but went creeping about through the woods endeavoring to steal upon his game, unconsciously carrying upon his shoulder an instrument that with so simple a contrivance as an elevated sight of proper grade might have brought it down almost as far as the eye could have seen it. And the game well knew the limited capacity of his gun, particularly the deer, which would frisk off to the distance of about three hundred yards and there stop, turn around, stamp their feet and "whistle" at him in apparent derision. Ah! that he had understood the real capabilities of his gun, and had suddenly invented and applied an elevated or long-range sight made after some of the approved modern plans, how he would have astonished them!

In those days of pioneer life in the States now no longer on the frontier, "match shooting" (it was not called target shooting, then) was always confined to a certain distance, sixty yards off-hand or one hundred yards with a rest. The marksman was permitted to take his own choice of modes. "Shooting matches" were very common in those earlier times, usually for beef. A fat ox was put up to be shot for at so much per shot, something on the plan of the modern raffle. When the amount asked for the animal had been made up, the shooting commenced. The best shot took first choice, which was one of the hind quarters of the ox, the second best took second choice, which was the other hind quarter; the third best took third choice, which was one of the fore quarters, and so on to the fifth choice, which consisted of the hide and tallow. Happy occasions, indeed, were those old "shooting matches," and splendid, indeed, was some of the shooting. A regular attendance upon numerous target matches of more modern times, with all the modern appliances, in the hands of marksmen with national reputations, has never shown us better shooting at sixty yards, off-hand, or one hundred yards with a rest.

General Directions.—Mr. Edward C. Barber, author of the "Crack Shot," says the greatest care and nicety is required in loading any kind of rifle, if we desire to have it shoot with accuracy. A few grains too much or too little powder will alter the range of the bullet, and the bullet itself, if not placed in the barrel exactly right, in the case of the muzzle-loader, will come out at an irregular angle,

Colt's Revolver.

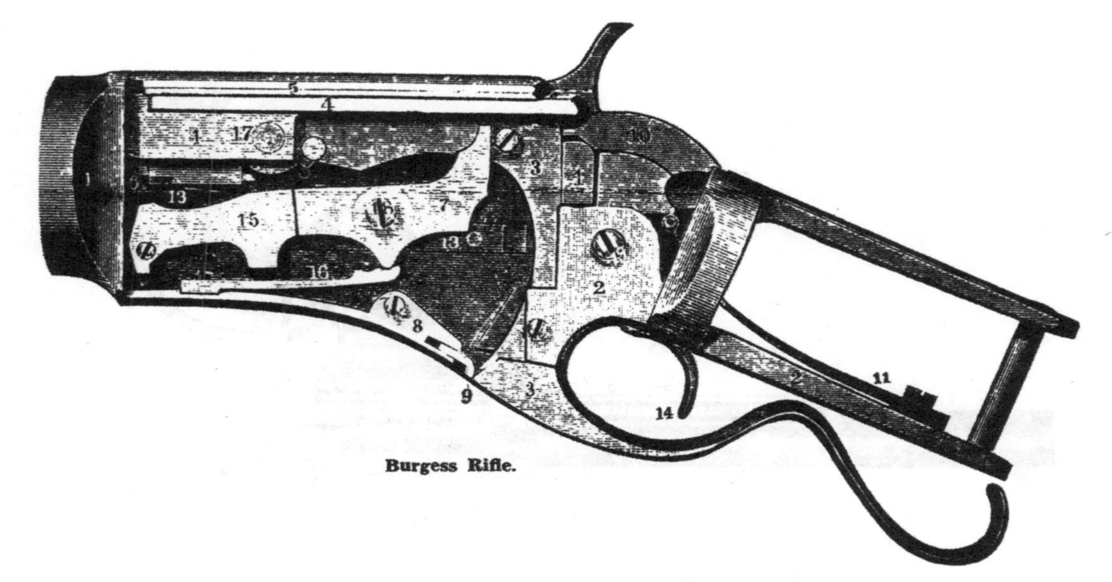

Burgess Rifle.

and, instead of going straight to the mark, will be turned sideways. This trouble is avoided by the use of a "starter," to be had at any gun store.

Supposing that a young man has just possessed himself of a rifle, but who knows nothing of its use save such information as he has been able to gather from mere theorists. He makes choice of a suitable place for taking his first practical lesson, where there is no danger of inflicting harm upon disinterested persons. He puts up his target and steps off fifty yards, or it might be better to measure it more accurately than by stepping.

Suppose the gun to be a first-class modern muzzle-loader. The target is now arranged; proceed to load. Grasp the barrel of the gun near the muzzle; turn it round so that the lock is outward, then pour from the flask the proper charge of powder, using the charger which the gunmaker has furnished. Be sure that the charger is exactly full—no more nor less. Pour the powder gently down the barrel, holding the latter upright so that none of the powder will lodge in the grooves or rifles. Get ready a "patch," which has been previously prepared by oiling on one side a piece of fine but substantial linen with sperm oil such as is used for sewing machines, and cutting out with a "patch-cutter," always to be had with a new gun. Place this patch over the muzzle, oiled side downward, and then set the bullet perfectly straight and true in the muzzle, and with the "starter" press it downward two or three inches, using the ramrod to force it home.

Avoid the common error of "ramming" home the bullet, for two reasons: firstly, because the bullet being jammed on the powder meals and grinds it, thereby depriving it of a portion of its strength, and, secondly, because injury is done to the face of the ball, which works against its taking a perfectly true and accurate flight. The old plan of making the ramrod rebound to prove that the ball was home, as mentioned in another chapter, was wrong. Nothing more than a moderate pressure is necessary, and if you are not willing to trust to this a mark on your ramrod, to come exactly to the muzzle when the ball is entirely down, will always tell the tale. Now place a cap on the tube or nipple, which is, doubtless, full of powder, and the "shootist" is ready for operations.

There are two modes of shooting with a rifle: off-hand, and with a rest, as has already been intimated. Choose the mode that suits best, and begin practice.

Off-hand Shooting.—Barber says the position which should be chosen for off-hand shooting is one that admits of a good deal of discussion. There is great difference of opinion on the subject, some good shots contending that they never could see any difference in their shooting, whether they were in one position or the other; while others maintain that it is absolutely necessary to good shooting that certain fixed rules should be adhered to. There are three recognized methods of firing, viz., the British or Hythe position, the Swiss position and the American position. In the first named, the rifleman stands perfectly erect, head slightly bent forward, feet at right angles to each other, the left advanced about twelve inches, the right arm raised well up, the left hand advanced so as to take a firm yet easy grip of the rifle, the butt of which is to be pressed firmly agains the right shoulder, the right hand grasping firmly the small of the stock. Captain Heaton describes the second method, or Swiss position, by stating that no particular manner of placing the feet is required. The whole body is kept perfectly rigid, the chest expanded as much as possible, against which the left elbow is allowed to rest, the rifle being held with the left hand as near the trigger guard as it can be placed. The Swiss rifles have a kind of handle provided for this purpose. The upper part of the body is thrown back. Before firing the Swiss marksman invariably takes a long, deep inspiration, which he holds until the bullet has left his rifle, when he breaks the suspension with a loud grunt of satisfaction if the shot happens to please him. In the American position, to draw again from Barber, the legs are kept wide apart, body slightly bent backward, the left shoulder a little back; with the left hand he grasps the rifle well out, bringing the arm nearly under the the barrel, so as to form a support; the right arm is thrown out square, similar to the style adopted in the English position. The butt of the rifle is not pressed against the shoulder, but in the hollow between the biceps muscle and the shoulder. Cleveland prefers this method to that of the English, but Barber does not, as he considers it more constrained than the other.

But, of course, great men must differ ; the world could not get along all right were it otherwise. The matter of method had best be left to stand as a matter of taste, or of feeling as to convenience to the marksman, as very good shooting has been done through all of them.

Having settled this point, bring the rifle up carefully into position, the eye being steadily fixed upon the object to be fired at; slowly raise the barrel until the sights and the object are in direct line, and the instant that this condition is fully apparent press upon the trigger, still keeping the eye steadily on the mark.

It is always best to hold the breath at the instant of firing ; and in pressing the trigger the forearm alone should act, the arm and wrist being stationary. No other movement of the body or any member thereof should take place between the time of securing aim and discharging the gun. The aim should be quickly taken—a long dwell, with wabblings on and wabblings off the mark is apt to do more harm than good. On this point Frank Forrester says: "Though it is necessary to get a sure aim before firing, it is not necessary to dwell on it before doing so. Every second between having taken true sight and the giving fire is a second lost, or worse than lost; for the longer the rifle is held to the face, the greater the tension of the muscles and nerves, and the likelier are both to shake and give way. The first true sight is always, with all firearms, the best sight, and a quick shot has as much or more advantage over a slow shot, with the rifle as with any other weapon." Barber says he considers "the *pull* of the trigger a very important consideration; it should not be too slight, so as to go off almost involuntarily, nor so hard as to require force, but so that, by a gentle pressure, commenced at the moment of taking aim, the slightest extra squeeze will cause the hammer to fall at the very instant when the aim is perfected."

Rest Shooting.—If the old-fashioned backwoods hunters shot with a rest at all that rest had nothing complicated about it, being usually only the side of a tree. The rifle was brought up against the side of a tree and pressed there with the left hand, which held it pretty much after the plan employed in the American method of off-hand shooting. If the object to be fired at was occupying an elevated position, as a squirrel among the branches of a neighboring tree, this kind of rest was a very easy and good one, but it was not so easy where a horizontal shot had to be made. In match-shooting with a rest the most common plan was to lie upon the ground, face downward, somewhat in the natural position of a swimmer, and put the gun out in front, its muzzle resting upon a small log or block of wood. These plans are still more or less in vogue in all regions where the old-style Kentucky rifle remains in common use.

The most popular modern rest, according to Barber, is to have a bench made about three and a half feet long and ten inches wide, with four stout legs standing out at considerable angle. The height should be about level with the breast when sitting down. At one end place a stout piece of wood about five or six inches high, crosswise, with notches cut in it to lay the barrel in. It should be well covered with cloth or some other soft material, and should be securely fastened to the bench. The end of the bench nearest the shooter may be hollowed out a little for the breast to fit in. This is a rest for target shooting—it would not be well suited for the hunter to carry around in the woods with him, of course.

The same authority tells how to make a cheaper rest, by tying three moderately stout sticks together near the top, and then throwing out the other ends upon the ground after the manner of the feet of a tripod. Place your coat in the crotch formed at the top to rest your rifle upon—that is all there is of it.

Having decided upon the kind of rest to be used, the question of rest-shooting is settled, as everything else is performed the same as in shooting off-hand. Most modern sportsmen object to rest-shooting to such an extent that no artificial rest is admitted at their target matches. Their reasons for such objections are that a rest is an inconvenient arrangement that could not be employed either in war or field-sports, and hence, people ought to learn to shoot well without it. And they do, but in many instances they shoot with a rest at last, making one of themselves by lying upon the ground and shooting off the knee or some other part of the person, or by setting the elbows upon the ground so as to brace with the gun as permanently as any artificial rest could possible be. The methods employed by the noted marksmen, Messrs. Fulton and Bodine, were of this character.

CHAPTER XXXVII.

ON USING THE SHOT-GUN.

Born Shooters.—Every man who uses a gun at all will feel an ambition to use it skillfully, and when he finds himself falling short of his aspirations he will apply to his gunsmith for instructions, for the gunsmith is expected to set the owner all right as well as his gun. There will be some difference in results to the gunsmith, however, for when the gun gets out of fix, and the gunsmith repairs the imperfections, the owner expects to pay for services rendered, but not so with reference to himself. He will expect the gunsmith to spend an hour or so in telling him how to shoot, but it will not occur to him that time is worth the same in dollars and cents spend it as we may, hence he will never think of tendering the slightest remuneration for the time consumed in giving him instructions. We have often thought that a chapter in some book telling about all there is to tell the novice on the subject of shooting would be worth a great deal to the gunsmith, as he could turn it over to his inquiring customers and go on about his work, leaving them to sift out from the "black and white" the information desired, taking their own time for it, and digesting everything in accordance with their own notions. And right here, it may be remarked, is a proper place to put in just such a chapter, which is done without further preface.

Some popular writer has said that, like the poet, the first-class shot with a gun, or the "dead shot." as he is often called, must be born such—he cannot be made. Good shooting is a fine art, and in none of the fine arts can perfection be acquired where there does not exist a natural talent, or natural capacity, if the term be better. Any man with fair calculation and a reasonably good mechanical eye may, by practice, become a very passable shot, but without this peculiar natural requirement, which no one can clearly explain, it will be impossible for him to ever excel as an expert marksman.

It is not often that a real born shot is met with—they are about as scarce as true poets and true painters. When one does meet with him one soon knows him, if there is any shooting going on. Perhaps he is at his first shooting match. He does not know himself as a "shootist," possibly. Curiosity alone, it may be, prompts him to try a shot, so he takes the gun, and wholly without study or previous experience, blazes away, and, to the astonishment of all present, shoots almost to perfection. It is in him as a gift. Some peculiar balance in his organization is the cause of it, and it is folly to be envious even in the least degree. Nor is it worth while to despair because such a peculiar balance of organization did not happen to fall to "our" lot. If there be a wish to succeed, a little patient study, industry and practice may soon bring the "shootist" up to the average at least, and that will leave no reasonable cause for complaint.

How to Shoot.—This part of the subject need not be brought down to the simple operation of merely discharging a gun, for it is supposed that every person with common sense, and old enough to handle a gun would know how to discharge it when loaded. What is meant, then, by "how to shoot," is how to shoot well, and to enable any one to do this, one of the most important requisites lies in taking aim on the object at which is expected to be shot. Most young gunners close one eye in this operation, which, according to the best authorities, is entirely wrong. A man will learn to take correct aim with a shot-gun much sooner by keeping both eyes naturally open than he will by holding one closed. Once got in the habit of shooting with a closed eye, it will be found a most difficult habit to break up—the "hiding eye" will "close up" just as the finger is being pressed upon the trigger. And with that "closing up" is very apt to come a deviation of the gun from the line of correct aim.

Some years ago Mr. Dougall, in his "Shooting Simplified," advanced many strong arguments in favor of shooting with both eyes open, basing them upon correct science. He says the person who takes aim with one eye closed has robbed himself of half his vision. The single open eye cannot see the whole of the object at which it looks, but only a part, or one side of it. Then, it requires the use of both eyes to see and calculate distance correctly.

One eye may outline a thing, but it calls for the employment of two eyes to give it a perfect perspective.

When an object is hastily caught within the range of both eyes, the sense of vision is instantly assured as to position of the object, its distance from the gun, and, if moving, the rate of speed at which it is going. By a mental operation the brain is promptly impressed with all this, giving confidence and, consequently, calmness. Here the main point favoring success has been attained—calmness and a strong belief that the shot is going to succeed. The moment when this is felt is the one in which to press upon the trigger. It means that a correct sight is secured, whether there be time to think about it or not, and hence an instantaneous discharge of the gun is almost sure to bring down the game.

Since beginning to write this book one of the authors interviewed a wonderfully successful sportsman with reference to his mode of taking aim at birds on the wing. "Why, bless your soul!" said he, "I never take aim at all. I throw my gun in range of the bird, look at the bird with both eyes open, and the moment a feeling comes over me that I shall kill the bird if I shoot, I pull the trigger, and it's about always my bird." So it is. But this expert is evidently mistaken with reference to taking aim: he takes aim mechanically. He thinks only about killing the bird, without thinking about taking aim, and in response to the securing of a perfect aim comes the feeling, unexplained in his thoughts, that if he shoots he shall kill the bird. It is simply a powerful concentration of thought, which is always of paramount importance in shooting. A mind scattering over all creation at the time of shooting is no more to be depended upon for good results than a gun scattering to all sides of a ten-acre field. There must be concentration in both cases. A man cannot buy goods, grow crops, swap horses, make poetry, edit a newspaper and kill birds on the wing with unvarying success all at the same instant.

Brewster on the Use of Two Eyes.—As the novice who has not devoted much thought to the subject of shooting, will be apt to feel some surprise at the idea of the use of both eyes being recommended in taking aim, the liberty will be assumed of quoting a paragraph from the writings of Sir David Brewster, offering it as evidence in substantiation of the foregoing position. In his able work on the Stereoscope he says: "When we look with both eyes open at a sphere, or any other solid object, we see it by uniting into *one* two pictures—one as seen by the right, and the other as seen by the left eye. If we hold up a thin book perpendicularly, and midway between both eyes, we see distinctly the back of it and both sides with the eyes open. When we shut the right eye, we see with the left eye the back of the book and the left side of it; and when we shut the left eye, we see with the right eye the back of it and the right side. The picture of the book, therefore, which we see with both eyes, consists of two dissimilar pictures united, namely, a picture of the back and left side of the book as seen by the left eye, and a picture of the back and right side of the book as seen by the right eye."

This argues that the sportsman who closes one eye at the time of taking aim at an away-going bird, really has a very imperfect view of it—but half a picture, as it were—hence the aim could not possibly be so perfect as in case where the picture was rendered more distinct by the use of both eyes, in accordance with the clear explanation of Sir David, who goes on to state:

"But though we see with one eye the direction in which any object or point of an object is situated, we do not see its position or the distance from the eye at which it is placed. In monocular vision we learn from experience to estimate all distances, but particularly great ones, by various tests, which are called the *criteria* of distance, but it is only with both eyes that we can estimate with anything like accuracy the distance of objects not far from us.

"The most important advantage which we derive from the use of two eyes is to enable us to see distance, or a third dimension in space. That this vision is not the result of experience as monocular vision is, is obvious from the fact that distance is seen as perfectly by children as by adults; and it has been proved by naturalists that animals newly-born appreciate distance with the greatest correctness."

Dougall's Reasoning.—Mr. Dougall says, in his

"Shooting Simplified," that "A thorough good gun will knock over a hare running broadside, with four or five shots at seventy yards distance, but full elevation must be taken, and the gun fired with the head well raised and the eyes kept steady on the aim, *not* taking sight along the rib, with the eye well down behind the breech, as has been erroneously recommended.

"Distance requires elevation in proportion. A rifle is fitted with graduated sights to meet this, but the elevation of the rib of a fowling-piece is fixed and immovable. But by a simple law of perspective, when you look at a hare (or any other object) seventy yards away, bringing mechanically the sight to bear upon it, you have the breech of the gun lower than if it were only forty yards off; whereas, if you adopt the one-eye system, you fire at exactly the same elevation at all distances. It would be as absurd to take a level aim along the rib at seventy yards as it would be to fire a rifle at a mark at two hundred yards with the sight set for one hundred.

"While everything has been done to increase the range of the fowling-piece, nothing has been done to give the elevation necessary to take full advantage of the increase of power. As long as the one-eye system of shooting is adopted, the object, if hit at all, will be struck only by outside weak pellets, and not by the effective central shot.

"The proper way is to throw the gun well up and into the shoulder; the setting off of the stock will then bring the gun right in front of the face; and, the head being erect, and both eyes fixed intently on the object, the line of motion is commanded, and the aim taken instinctively. The central pellets have thus an allowance given them to compensate for distance and the motion of the object. You look along the imaginary line, higher at the breech according to distance, and at this elevation the gun is fired, exactly as a rifle target-shooter sets his breech sights to a given distance.

"How does a man drive a nail? Certainly not by closing one eye and looking along the hammer; but with both eyes open, he mechanically balances the hammer and strikes instinctively, never, if accustomed to the use of the tool, missing his aim. It is the same in shooting."

Coming directly to the subject of employing binocular vision in taking aim to shoot, Mr. Dougall quotes from a paper in *Once-a-Week* to the effect that monocular vision, while much employed for this purpose, cannot at all be depended upon. To prove this position, place upon a table an empty small-mouthed vial, and taking another similar vial full of water in one hand, shut an eye and approach the vial upon the table; when apparently near enough, stretch out your arm quickly and endeavor to pour the water from the full vial into the other, still keeping the eye closed. You will be very apt to find, as the water comes down, that it is missing the mouth of the empty vial on account of a miscalculation, due to monocular vision. Now repeat the operation with both eyes open, and if care is exercised success will be the invariable result. A similar miscalculation will be shown to the person who endeavors to approach and snuff a candle with one eye shut.

Mr. Dougall thinks there can be no reasonable question as to the advantages of learning to use the shot-gun with both eyes open. This has been proven time and again by the most rigid tests. It is even a settled fact that the nearer the eyes of an individual set together in the head the less he is likely to shoot well. "And yet," says Mr. Dougall, "how strange it is to find sportsmen who would still further narrow this fine provision of nature into the diameter of one retina only. Throwing the fowling-piece into a line with the object of aim by an instinctive effort, keeping both eyes firmly fixed on and following the flight of the object, is the first great principle in shooting well."

Gloan on Taking Aim.—The clever author of a neat little book entitled "The Breech-Loaders," tells us that when the shot leave the gun the powder which propels the pellets has started them with sufficient force to keep them up for a short time against all natural resistances acting upon them, but finally gravitation, which is pulling upon them all the time, begins to tell, and carry them downward from the line upon which they set out.

"The shot have a journey to perform after they leave the gun, and before they reach the bird. It may be a long journey or a short journey, according to the distance of the bird; but still it is a journey, and it takes some time to do it in. While the shot are traveling on their way, the bird is flying on *his* way. If the bird is flying across the shooter, and the aim is at the bird, naturally, by the time the shot get to the point of aim, the bird has gone on beyond it, and is untouched by the shot. And if the distance is great, gravitation has affected the shot and pulled them down below the point of aim. Possibly, too, the wind is strong, and has blown them a little to one side. So that, assuming that a sportsman aims steadily and exactly at a cross-flying bird, sixty yards distant, going a mile a minute, the gun making a pattern good enough to kill, what results?

"When the shot arrive at their point of destination they are from eight to ten feet behind the point to which the bird has flown; and they are from ten to twelve inches below the line upon which the bird was flying. If the wind is high they are blown aside, even on the lower line, and the other pellets become harmless if they hit. The bird escapes, as a matter of surprise to the young sportsman, who is confident that he 'covered it exactly.'

"He did cover it, literally, and exactly, and that was the cause of the miss. If he had aimed the length of a fence rail ahead of the bird and half the length above it, he would probably have brought it down. As the shot was, however, the bird was sure to be lost.

"An old shot will shine on range and allowance. His eye will measure distance as though with a tape-line. He will estimate velocity as with a registering instrument. He makes his cheek an index of the wind, and before his gun is at his shoulder he has decided with unfailing skill where the aim must be, and there he plants the load. If the bird does not fall it is the gun's fault, not his.

"By the binocular vision these difficulties, which are so trying to the novice, are the more readily overcome. The eyes take in the flight of the bird, and convey the rate of speed at which it flies. The full distance of the whole perspective of the landscape is made palpable to the sense, and the finger responds to the call, which is made all the more quickly and all the more truly because of the certainty which the eyes impart."

CHAPTER XXXVIII.

ON USING THE PISTOL.

Natural Talent.—The number of persons who are really good shots with the pistol is smaller than one would be apt to suppose after considering how many weapons of this kind are in every-day use. They are almost as common as pocket-knives, and some of them are capable of shooting reasonably well at considerable length of range, and yet not an average of one man in five hundred, who owns a pistol, could be found, perhaps, who could put fifty per cent. of his bullets through a hat set up for a target ten paces away. The fact is, the pistol, while capable enough, if well made, is the most difficult of all our fire-arms to manage, so far as relates to good performances. There are men who can take a good revolver and shoot a chicken's head off every time, ten or fifteen paces, but of such men there are not very many. And none of them have ever communicated how they happened to become such fine shots with the pistol. In some cases they had practiced a good deal, but not more than had hundreds who were but comparatively poor performers. To come squarely down to the point at once, the peculiarity which made them good shots with the pistol was a "born-gift," as in the case of the best shots with the shot gun. Any man who practices with the pistol, in accordance with the established rules governing its use for best results, may soon become a fair shot, but it calls for more than mere practice to make him an excellent shot.

Taking Aim.—The best shots do not take aim by sighting along the barrel of the pistol, holding it out at arm's length after the manner of the wooden figure standing in front of the city shooting-gallery. They do not close one eye and turn sideways to the object of aim like the ideal duelist, but they hold out the pistol, look at the object (not the pistol), with both eyes open, and blaze away, usually putting the bullet about where they want it to go. There is really no aim-taking in the case, any more than there is in the case of a boy playing at marbles. Indeed, shooting a pistol to the best advantage is very much on the same principle as shooting a marble. The boy takes the marble properly between his thumb and first finger, holds out his hand in the direction of the marble to be shot at, but considerably below his line of vision, looks at the object-marble with both eyes open and "flips" in obedience to the promptings of a kind of unconscious calculation as to distance, force at command, effect of gravitation, and so on. The marble "flipped" curves out on its way, and, if shot from the hand of a skillful player, strikes its mark with astonishing certainty. Just so with the bullet sent from the pistol; under the management of a skillful performer it goes in obedience to an unconscious calculation, and not in obedience to the squinting of one eye along the barrel. Sight-taking won't do in either case; the good marble player would be a hopeless failure if he held up his arm to his line of vision and took sight every time he went to "shoot"—the pistol-shooter who performs upon the same plan is invariably a marksman of sterling uncertainty, to say the least.

Cane Aiming.—Some people are so deficient in the species of calculation necessary to successful pistol-shooting, on the plan suggested in the foregoing, that they cannot do much at it. Such as these have some excuse for taking sight, but holding the pistol out at arm's length and sighting along the barrel or through its "sights" rarely gives them more than very little certainty. The best method of actually taking sight with a pistol is performed in connection with a rod some three feet long—usually with a walking cane. Grasp the grip of the pistol in the right hand, in the usual way, and take the cane in the left hand. Bring the handle of the cane up against the shoulder like the breech of a gun, pass the pistol down along the side of it till the barrel reaches the left hand, and both hands are in easy position. Hold the cane between the thumb and first finger of the left hand, letting them pass beyond it and grip the barrel of the pistol between the end of the thumb and the turned-up end of the finger. Let the thumb and first finger of the right hand also grip the cane beyond the "grip" of the pistol. The aim of the pistol should range a little to the right of the direction pointed by the cane, which it will very naturally do.

This plan steadies the pistol and affords as fine an opportunity of taking perfect sight as one could have with a rifle. A little practice with it, to enable one to arrive at a certain conclusion as to the rise or fall of the bullet, will soon pave the way for pretty fair shooting. A kind of clasp with which to fasten the pistol to the cane is now on the market, and may be made to work very well, though some would always prefer holding the pistol with the hands, in the manner just described.

The Best Pistols to Use.—It is not advisable to say a recommendatory word about any particular make —how could it be done, under the above heading, when there are twenty or thirty really good pistols now before the the public under the brand of the same number of different manufacturers? The best pistol for any person to use is any good pistol that this person happens to like, and no other kind. All pistols do not shoot alike, and, hence, when any one has practiced with a certain kind until accustomed to its peculiarities they had better stick to it, as a change would be apt to throw at least some derangement in the shooting calculations, putting them under the necessity of a repeated practice. All the best shots invariably stick to some particular make of pistol, and usually to some particular size.

In making choice of a size it is best to be governed by the character of work the pistol is desired to perform. The large pistols shoot stronger, and, as a general rule, with greater accuracy than the small ones; still, comparatively small pistols are sometimes known to shoot reasonably well. They are intended only for short range, however, and hence must not be depended upon when a good performance of long-range pistol shooting is desired. The large pistol has many advantages over the small one, while the latter can claim but two over the former. These two consist in its lightness, fitting it to figure as a pocket pistol, and in the lesser cost of its ammunition.

CHAPTER XXXIX.

VOCABULARY OF MECHANICAL TERMS USED BY GUN-MAKERS.

Action.—The iron bed attached to the stock of a breech-loading gun, into the recess of which the lump descends and is secured. The term is used generally as "side action," "snap action," etc. The word is also used to indicate the different form of gun locks, as back-action, bar-action, front-action, etc.

Anneal.—To render more soft, as in the case of iron and other metals.

Auxillary Rifle.—A rifle-barrel some twenty inches in length, and so arranged that, like a cartridge, it may be slipped within the barrel of a breech loading shot-gun, thus at once converting the shot-gun into a rifle. The rifle-barrel, charged with its cartridge, may be placed in the shot-gun in a moment and at pleasure.

Back-action Lock.—A lock that is located entirely back of the barrel, being bedded in the stock alone.

Bar-action Lock.—When the lock is bedded partly back of the barrel and partly along side of it.

Barrel.—The iron or steel tube of the gun through which the charge passes in the act of firing.

Barrel loop.—A metallic loop under the barrel,

through which a small bolt passes to hold the barrel into the stock.

Bents.—The notches in the tumbler of a gun-lock.

Black-Walnut.—A tree, native to North America, whose wood is extensively used in the manufacture of fine gun stocks; the *Juglans nigra* of botanists.

Binocular Vision.—Seeing with two eyes.

Bolt.—The part which, in a breech-loader, passes into the lump of the barrel and holds it into the action when the gun is closed.

Bore.—The interior of the barrel along which the charge passes.

Bores are made of the following forms: True cylinders; cylinders enlarged at the breech; cylinders enlarged or freed at the muzzle; tapered to narrow at the muzzle; narrowed to close at the muzzle; cylindrical, with ring cut out near muzzle; narrowing the muzzle with depth cut out, modified, etc. Bores are also made elliptical, hexogonal, polygonal, etc.

Brazing.—Soldering iron with brass or copper as a solder.

Breech.—In earlier days all that portion of the gun back of the lock was considered *the* breech, but now a gun is regarded as having two breeches: the breech of the barrel, the place where the cartridge is inserted, as in the case of the breech-loaders, and the breech of the stock, being that part which comes against the shoulder.

Breech-bolt.—A small iron bar used in some

make of guns to assist in holding the barrel secure to the action.

Bridle.—That piece in the lock connected with the tumbler as a kind of cap.

Browning.—A rust produced on the surface of gun-barrels by means of acids.

Bump.—The corner of the stock at the top of the heel-plate.

Burnisher.—A piece of smooth and hardened steel used in polishing the surface of metals.

Calibre.—The diametrical measurement of the bore of a gun barrel. Breech loaders are made of 10, 12, 14, 16 and 20 calibre. Muzzle loader of every variety of measurement.

Cap.—The metal covering placed on the end of a pistol handle. Also the small cup-like contrivance put on the nipple upon which the hammer strikes to fire the gun.

Carbine.—A short form of rifle; so made to be easily carried by persons who used them mounted on horses.

Cartridges.—The ammunition for a gun, contained in metal or paper cases. They are sized to regular numbers, as gauge 10 or 12, etc., and are of two kinds, central-fire and rim-fire.

Case-hardening.—A hardened, steel-like exterior given to iron by heating it in connection with animal charcoal, and then plunging while hot in cold water.

Central-fire.—Setting off the cartridge by striking it in the centre, where the fulminate is placed.

Chamber.—The enlarged space in the breech of the barrel wherein the cartridge is placed, or where the charge rests in the case of a muzzle-loader. The bores intended to receive the charge in the cylinder of a revolver. In loading a gun with coarse shot, if they rest in the barrel side by side in regular layers or strata, we say they chamber; but if they are a little too large for this, so that some of the shots must lie above the common level for want of space between other shots and the side of the bore to admit of their going down, we say the gun will not chamber shot of that particular size. A gun is not supposed to shoot shot to perfection which she cannot chamber.

Charger.—A small measure employed for measuring powder in loading a gun or cartridge-shell.

Chequer-work.—The chequered carving as made on the stock of a gun.

Cherry-mould.—A small spherical cutting-tool, used for enlarging the interior of bullet moulds. It may be bought of houses dealing in gunsmith's materials, or it may be made by dressing a piece of soft steel down to proper shape, cutting file-teeth upon it and then hardening in the usual way. To use the cherry, close the mould upon it and then turn it round and round until the interior of the mould is cut out to the required size and shape.

Cherry Tree.—A North American tree, growing to about medium size and furnishing a hard, reddish and most beautiful wood, highly prized for fine gun stocks. It is now getting to be quite scarce. Botanical name, *Cerasus serotina.*

Choke-bore.—A gun-bore slightly larger at the breech than at the muzzle.

Choke-dressing.—Dressing out the bore of a gun so as to make it slightly larger at the breech than at the muzzle.

Clamp, Mainspring.—A mainspring clamp is a kind of vise used by gunsmiths for clamping the mainspring preparatory to taking it from the lock.

Cock.—In flint-lock guns, that part of the lock which holds the flint. The name is also often applied to the hammer of percussion and other locks of more modern make. When the hammer has been pulled back to its last catch, we say the gun is cocked, or at full-cock; when pulled back to the catch next preceding the last, we say the gun is half-cocked, or at half-cock.

Comb.—That portion of the stock upon which the cheek rests at the time of firing.

Cone.—See Nipple.

Counter-sink.—The reccess in the chamber in which the rim of the cartridge fits.

Cross-Fire.—We say a rifle "crosses fire" when it plays the balls on the same level without varying upward or downward.

Curled Maple.—This is not a species of growth, but an unexplained condition to be met with in the wood of the maple, most commonly in that of the sugar or hard maple (the *Acer saccharinum* of botanists), though occasionally in *Acer rubrum*, or red maple. The grain of the wood lies in regular waves, presenting a most beautiful appearance when nicely dressed up. It is very popular for fine gun stocks.

Cylinder.—That part of a revolver in which the charges are placed. In the older make of percussion lock guns a short plug screwed into the side of the barrel at the breech, in which was placed the cap-tube or nipple, and through which the fire from the cap was communicated to the charge.

Damascus.—The variegated appearance on gun barrels, produced by welding together metals dissimilar, as steel and iron, and then, while heated, twisting these metals into various tortuous forms and re-welding. The colors of the dissimilar metals are brought out by browing mixtures.

Direct Fire.—That arrangement in a breech-loader by which the plunger lies and strikes the ignition horizontally.

Dog.—That part of the gun-lock acted upon by the trigger to release the tightened mainspring and set the hammer in motion. Earlier gunsmiths called it by this name, but it is now usually called the sear.

Double Triggers.—Often called set-triggers. A pair of triggers arranged to a rifle, occasionally, to admit of setting it off with but slight pressure. The triggers are located one in advance of the other under the guard. To operate pull upon the rear one until it "clicks" and is "set," after which cock the gun. The slightest pressure upon the front trigger springs the "set," which acts suddenly upon the sear, releasing the mainspring.

Drop.—Distance measured from the top of the butt of a gun stock to a line drawn rear-ward from the top of the barrels, usually from 2 to 3½ inches.

Elevated Rib.—The raised rib on top of and between the barrels of a shot gun.

Escutcheons.—Pieces of metal, through which the bolt to hold the barrel to the stock, is passed.

Extractor.—An automatic working rod in central fire guns, by which the empty cartridge is partly withdrawn from the chamber.

False Breech.—A piece of iron permanently screwed to the stock to fit squarely against the breech of the barrel. In the modern muzzle-loader the barrel is secured against it by hooks. It is also called a patent breech, also a standing breech.

Fastenings.—Mechanism for holding the barrel of breech-loaders securely to the frame or action when the barrel is in position for firing.

Flash.—In the days of the old flint-lock a gun was said to "flash" when the priming ignited in the pan but failed to fire the charge.

Flux.—A substance or mixture used to facilitate the melting of metals or minerals, as glass, borax, and the like.

Fore Piece.—That portion of the stock lying under the barrel, forward of the lock, called also fore-end and fore-arm.

Fore Sight.—The sight located nearest the muzzle end of the barrel.

Forge.—A furnace with its accompaniments where iron or other metals are wrought by heating and hammering. When a piece of metal is hammered into some required shape, the operation is termed "to forge it."

Fowling Piece.—A smooth bored gun, used for hunting small game, shooting shot or small pellets.

Freeing.—Slightly enlarging the bore of a gun at the muzzle.

Frizzen.—In the old flint-lock the steel plate that covers the pan and stood up in front of the flint, against which the flint struck to produce fire to ignite the priming.

Grip.—A name usually applied to the round part of a gun stock just back of the locks. It is also applied to the handle of a pistol.

Guard.—The piece of metal which curves around the triggers and protects them.

Half Stock.—A gun stock that does not extend the full length of the barrel.

Hammer.—That part of the gun-lock that strikes the plunger or cap, or other form of ignition. See cock.

Hammer-Gun.—A gun whose lock works with a hammer.

Hammerless Gun.—A gun whose arrangements for setting off the ignition are contained inside the breech mechanism, and not visible when the arm is ready for use.

Handle.—See grip.

Hazel Nut.—A small shrub growing abundantly in many portions of the United States. The *Cory-*

lus of botanists, divided into two species, ***Americana*** and ***Rostrata.***

Head.—In a gun stock, the part where the breech end of the barrel rests against.

Heel Plate.—The metal piece terminating the breech end of a gun stock.

Hind Sight.—The sight upon the barrel, nearest the breech.

Hinge Pin.—A pin fixed in the action on which the barrel plays.

Ignition.—Any chemical combination which can be caused to explode and fire the charge, as in a cap or cartridge, for instance.

Kentuckg Rifle.—A form of rifle, once very popular with Western hunters, and now used to some extent. It is muzzle loading, and the great length of the barrel was one great peculiarity.

Kick.—When a gun rebounds at firing the term is used "it kicks."

Land Space.—The space in the bore of a rifle between the grooves.

Lever.—The bar or rod the working of which locks or unlocks the action of a breech-loader, enabling the operator to open or close the gun. As top-lever, side-lever, under-lever, etc.

Lock Plate.—The flat plate to the inside of which all the other parts of the gun-lock are secured.

Loop.—The projection under the barrel to which the fore end is fastened. See barrel loop. They are of two kinds, wire and bolt loop.

Long Fire.—When a noticeable space of time intervenes between the striking of the hammer and the explosion of the charge, hence the term, the gun has made "long-fire."

Lower Rib.—The rib underneath and between the barrels of a shot gun.

Lump.—The iron piece soldered to the barrel of a breech-loader, which descends into the action and is there secured preparatory to firing.

Magazine Rifle.—A rifle provided with an interior magazine for containing cartridges, and so made that they are passed automatically into a chamber ready for firing.

Mainspring.—The large spring in the gun-lock which imparts action and power to the hammer.

Monocular Vision.—Seeing with only one eye. When one eye is closed, as some do in taking sight with a gun, it is a case of monocular vision.

Mould.—An implement for moulding bullets. The plural form is generally given to it, as bullet moulds.

Musket.—A form of gun, smooth bored and formerly used for military purposes. When grooves are cut in the interior of the barrel, it is called a rifle.

Nipple.—In a percussion-lock gun, the tube upon which the cap is placed. In the central-fire breech-loader, the tube through the standing breech in which the striker or plunger works.

Nipple Wrench.—An implement used for screwing the nipples into position or out. It is often called a tube-wrench.

Oblique Fire.—Indicates that the plungers of a breech-loader lie and strike the ignition obliquely.

Pan.—A small pan-like outside on the flint-lock, which holds the priming, and in which the latter is ignited by a spark from the flint striking the frizzen.

Patent Breech.—See false breech.

Pepper Box Pistol.—One form of revolver pistol, in which the barrels are made full length from one piece of metal. The rotation of the barrels and the action of the lock to fire the arm was produced by pulling the trigger.

Picker.—A small wire implement hung to the shot-pouch of the hunter in the days of the old flint-lock, and used when occasion required for picking priming into the touch-hole of the gun.

Pipes.—Short tubes attached to a barrel or to a rib attached to the barrel to receive the ramrod and hold it in place.

Pistol.—A small variety of fire-arm, so made as to be easily carried in the pocket or a holster, and readily manipulated and fired with one hand.

Pistol Grip.—A gun stock whose grip inclines to turn down like the handle of a pistol, is said to have a pistol grip.

Play.—A rifle which does not shoot with regularity is said to play its balls..

Plungers.—The pins which are struck by the hammers, in breech-loaders, and which in turn strike and explode the ignition.

Powder Bed.—The chamber, in a muzzle-loader, where the powder lies when the gun is charged.

Priming.—The powder in the pan of a flint-lock gun.

Proof Marks.—Impressions of stamps made in gun barrels to indicate that they have been proved.

Proving.—Firing gun barrels with very heavy charges of powder and balls to ascertain if they are of proper strength.

Ramrod.—A rod with which the tightly fitting portions of the charge are pushed home in loading a muzzle-loader.

Rebounding Lock.—A lock which has the top of the mainspring and crank of the tumbler lengthened to such an extent that when the trigger is pulled the hammer delivers its blow and immediately rebounds to the half-cock.

Rib.—The metallic strip lying between and connecting the barrels of a shot-gun. See lower rib and upper rib.

Rifle.—A gun having grooves cut parallel with each other along the interior of the barrel. They usually take a more or less spiral course for the purpose of imparting to the bullet thrown a whirling or twisting motion on its flight through the air. The grooves thus cut are sometimes called rifles.

Rifle.—A gun with grooves cut in a twisted or spiral-like manner on the interior of the barrel, for the purpose of giving the projectile a rotary motion on its axis during its flight. The design being to give greater accuracy to the course of the bullet.

Rifle Cane.—A metallic walking staff, which is virtually a rifle, capable of shooting with much force. The lock works internally, and everything is so arranged as to pretty effectually conceal the true character of the arm, it, at a casual glance, presenting only the appearance of a neat walking-stick.

Rifle Guide.—An implement used by the gunsmith to guide the course of his rifle-saws in cutting grooves in the bore of a barrel.

Rifle-Saws.—Short files made to fit in the grooves of a rifle. They are usually attached to a rod, near the end, and drawn to and fro through the gun for the purpose of filing the grooves down to greater depth, where such a thing is required. In cases where new grooves are to be cut in a smooth-bore, the rod passes through a rifle-guide, which forces the saws to take the proper twist through the barrel.

Rim-Fire.—A cartridge whose ignition is around the rim instead of in the centre, and which, consequently, can be used only by some arm striking the cartridge at the rim.

Rouge.—A fine powdery material, used for putting a high polish upon the surface of well-finished metals. It is usually applied by rubbing in connection with soft leather, either in the form of a buff or otherwise.

Saturated Solution.—A liquid holding in solution as much of some particular soluble chemical as it will dissolve. For instance, if salt be put in water until a portion remains undissolved at the bottom of the vessel, there is in the liquid a saturated solution because it holds in suspension all the salt that it can dissolve.

Scatter.—When a shot gun throws the pellets

over a range of space unusually wide, it is said that it scatters.

Scroll Guard.—An extension downward from the trigger guard, to steady the hand. It is designed to answer the same as pistol grip.

Sear.—Sometimes called dog, which see.

Sear-Spring.—The small spring in a gun-lock which presses the sear into the notches of the tumbler.

Set-Triggers.—See double-triggers.

Side-Lever.—A lever which works at the side of a breech-loader.

Side-Screw—The long screw holding the lock to the stock.

Slack-Tub.—A vessel containing cold water, to be used in suddenly cooling hot metals, as in hardening steel, for instance.

Smooth Bore.—A gun for throwing single bullets, made on the plan of a rifle, but having no grooves in the bore. It is sometimes called a "smooth-bore rifle."

Standing Breech.—See false breech.

Steady-pin.—The small projection on the mainspring which fits into the lock-plate.

Strap.—The metal strip in a breech-loader which runs from the breech-works down the stock, in place of the tail, or the old fashioned breech-pin.

Strikers.—See plungers.

Sugar Maple.—A tree indigenous to the United States, whose wood is extensively used in the manufacture of gun-stocks. See curled maple.

Swivel.—The small piece in a lock connecting the tumbler and the mainspring.

Tear.—When a bullet makes a hole larger than its own diameter, particularly in the flesh of an animal, the gun from which it was shot is said to tear.

Tenons.—Iron projections on the lump of a breech-loader, to fit into corresponding spaces in the action.

Thimbles.—The metallic loops on the under side of a muzzle-loader, made to hold the ramrod when not in use.

Toe.—The extremity of the breech which rests nearest the armpit when in the act of taking off-hand aim.

Top Lever.—The lever of a breech-loader, which works on the upper side of the gun, just back of the hammers.

Trigger.—The small lever under the gun, upon which is pressed with the finger to release the confined mainspring and allow the hammer to descend.

Trigger-Plate—The iron plate in which the trigger works.

Trigger Spring.—A small spring to keep the trigger pressed close to the sear.

Tube.—The modern gunmaker calls the gun-barrel a tube ; in old times the only tube known to the gunsmith was that projection upon which the percussion cap was exploded. See nipple.

Tube.—See nipple.

Tumbler.—That part of the lock directly connected

with the hammer, and in which are the two set notches.

Tumbler-Screw.—The screw on the outside of the lock, passing through the hammer and holding it securely in its connection with the tumbler.

Upper Rib.—The rib above and between the barrels of a double-barrel shot-gun.

Vent.—A small hole in side of the gun breech communicating with the interior or powder chamber.

Vise.—An implement for clamping or holding.

White Maple.—The *Acer dasycarpum* of botanists —a near relative of the sugar maple. Common in many parts of the United States. Called soft maple in some localities.

Whole-Stock.—A gun-stock extending the entire length of the barrel.

Wiper.—A long ramrod used only in wiping out and cleaning the bore of a muzzle loader. Also a small spiral implement made to screw on the end of a ramrod for the purpose of boring into and drawing a wad from a gun, or for holding material for wiping. Sometimes called a wormer.

Wormer.—See wiper.

CHAPTER XL.

VOCABULARY OF CHEMICALS AND SUBSTANCES USED IN BROWNING, VARNISHES, &C.

Acid, Gallic.—Acid produced in yellowish colored crystals, derived from nut-galls or oak-apples. Soluble in water and alcohol. Nut galls are an import ingredient in the manufacture of good black ink.

Acid, Muriatic.—Called also Hydrochloric Acid and sometimes spirit of salt. Made by the action of sulphuric acid on common salt (chloride of sodium). Mingled with half its volume of Nitric Acid it forms Aqua Regia.

Acid, Nitric.—Sometimes called Aqua Fortis. Made by the decomposition of Nitre, or saltpetre by strong sulphuric acid.

Acid, Sulphuric.—Called oil of vitriol, made from sulphur and nitre or saltpetre.

Acid, Hydrochloric.—Called Muriatic Acid, which see.

Alcohol.—The product of the fermentation of sugar, and is contained in all fermented liquors. It is a colorless fluid, boils at 173° F. and burns without smoke. The volatile oils and resins are dissolved by it, as well as many acids and salts, the caustic alkalies, etc. The resulting compounds of the acids upon alcohol are called ethers.

Alkanet Root.—The root of a species of Bugloss.

It affords a fine red color to alcohol and oils, but a dirty red to water. The spirituous tincture gives to white marble a beautiful deep stain.

Annatto.—Also spelled Anotta and Anotto. A red coloring substance obtained from the pulp of the seed-vessel of the plant *Bixa orellana.* It dissolves better and more readily in alcohol than in water.

Antimony, Chloride of.—Called also Butter of Antimony and Sesquichloride of Antimony. Made by distilling the residue of the solution of sulphuret of antimony in strong hydrochloric acid, or by distilling a mixture of corrosive sublimate and antimony. It is highly corrosive. In medicine, used as a caustic.

Antimony, Butter of.—See Antimony, Chloride of.

Aqua Fortis.—Called also Nitric Acid, which see.

Aqua Regia.—Made by mixing one part nitric acid in two muriatic acid, by measure; keep the mixture in a bottle in a cool, dark place.

Asphaltum.—Native bitumen, will dissolve in turpentine with gentle heat.

Benzoin, Gum or Gum Benjamin.—A gum extracted from the tree, *Styrax benzoin,* which grows in the East Indies. It fuses at a gentle heat, can be dissolved in alcohol and imperfectly dissolved in ether. It is employed as a varnish for toilet and other articles, which give out an agreeable smell when warmed by the heat of the hand.

Blue Vitriol.—Sulphate of copper. A salt formed by sulphuric acid in combination with copper. It is soluble in cold or warm water, used much in dyeing and exciting galvanic batteries.

Brimstone.—See sulphur.

Brimstone, Black.—Crude sulphur.

Burnt Umber.—Umber is a mineral of brown color from the Island of Cyprus. Two kinds are found in the market, raw and burnt.

Butter of Antimony.—See antimony, chloride of.

Camphor.—A solid concrete substance, *Laurus camphor* or Indian laurel tree, which grows in the East Indies, China and Japan. Soluble in alcohol, ether, oil and acetic acid.

Chloride of Antimony.—See antimony, chloride of.

Chloride of Mercury.—Called corrosive sublimate, which see.

Chloride of Iron.—See muriate of iron.

Copal.—The concrete juice of a tree growing in South America and the East Indies. Strictly speaking, it is not a gum or a resin, but rather resembles amber. It may be dissolved by digestion in linseed oil with heat little less than sufficient to boil the oil. The solution, diluted with oil of turpentine, forms a transparent varnish. It also dissolves in ether, and the ethereous solutions may be mixed with alcohol.

Copperas.—Sulphate of iron or green vitriol. A salt made by the decomposition of iron or iron pyrites in oil of vitriol. Dissolved in water, is the basis of black dyes, and is used in making ink, &c.

Copper, Sulphate of.—Called blue vitriol, which see.

Corrosive Sublimate.—Chloride of mercury. A

salt prepared by the decomposition of sulphate of mercury by common salt. It is a deadly poison. It is soluble in alcohol, ether, in two or three parts of hot water and in about 15 parts cold water. It melts and sublimes about 600°. The white of eggs is an antidote for the poison.

Damar or Dammar.—A gum obtained from the agathis or dammar tree, allied to the pine trees, growing in the East Indies. It is soluble in alcohol and in oil of turpentine.

Dragon's Blood.—The inspissated juice of various plants, of a red color, used for tinging varnishes, tooth tincture, staining marble, &c.

Ether, Nitric.—Mode of distilling equal parts of strong nitric acid and alcohol with a few grains of urea. It is liquid, colorless, of sweet taste, and insoluble in water. It boils at 185° F. The vapor explodes at moderate heat.

Elemi.—A resin obtained from plants grown in the East Indies and South America. In making lackers, it is used to give toughness to the varnish.

Fustic.—The wood of a tree growing in the West Indies. Used for dyeing yellow.

Gallic Acid.—See Acid, gallic.

Green Copperas.—Sulphate of iron. See Copperas.

Green Vitriol.—Copperas, which see

Hydrochloric Acid.—Muriatic Acid, which see

Iron, Chloride of.—See Muriate of Iron.

Iron, Muriate of.—See Muriate of Iron.

Iron, Sulphate of.—See Sulphate of Iron.

Iron, Sesqui-Chloride of.—Perchloride of iron or permuriate of iron. Made by dissolving rust of iron in muriatic acid and then crystalizing. It forms red crystals. Soluble in water, alcohol and ether. Very corrosive.

Logwood.—The wood of a tree growing in Central America. The extract is used in dyeing black color.

Madder.—A plant of the genus Rubia, one species of which is used in dyeing red.

Manganese, Sulphate of.—A beautiful rose-colored salt, used to give a fine brown dye.

Mastic.—A resin exuding from the mastic tree. It is in yellowish-white, semi-transparent tears. Used as an ingredient in varnishes.

Mercury, Quicksilver.—A metal fluid at ordinary temperatures. Congealable at about 40° below zero. Boils at 660° and forms a colorless dense vapor. It is used in barometers and thermometers, and in alloy with tin in coating mirrors. It unites with chloroform, forming calomel and corrosive sublimate. The only acids that act on it are sulphuric and nitric. To unite with the latter it must be heated.

Mercury, Chloride of.—See Chloride of Mercury.

Mercury, Horn.—Called Chloride of Mercury.

Mercury, Muriate of.—Chloride of Mercury.

Muriate Tincture of Steel.—See Muriate of Iron.

Muriate of Iron.—Called Chloride of Iron. Made by dissolving iron filings in muriatic acid and crystalizing by evaporation. Crystals of green color being the result.

Nitrate of Silver.—Made by dissolving silver in nitric acid and evaporating the solution in crystals. Will dissolve in warm water. Is used for indelible ink to mark clothing and in photography. When fused and cast in small sticks is called lunar caustic.

Nitric Acid.—See Acid, nitric.

Nitric Ether.—See Ether, nitric.

Oil of Vitriol.—See Acid, sulphuric.

Pearlash.—Carbonate of potassa. An alkali obtained from the ashes of trees by leaching. When evaporated to dryness in iron kettles it is called potash, but when calcined to burn off the coloring matter it is called pearlash.

Potash.—See Pearlash. Sometimes called salts of tartar.

Pumice Stone.—A substance resembling the slag from furnaces, ejected from volcanoes. The pulverized material is used to remove the gloss and imperfections on varnished surfaces by rubbing with a woolen cloth and water.

Quicksilver.—See Mercury.

Rotten Stone.—A soft stone used for fine grinding and polishing. Generally used after pumice stone, and is applied with a soft woolen cloth and sweet oil.

Salts of Tartar.—See Potash.

Sandarac.—A resin that exudes from tree growing in Africa. Fusible by heat and soluble in alcohol. Used in varnishes.

Sesqui-Chloride of Iron.—See Iron, Sesqui-chloride of.

Shellac.—Lac is a resinous substance produced mainly from the banyan tree of the East Indies. It is the product of an insect. Stick lac is the resin in its natural state; seed lac when broken up, cleaned of impurities and washed; shellac when it is melted and formed in thin flakes. United with ivory-black or vermilion it makes sealing wax. Dissolved in alcohol it makes lackers and varnishes.

Silver, Nitrate of.—See nitrate of silver.

Soda.—Common. See potash.

Spanish Whiting.—Ground chalk carefully cleaned from all stony matter.

Spirits of Nitre.—An alcoholic solution of nitrous ether.

Steel, Tincture of.--See muriate tincture of steel.

Sulphate of Iron.—Copperas or green vitriol. See copperas.

Sulphate of Manganese.—See manganese, sulphate of.

Sulphur.—Often called brimstone. A mineral of yellowish color. Soluble in turpntine, fat oils, bisulphuret of carbon and hot liquor of potassa. With oxygen it forms sulphuric and sulphurous acids, and with the metals it combines as sulphurets or sulphides. It is an essential ingredient in gunpowder, and the gas arising from its combustion is employed in bleaching straw and woolen goods.

Tartar, Salts of.—See potash.

Turpentine.—An oleo-resinous substance as flowing from several species of pine, larch and fir trees.

Oil of turpentine is obtained by distilling the crude turpentine.

Umber, Burnt.—See Burnt Umber.

Venice Turpentine.—A liquid resin which exudes from the larch tree. The Venice turpentine usually met with is turpentine to which is added a quantity of black melted resin.

Verdigris.—A green oxide of copper, very poisonous. The white of eggs is an antidote for the poison, when taken into the stomach.

Vitriol, Blue.—Called sulphate of copper. See Blue Vitriol.

Vitriol, Green.—Sulphate of iron. See Copperas.

Vitriol, Oil of.—See Acid, sulphuric.

Whiting, Spanish.—See Spanish Whiting.

CHAPTER XLI.

CALIBRES OF GUNS, RIFLING, TWIST OF RIFLING, ETC.

European Guns.—The Enfield Rifle; Muzzle Loader, Cal. 577; 3 grooves; regular twist, slightly deeper at breech than at the muzzle; rifling one turn in 6 feet 6 inches.

The Purdy Rifle, Muzzle Loader; Cal. 650; 4 grooves; increasing twist, commencing at one turn in 6 feet and ending at one turn in 4 feet 9 inches.

The Wilkinson Rifle, Muzzle Loader, Cal. 530; 5 grooves with a regular twist of one turn in 6 feet 6 inches.

The Lancaster Rifle, Muzzle Loader. Bore smooth and elliptical diameter at muzzle; greater axis, 550; lesser axis, 540; greater axis at breech, 557; lesser axis, 543. The twist is one quarter turn in whole length of barrel. Length of barrel, 39 inches.

The Snider Rifle, Muzzle Loader; Cal. 577; 5 grooves, one turn in 4 feet.

The Whitworth Rifle, Muzzle Loader. Polygonal or hexagonal form of bore. Rifling, one turn in 20 inches. Bore, 564 across the flats. 568 across center of flats.

The Jacobs Rifle, Muzzle Loader; 4 grooves; loads and grooves equal. Rifling four-fifths turn in 24 inches.

The Turner Rifle, Muzzle Loader. Bore, 568. Rifling Turner's Patent, one turn in 4 feet.

The Rigby Rifle, Muzzle loader. Rifling 6 grooves; one turn in 4 feet.

The Boucher Rifle, Muzzle Loader. Bore hexagon with angles, rounded off so as to form shallow grooves, 608 deep in center. Bore, 570. Rifling one ture in 3 feet 3 inches.

The Prussian Needle Gun, Breech Loader. Rifling 4 grooves, one turn in 40 inches.

The Chassepot Rifle, Breech Loader; Cal. 433; rifling 4 grooves, turning from left to right, one turn in 21½ inches.

The Snider-Enfield, Breech Loader. Rifling 3 grooves slightly deeper at breech than at the muzzle, one turn in 78 inches. Diameter, 577. Depth of rifling at muzzle, 05. At breech, .13. Width of grooves three-sixteenths inch.

Westley Richard's, Breech Loader. Bore octagonal form. Rifling one turn in 20 inches.

Regulation Minie Rifle, Muzzle Loader. Rifling one turn in 6 feet 6 inches.

American Guns.—The Peabody-Martine Rifle, Breech Loader. Rifling 7 grooves, one turn in 22 inches, gain twist, lands and grooves of equal width.

Maynard Rifle, Breech Loader. Rifling 3 grooves, one turn in 5 feet, lands and grooves equal width; depth, .01.

Sharp's Rifle, Breech Loader. Lands and grooves equal width. Rifling one turn in 20 inches.

Bown & Sons' Kentucky Rifle, Muzzle Loader. Standard number of grooves 7, but made with 4, 5,

6, and 7 grooves, same width as lands. Even twist one turn in 42 inches. Gain twist commences at 9 feet and ends at 6 feet.

Powel & Son's Breech Loading Rifle, 6 and 7 grooves, one turn in 36 inches.

Steven's Rifle, Breech Loader. Regular twist, one turn in 26 inches.

Springfield, U. S. Rifle, Breech Loader, Cal. 45. Rifling 3 plain concentric grooves. Lands and grooves equal width. Uniform twist, one turn in 22 inches, depth .005.

Frank Wesson's Rifle, Breech Loader. Long and mid-range guns using long slugs, even twist, one turn in 18 inches, grooves 6, lands and grooves equal width. Short range guns, using slugs having short bearing, increase twist commencing on 6 feet, and ending on 2 feet, 5 and 6 grooves, lands and grooves of equal width.

Wesson's Muzzle Loading Rifle. Barrel 2′ 8″ long. Rifling one turn in 3′ 6″. 6 grooves; space between grooves equal to interior surface presenting a dovetail appearance. Groves not so wide as spaces.

The Whitney Arms Co.'s Guns, Breech Loading, comprising the Whitney, Kennedy, and Phœnix systems. Rifling 6 grooves, one turn in 22 inches. Lands and grooves of equal width.

Marston's Rifle (Toronto, Canada), Muzzle Loader, number of grooves 6, lands and grooves equal width; regular twist, one turn in 30 inches; depth of groove 15-thousandths inch, slightly freed at breech.

Pistols.—Colt's Army Pistol, Breech Loading Revolver, Cal. 45. Rifling 6 grooves, twist uniform, one turn in 16 inches; depth .005.

Schofield, Smith & Wesson Revolver for Army Use, Breech Loader. Bore, .435. Number of grooves 5, uniform twist, one turn in 20 inches. Depth of rifling .0075.

CHAPTER XLII.

DIRECTIONS FOR TAKING APART AND ASSEMBLING RIFLES, DOUBLE-BARRELLED SHOT GUNS AND PISTOLS, OF THE MOST NOTED MAKERS IN THE UNITED STATES.

The Ballard Rifle.—(Made by the Marlin Arms Co., New Haven, Conn).

To Take Apart.—1, take the sight from the barrel; 2, take off the stock by unscrewing butt-plate; and turning out the long tang screw ; 3, drop the lever and take out lever screw ; take out the extractor then the block ; 4, unscrew the barrel from the frame and take the tang from the frame ; 5, take the screws from the lock and pry the plates apart.

To Assemble.—Proceed in reverse order.

The Burgess Repeating Rifle.—(Made by Whitney Arms Co., New Haven, Conn).—1, receiver ; 2, bottom tang ; 3, lever ; 4, breech-block ; 5, top lever ; 6, ejector ; 7, carrier-block ; 8, bottom plate ; 9, bottom plate snap ; 10, hammer ; 11 main-spring ; 12, hammer-screw ; 13, side loading spring cover as seen from the back ; 14, trigger.

To Take Apart.—1st, take out the bottom plate screw, and remove the plate; 2d, take out the top cover screws and slide the cover back against the hammer, having depressed the lever sufficiently to let it pass by, then pull back the hammer as far as possible and take the cover out ; 3d, take out the carrier screws, there being one on each side of the upper rear portion of the receiver, and the stop screw on the upper front left hand side of the receiver, then the lever, breech-block, extractor and carrier can be taken out through the top.

To Disengage the Lever from the Breech Block.—Take out, 1st, the firing pin screw; 2d, the firing pin; 3d, the ejector from the side of the breech-block; 4th, the large pin from either side. In assembling, replace the pin in exactly the same position it was when taken out.

To Assemble.--1st, place the lever, breech block, extractor and carrier in their proper position, relatively to one another, as they were when taken out, with the projection on the breech-block inside, and under the front part of the carrier. 2d. Replace the above parts taken together in the receiver, passing the handle of the lever first through the top, put in the carrier side screws and the stop screw. 3d. cock the hammer, slide the top cover into place, the breech being left half way open, then put in the screw; 4th, close the breach and screw the bottom plate to place.

Burnside's Breech Loading Rifle.—To clean the gun, unlatch the guard and drop the chamber; press down the small spring bolt at the guard joint with the finger nail, while the lever of the joint-bolt is turned out of place and taken from the joint. To detach the movable breech-pin from the chamber, press it back with the thumb and forefinger of the left hand; hold the bolt in this position with the thumb nail of the right hand inserted in the notch of the bolt, while with the fore finger of the same hand, the breech-pin is pushed into the chamber, and the head or button of the spring-bolt is turned from its place, when the breech-pin may be removed. Every part of the arm, except the lock is now exposed to view. Put together in reverse order of taking apart.

The Evans Magazine Rifle.—(*Made by the Evans Magazine Rifle Co., Mechanics Falls, Me.; Merwin, Hulbert & Co., agents, New York City.*)—To load the magazine, introduce the cartridge through the opening in the butt plate. Each complete movement of the lever forward carries the cartridge to its chamber. Repeat the motion till the magazine is full.

To use as a single loader, drop the lever to right angle with the barrel and insert the cartridge directly in the chamber.

The full motion of the lever forward discharges the empty shell, the return places the loaded cartridge in position, when the arm is ready for discharge.

Semi-Hammerless.—The American Arms Company are now producing a gun at a low price called the semi-hammerless single gun, for which the manufacturers claim that it combines the advantages of a hammerless without the danger of the self-cocking principle. To cock the gun press down the little lever on the side. The lock-plate is easily removed to get at and oil the lock. Its construction is such that no water or dirt can penetrate to the lock.

The Hotchkiss Magazine Gun.—(*Made by Winchester Arms Co., New Haven, Conn.*)—To remove the magazine cut off, turn the notched end to the front; place the point of a screw-driver under the rear end and bear down gently, slightly supporting the front end against the pressure with the fingers of the left hand. To remove the breech-bolts press on the trigger and at the same time unlock the bolt and withdraw it. N. B.—The bolt can be removed in the following manner: unlock and draw back the bolt until the cocking piece just clears the receiver; then, letting go the handle, take hold of the cocking piece and turn it down to the right until the projection on the bolt-head leaves the groove under the front end of the locking-tube. The latter may then be drawn out at the rear, and the head at the front of the receiver. To return the bolt, the head must be inserted from the front and the part from the rear, unless the cut-off be removed To remove the magazine-spring and cartridge-follower, insert the point of a screw-driver in the hole at the rear of the magazine tube, and draw out the tube. The barrel cannot be removed until the magazine has been taken out. Remove then the trigger spring screw and spring, the cartridge stop pin and stop, the trigger pin and trigger using a punch to drive out the pin. Remover the trigger catch pin and catch, using the point of a screw-driver in the notched end of the pin to draw it out.

To dismount the breech-bolt, remove the bolt-head, which can be done by holding the cocking-piece firmly in the left hand, and with the right turn down the handles as in the act of locking the bolt; the head will then slip off. Turn out the firing-pin screw; slip the bolt-head partly on the projecting end of the firing-pin, and use it as a wrench to unscrew the pin; the main-spring may then be removed. Remove the extractor by tapping gently on its projecting end with a piece of wood.

To assemble, proceed in the reverse order.

Howard's Sporting Rifle, "The Thunderbolt."—To clean the lock, take out the screw that attaches the back end of the yoke to the breech piece; unscrew the barrel; then take the nut from the back end of the sliding breech-pin, which with the mainspring and hammer, constitute the lock.

In using, if the operator does not wish to have the piece cocked, he has only to hold the trigger back while closing the guard, and it will not be cocked. To cock it from this position, he has only to open the guard a short distance, and close it. If he wishes to load and fire rapidly, it will cock itself. If in no haste, or does not wish it cocked, he has only to hold back the trigger, while closing its guard.

The Kennedy Magazine Gun.—(Made by Whitney Arms Co., New Haven, Conn.)—Directions for taking apart:

1. Take out the two side screws, on the left side of the receiver, that are nearest together. 2. Remove the bottom plate and carrier block through the bottom of the receiver. 3. Full cock the hammer

and take out the extractor screw from top cover, then depress the lever sufficiently to let the cover pass over it, pull back the hammer as far as possible and slide the cover out over it. 4. Remove the breech-block and lever together through the the top of the receiver.

To disengage the breech-block: 1. Take out the firing-pin screw. 2. The firing pin. 3. The ejector from the side of the breech-block. 4. The large pin from either side.

To assemble, put the parts together in reverse order from which they were taken out.

Marlin's Magazine Rifle—(Made by Marlin Arms Co., New Haven, Conn.)—Figure No. 1 shows the arm in a closed position. A, represents the Lever; B, the Bolt; C, Extractor; D, the Carrier Block; E, the Ejector; F, the Carrier Block Spring; G, the Hammer; H, the Trigger; I, the Firing Pin.

To take the action apart: 1. Take out the lever pin screw, and drive out the lever pin, allowing the lever to be removed. 2. Take out the tang screw (this allows the stock to be removed), hammer screw, and front pin that goes through trigger strap; now remove the trigger strap with lock work attached. 3. The bolt can now be slipped out.

To assemble the action, put the parts into the receiver in reverse order from that in which they were taken out.

Maynard Rifle, Self-Priming Model.—(Made by Mass. Arms Co., Chicopee Falls, Mass.)—To detach the barrel: Loosen the lever at its rear end and move it forward. There is a button that keeps the magazine closed; turn this button downward and forward as far as it will go; then pull it out as far as it will come; this will detach the lever from the breech-piece, so that it will come partly out of it; unhook the barrel, and the lever will pass quite out of the breech-piece. To attach the barrel reverse the operation.

To remove the nipple: On the left side, opposite the nipple, is the screw which fastens it; take out this screw; put a stick of hard wood in the screw-hole; strike the stick a little and the nipple will be driven out.

To dissect the rifle for a thorough cleaning: There are four screws on the under side of the gun, behind the hole where the lever is pivoted. Take out the two farthest back, and the stock may then be drawn back so as to separate it from the breech-piece.

To adjust the joint between the end of the barrel and the breech-piece: There are two screws visible on the under side of the breech-piece, forward of the lever. They are to adjust the joint to the thickness of the flange of the cartridge. To do this: First, turn the screw nearest the lever once round to the left; now raise the butt-end of the barrel, put in a cartridge, and observe as you bring the butt end down again whether the joint is too close, so as to pinch the flange, or not close enough to hold it firmly. The exact degree of tightness allows the lever to work easily, but holds the barrel perfectly firm. This degree will be found by turning the forward screw to the right or left. Having found this degree, turn the rear screw to the right, tightly, and the joint is adjusted.

The Peabody-Martini Rifle.—(*Made by Providence Tool Co., Providence, R. I.*)—1. Butt Stock. 9. Stock Bolt. 10. Receiver, or Body. 11. Trigger Spring. 12. Screw for Locking Bolt Spring and Trigger Spring. 14. Stop Nut. 15. Block Axis Pin. 16. Striker, or Firing Pin. 19. Block. 25. Tumbler. 26. Indicator. 27. Block Lever. 28. Extractor. 29. Tumbler Rest. 30. Tumbler Rest Axis Screw. 31. Extractor Axis Screw. 32. Guard. 33. Trigger. 34. Trigger Axis Screw. 35. Swivel. 36. Swivel Axis Screw. 46. Barrel. 47. Fore, or Tip-Stock. 48. Cleaning Rod.

To dismount body or receiver: Turn keeper-screw so the groove in head will allow block axis pin to drop out; open the breech, and with the thumb press with force on front end of block, and, at the same time, raise the lever; turn the keeper-screw so as to allow the tumbler axis to be pushed out. This also relieves the tumbler. Take out extractor axis screw.

To assemble body: Put lever back to its place in assembled guard and insert both in the body. Drop in extractor and turn in extractor axis screw. Put tumbler in place and put in tumbler axis, point upright and secure keeper screw. With the right hand raise the lever so as to touch the lever catch, then, with the first finger, pull the trigger back, and with the thumb push the trigger axis forward, and drop in the assembled block, the front end entering first.

Apply a little force to back end of block with the left hand, moving the lever a little at the same time with the right hand, and the block will drop into place. Insert block axis pin and secure it with the keeper screw.

To dismount guard: Take out tumbler rest axis screw, relieving tumbler rest. Take out trigger spring screw, relieving trigger spring and locking bolt spring. Take out trigger axis screw, relieving trigger. Take out locking bolt screw, if found necessary.

To assemble guard: Hold trigger in place and turn in trigger axis screw. Restore locking bolt and thumb piece to place and turn in screw. Restore locking bolt spring and trigger spring and turn in trigger spring screw. Insert tumbler rest and turn in tumbler rest axis screw. The parts are now ready to be attached to the body, or receiver.

To dismount block: Turn keeper screw on end of block and take out stop nut. The firing pin and coil spring will then drop out.

To assemble block: Restore firing pin and coil spring. Turn in stop nut, and turn keeper screw to secure it.

The firing pin has a rectangular slot near one end. This slot is longer on one side than on the other. The long side should be so placed as to admit end of the tumbler freely.

The Phœnix Breech-Loader.—(Made by Whitney Arms Co., New Haven, Conn.)—No special directions are necessary for dismounting and assembling the Phœnix system. The breech-block is taken out by loosening the screw that holds the pin, and then taking out the pin. After the breech-block has been removed let the hammer down as far as it will go, which relieves it from the pressure of the main spring, and it can then be easily removed by taking out the screw which holds it.

The Remington Breech-Loading Rifle.—(Made by E. Remington & Sons, Ilion, N. Y.)—Explanation of parts and technical names: AA. Receiver. B. Breech Piece. C. Hammer. D. Locking Lever. a. Main Spring. bb. Pins. c. Trigger. d. Lever Spring. e. Trigger Spring. f. Firing Pin. g. Extractor.

To remove the breech piece and hammer: Loosen the button screw until the button can be removed from the heads of the breech and hammer pins. Cock the hammer, push out the breech pin, take out the breech piece, let down the hammer as far as it will go (which leaves the main spring resting upon a stationary pin, and obviates the necessity of using a main spring vise in readjusting the parts). Remove the hammer pin and take out the hammer.

To replace the hammer and breech piece: Lay the arm down on the right side, press upon the trigger at the same time replacing the hammer with the thumb piece forward and downward, until the hole in the hammer and receiver correspond. Replace the hammer pin, cock the hammer, replace the breech piece, insert breech pin in receiver, and by pressing on the pin at the same time pressing down the breech piece and working it back and forth slightly the pin will enter. Adjust the button and tighten the button screw.

To take the entire arm apart: Take out the extractor screw, open the breech, remove the extractor, take out the breech piece and hammer, as described. In military arms remove the wiping rod by unscrewing the same, remove the bands, separate the tip stock from the barrel at the muzzle, until it is liberated from the stud upon the under side of the barrel when it may be withdrawn from the receiver; take out the tang screw and remove the butt stock.

To detach the guard strap: Take out the two side screws which pass through the guard strap, always removing the rear screw first. Unscrew the barrel from the receiver, taking care that the extractor has been removed before unscrewing the barrel.

To assemble the arm: Screw the barrel into the receiver, until the mark on the top of the barrel and receiver correspond. Replace the extractor and screw, place the forward end of the guard strap in the receiver, putting in the screw. See that the main spring is in the center of the guard strap, press the rear end in until the screw will enter. Replace the hammer and breech piece, as previously described. Replace butt stock and tip. In putting on the bands of military guns, see that the letters upon them are upon the same side with the band springs. Replace the wiping rod by screwing it in.

The locking lever, attached to the guard strap, serves a double purpose: one end locking the sear, or trigger, when the breech is open to receive the cartridge, which effectually prevents accidental discharge, the other end working in a groove on the under side of the breech piece, serving to close the breech piece and keep it closed in the act of firing.

The Remington Magazine Gun; Keene's patent.—(Made by E. Remington & Sons, Ilion, N. Y.) To remove the breech, turn the large screw at the right hand side of the stock below the hammer to the right until the carrier (which should be in its lower position at the time) drops free of the bolt and allows it to be withdrawn. N. B. The screw referred to is cut with a left hand thread. To separate the rear end of the bolt and firing pin from the front end, bend back the hammer and twist it around to the right until the shoulder on front end of rear cap slides back in the groove in breech bolt. To reassemble it reverse the operation described. To take out the extractor, press back the extractor bolt, using the hooked end of the screw-driver for this purpose, thus releasing the rear end of the extractor, which may then be lifted out of its seat. Care should be taken not to let the extractor be thrown out by the spring when released. To remove the stock, take off the bands; take out the screw at the end of the metal tip, and remove the tip-stock by slipping it forward over the magazine tube. Unscrew the magazine tube, take out the tang screw, remove the guard bow, and take off the butt stock. The barrel should never be unscrewed except with proper appliances to avoid injuring the receiver.

To assemble the parts, reverse the operations described, taking care in screwing in the magazine tube that the follower does not catch against the cut-off and interfere with replacing the tube.

Remington No. 3 Rifle,—(Hepburn's Patent, made by E. Remington and Sons, Ilion, N. Y.)—Remove the upper screw on the left hand side, and the breech block may be taken out. To take out the hammer, remove the upper screw and slip the hammer forward into the breech block hole. To take out the extractor, remove the forward screw on left hand side. The lever which operates the breech block passes through the rocker sleeve with a square stud and is held in place by a set screw directly under the fore stock, which must be removed if it is ever desired to take off the lever. If necessary to remove the guard it can be done by taking off the butt stock and taking out the side screws in the usual way. The barrel should not be unscrewed from the frame except with proper appliances. When necessary to unscrew the frame, the extractor should be taken out and the breech block and guard put back in place, before putting on the wrench.

Sharp's Rifle, (old model using paper or linen cartridge, also model of 1874 using metallic cartridge; made by Sharp's Rifle Co., Bridgeport, Conn.)—To take the arm apart: Relieve the lever key from pressure of spring by throwing down the lever guard, the key can then be taken out and the slide with lever guard attached, removed.

To replace, put slide in place, leaving guard down, then insert lever key, turning the key to place.

To take off the lock, give four or five turns to the side screws; tap their heads gently with the handle of the screw-driver to start the lock from its bed, the side screws can then be taken out and the lock removed. To replace the lock, press it firmly into its bed, before entering the screws and then turn them up close.

Sharp's Rifle, (Borchardt's Patent model of 1878; made by Sharp's Rifle Co., Bridgeport, Conn.)—Plate 3—AAA, receiver; BB, slide; CC, sear; D, firing bolt; E, cam; F, extractor; G, connection, H, trigger; K, safety catch; L, safety lever; MM, lever; NN, mainspring; O, lever spring; P, barrel stud; R, ramrod stop, military; S, ramrod, military; T, swivel, military; UU, barrel; VV, forearm; W, link; X, butt-stock bolt; 1, lever pin; 2, lever screw.

To take the arm apart: Loosen the rear screw under the barrel, and this will relieve the pressure of the lever spring. Cock the gun by opening and closing. Bring down the guard lever half way. Take out the lever pin on which the lever rotates. This pin is held in place by a small screw directly above it. Turn this screw to the left until the circular cut in its side is on a line with the lever pin, and the latter can then be removed. Pull lever out of the joint. Replace lever pin so as to hold extractor in place. Remove screw which connects lever and link, through hole in left side of link.

Take out lever. Push slide up and out, and then take out extractor.

To strip the slide, uncock it and push out sear pin and remove sear. Take out pin at rear end of slide. Take out slide plug and mainspring. Drive cross pin out of firing bolt and remove same. Remove link by taking last screw out of slide. To remove trigger, safety and safety lever, drive out trigger pin and safety pin above it. Pull back safety catch and pull out trigger. Push forward safety catch as far as it will go, and it will drop out, together with the safety lever above it.

To assemble, replace safety catch, safety lever and trigger. Assemble slide and cock it. Push safety catch into notch of trigger. Put in extractor and lever pin. Insert slide and push it down, keeping extractor close to its place, in base of barrel. Attach lever. Take out lever pin, bring lever into the joint, replace the pin, and secure it by giving small screw above it half a turn to the right. Tighten the screw which was loosened under the barrel.

Never use a hammer or other force either in taking apart or assembling this system. If the parts are in proper position, everything will go into place easily.

The U. S. Muzzle Loading Rifle and Musket.—To take apart: Draw the ramrod; turn out the tang screw; put the hammer at half cock; partially unscrew the side screw, and with a light tap on the head of each screw with the handle of the screw-driver or a light wood mallet, loosen the lock from its bed in the stock, then turn out the side screws and remove the lock with the left hand. Remove the side screws and take off the bands. Take out the barrel by turning the gun horizontally, barrel downward, holding the barrel loosely with the left hand below the rear sight, the right hand grasping the stock by the small; if it does not leave the stock, tap the muzzle on the top side against the work bench which will effect loosening it at the breech.

To assemble, put together in the inverse order of taking apart. Squeeze the barrel in place with the hand; give the butt of the stock a gentle tap on the floor to settle the breech end of the barrel against the head of the stock.

Springfield Breech Loading Rifle (*made at Springfield, Mass. by U. S. Government; adopted by U. S. Government.*)—A, Bottom of Receiver; B, Barrel; C, Breech Screw; E, Hinge Pin; F, Cam Lock; G, Cam Latch Spring; H, Firing Pin; I, Firing Pin Spring; J, Extractor; K, Ejector Spring and Spindle; L, ejector Stud; M, Lug of Extractor.

To dismount the breech loading parts: 1. Remove the hinge pin by pressing on its point with a small-sized punch until the end carrying the arm projects sufficiently to enable it to be grasped and removed by the fingers. 2. Remove the breech block carefully, so as not to allow the extractor and ejector spring to fall out. 3. Remove the extractor and ejector spring. 4. Remove the cam latch by unscrewing the breech block cap screw, and loosen the cap with the point of a screw driver. 5. Remove the cam latch spring. 6. Turn out the firing pin screw, then take out the firing pin and spring from the breech block.

To assemble: 1. Insert the firing pin screw in the breech block, then the firing pin, and then replace the firing pin screw. 2. Insert the cam latch spring in its place. 3. Replace the cam latch and the breech block cap; turn the cap screw well down. 4. Insert the ejector spring in its place. 5. Replace the extractor in such a position in the breech block that the small recess in the back of the extractor will be in a position to be presented to the point of the ejector spring spindle. 6. Insert the breech block. After seeing that the point of the spindle has entered the recess in the back of the extractor, strike the breech block over the thumb piece and head of the firing pin, a smart blow with the palm of the hand, forwards and downwards, this will cause it to enter sufficiently to hold it in place. Then press it into position by grasping the block and receiver with the fingers and thumb, the thumb uppermost, and squeeze it home. 7. Insert the hinge pin by striking it a sharp blow with the palm of the hand. See that the stud in the arm enters the recess cut for it on the side of the receiver.

Should the thumb piece interfere with the head of the hammer in raising the breech block, it is probable that either the tumbler or sear screw is too loose or broken.

Whitney Breech Loading Gun (made by Whitney

Arms Company, New Haven, Conn.)—To take apart: 1. Give the screw in the side of the frame or receiver (that holds the two fulcrum pins) a few turns to release the flanges or heads of the two pins, then turn them away from the screw a little. 2. Place the hammer on the half-cock, open the breech half way, and press the locking shoulder back with the screw driver until it is held by the catch on the locking lever made for the purpose. 3. Knock out the pin that holds the breech block, and take out the breech block, lever and cartridge extractor at the same time. 4. Bring the hammer to full-cock, so as to release the locking shoulder, and then uncock it, pressing it forward so as to relieve the tension of the springs; knock out the large pin, and take out the hammer and locking shoulder together.

To assemble: 1. Draw back the trigger to its usual place and insert the hammer and locking shoulder (placed together, as when taken out) into the receiver, pressing them forward so as to relieve them from the tension of their springs; then insert the hammer pin, half-cock the hammer, and press back the locking shoulder until it is held by the catch on the locking lever. 2. Insert the lever, breech block and cartridge extractor placed together, put in the fulcrum pin, turn the heads or flanges of the two pins to their places against the binding screw, and turn it up to its place. 3. Open the breech in the usual way, or simply bring the hammer to full cock, when the locking shoulder will be released and the piece ready to operate. The ramrod is held in place by being screwed into the steel on the lower side of the barrel.

Whitney New System Breech Loading Gun (*made by Whitney Arms Company, New Haven, Conn.*)—1, Receiver or Frame; 2, Bottom Tang; 3, Barrel, 4, Breech Block; 5, Hammer; 6, Breech Block Fulcrum Pin; 7, Hammer Fulcrum Pin; 8, Extractor; 9, Mainspring; 10, Trigger; 11, Stud.

To take appart the lock work: 1. Give the screw in the side of the frame or receiver (that holds the two large fulcrum pins) a few turns to release the flanges or heads of the two pins, then turn them away from the screw a little. 2. Place the hammer on the full cock, open the breech half way, knock out the pin that holds the breech block and the extractor screw in the side of the receiver, then take out the breech block and cartridge extractor at the same time. 3. Uncock the hammer, pressing it forward so as to relieve the tension of the spring; knock out the large pin and take out the hammer.

To assemble the lock work: 1. Draw back the trigger to its usual place, and insert the hammer into the receiver, pressing it forward so as to relieve it from the tension of the spring; then insert the hammer pin and cock the hammer. 2. Insert the breech block and cartridge extractor, placed together, put in the fulcrum pin, turn the heads or flanges of the two pins to their places against the binding screw, and turn it up to its place; then put in the extractor screw.

Winchester Magazine Gun.—(*Made by Winchester Arms Co., New Haven, Conn.*)—To take apart:

To take out the barrel: Take out the two tip screws, the magazine ring pin, pull out the magazine tube, and take off the forearm; then, before unscrewing the barrel from the frame, the breech pin must be thrown back by moving the finger-lever forward, otherwise the attempt to unscrew it will break the spring catch that withdraws the cartridge, and ruin the breech-pin.

To remove the breech pin model of 1866: After removing the side plates and links, the spring-catch must be next taken out, which is done by moving the breech-pin back so that the pin that holds the spring catch will be in a line with a corresponding hole through the frame; then with a small steel wire punch out the pin, then move the breech-pin forward and take out the spring catch; the piston can then be unscrewed with pliers or hand vise, first setting the hammer at full cock, or taking it out.

In models of 1873 and 1876: After removing the side plates and links, take out the link pin and retractor; the piston can then be pulled out with the fingers, first removing the hammer or setting it at full cock. Should the main spring require strengthening it can be done by turning up the strain-screw, which will be found directly under it, on the under side of the frame.

Remington's Rifle Cane.—(*Made by E. Remington & Sons Ilion, N. Y.*)—Directions for using: To load, unscrew the handle or breech from the body of the cane ; insert the cartridge and replace the handle, drawing back the handle will cock the piece ready for firing, when pressing on the trigger-knob underneath will discharge it. Do not press on the trigger-knob when the piece is being cocked.

The lock-case or breech may be closed by a slight pressure upon the spring sight.

For hunting or target practice, remove the tip or ferule at the muzzle. If it is required to use the arm suddenly, as for self-defense, it is not necessary to remove the tip.

To remove the lock-case, remove the ferule under the handle by driving it down, take out the pin under the ferule, draw out the handle, draw the cane to full cock and press down and back the trigger, unscrew the lock from the barrel and push the cock out at the top end of the case.

In replacing the lock be careful to get the slot on a line with the guide inside of the case, and press down the sight spring.

Billings' Breech Loading Shot Gun.—(Made by Billings & Spencer, Hartford, Conn.)—This arm is provided with a backward and upward moving breech block in the rear of the cartridge, the breech block turning backward upon the hinge, which is a more natural motion than a forward turn.

To open the breech for loading, half cock the piece ; draw the locking bolt with small handle on right side, and pull towards you ; this retracts the firing pin, also extracts the shell automatically at the same time.

The Fox Breech Loading Shot Gun.—(*Made by American Arms Co., Boston, Mass.*)—To take apart: To detach the barrels, first open the gun as if for loading, which is done by pressing forward the thumb-piece on the top of the stock; then with the left thumb at a point about two inches from the end of the barrels, press the barrels towards the right and the gun is in position to load. Next turn the gun over in the right hand, holding it by the small of the stock, the end of the stock under the elbow supporting the weight of the gun; with the left thumb press the extractor home, and, with the thumb placed on the extractor spring, as close up to the fore end as convenient, press down the extractor firmly, and gently swinging the stock to the right until the detachment is obtained.

To attach the barrels again, grasp the barrels with the plate up, so that the large screw at the head of the plate comes about at the center of the hand; be sure that the extractor is home. Place the opening for the screw which is in the breech-plate, over the screw, with the stock at an angle of about forty-five degrees with the barrels, at the same time put the left thumb on the end of the fore end, holding it firmly and flat on the plate, the stock-plate covering the guide-pin next the screw on the barrels, but not the pin on the extractor; gently move the stock until the two plates come into perfect contact, when the barrel will swing into position.

To remove the extractor, detach the barrels from

the stock, lay them on a table with the plate up and muzzle from gun; pull out the extractor as far as it will come readily, then turn it to the *left* until the short arm strikes end of the barrels; now draw it straight out, meanwhile holding a finger over the extractor button to prevent its springing out and getting lost, when the button and locking stud will fall out of their own weight.

To replace the extractor, lay the extractor button in its cavity and slide the long shank of the extractor through it, then place the locking stud in position, holding it snug against the rear end of its seat, run the extractor into it, solid home, and turn to the *right* till the short arm is opposite its hole, when push straight in.

To take out firing pins, remove the screw holding them, which will be found in the breech-piece at the rear of the scroll-fence.

The Lefever Hammerless Gun.—(Made by Daniel Lefever, Syracuse, N. Y.)—Locks are rebounding.

To take apart: To take off the lock, see that both hammers are down; take out lever-screw; remove lever; turn out lock plate screw and drive off right hand lock by tapping on head of lock plate screw; take out the screw and insert in sear hole, and drive off left hand plate.

To take out the hammers, turn *in* the screws in bottom of the frame until the mainspring will allow the hammer to drop back far enough to allow its being lifted out of the frame. In putting back, be careful to press the projection on the lever on top of the spring that holds it, up to place, before putting the lever-screw in.

Parker Double-barreled Breech-loading Shot Gun. (Made by Parker Brothers, Meriden, Conn.)—1. Finger piece. 2. Guard. 3. Lifter. 4. Locking bolt screws. 5. Locking bolt. 6. Barrel lug. 7. Trip. 8. Trip spring. 11. Extractor. 13. Joint Roll. The finger piece is solid and a part of lifter.

Pressing up the finger piece in front of guard raises the lifter, and its beveled side coming in contact with the locking bolt screw, acts as a wedge to draw the locking bolt from the mortise in the lug, and releases the barrels so that they tilt upward ready to receive the cartridges. When the bolt is back to the position shown in Fig. 2, the small hole which is drilled in the under side of the bolt comes directly over the trip, which, by the assistance of the trip spring, is made to enter the hole in the bolt and thereby hold it in position.

For cleaning, it can be very easily removed by taking off the locks and removing the locking bolt screw from the end of the locking bolt, then press down on the trip, which will allow the lifter to be withdrawn without removing either stock, guard or trigger-plate.

To replace the plunger: Withdraw the cone with a common screw-driver, by pressing it against the plunger until the screw-driver enters the slot. After removing the plunger and spring, be careful to replace them with spring at side of plunger.

Remington Double-barreled Breech-loading Shot

Gun. (*Made by E. Remington & Sons, Ilion, N. Y.*) —A, thumb piece; B, lever, engaging locking bolt; C, pivot of lever B; D, locking point; H, joint check; K, pivot pin; L, joint check screw, limiting motion of barrels; M, hammer lifter; N, extractor; O, wire, a shoulder of which rests against P; P, shoulder of dog engaging locking bolt; S, snap action spring.

To take apart: To remove the barrels, take off the tip-stock, full cock both hammers and press the thumb-piece (between the hammers, and used for unlocking the barrels for loading) upward as far as it will go. The barrels can thus be detached.

In Fig. 3, the locking bolt is drawn as far as the shoulder P will allow it to move. This shoulder P is formed on one side of a little dog, in the other side of which is a corresponding shoulder, resting against the wire O. So long as the tip-stock is in place this dog cannot yield or permit the locking-bolt to be drawn far enough to allow the joint-check to come out of the mortise in the frame; but when the tip-stock is removed, the wire O can slip part way out, as in Fig. 4, allowing the shoulder P to move back, so that the locking-bolt can be drawn back clear of the joint-check—thus releasing the barrels.

The Roper Four-shooting Shot-gun and Rifle. (*Made by the Billings & Spencer Co., Hartford, Conn.*) —A, frame; B, receiver; B^1, hinged lid of receiver; C, hammer; D, plunger; D^1, head of plunger; E, plunger link; F, cartridges; G, carrier in which shells are placed; H, lever to revolve carrier; I, mainspring; J, sear; *a*, ratchet; *b*, stirrup; *c*, link connecting hammer with mainspring; *d*, pin of lever H; *e*, pivot of carrier G; *f*, firing pin; *h*, elastic tail of lever H.

To take apart: To take the gun apart, *turn in* the set screw on under side of cylinder forward of the guard plate screw, until it comes to a stop. Then bring the hammer to cock notch and unscrew the cylinder from breech. N. B.—This set screw turns *in* to take the gun apart, and turns *out* to fasten the cylinder.

In putting the gun together, screw up the breech until the set screw can be replaced. This screw should be turned sufficiently tight to prevent any looseness of the breech.

To take off the stock and expose the lock, take out the long screw that runs through the small, rear end of receiver on top, and the screw in the guard plate which fastens it to the receiver underneath in front. Then remove the stock, and the working parts are exposed and can be readily cleaned and oiled. The firing pin should be detached occasionally, cleaned and oiled, as its easy working insures certain fire. To do this, take out the small screw in the top of the hammer and remove the piston entirely from the receiver, and the piston and firing pin are readily separated. In replacing the piston, care should be taken to put it in right side up the retractor spring being at the bottom. Never attempt to take out the screw which fastens the link to the piston, until the firing pin is detached.

Colt's Revolver For Army Use, Cal. 45.—(Made by the Colt Pat. Fire Arms Co., Hartford, Conn.)— A, barrel; B, Frame; B^1, recoil plate, C, cylinder; DD, firing pan; D^1, center pin bushing; E, guard; F, back strap; G, hammer; H, main spring; I, hammer roll and rivet; J, hammer screw; K, hammer cam; L, hand and hand spring; M, bolt and screw; N, trigger and screw; O, hammer notches. P, firing pin and rivet; Q, ejector rod and spring; Q^1, ejector tube; R, ejector head; S, ejector tube screw; T, short guard screw; U, seat and bolt spring (combined) and screw. V, back strap screw; W, main spring screw; X, front sight; Y, center pin catch screw.

To take apart: To dismount the pistol, half-cock the hammer, loosen the centre pin catch screw; draw out the centre pin, open the gate, and the cylinder can then be withdrawn. To remove the ejector, turn out the ejector tube screw, then push the front end away from the barrel and pull it towards the muzzle. The stock can be removed by turning out the two screws just behind the hammer, and that at the bottom of the strap. Remove the main spring and trigger guard; the parts of the lock can then be readily separated. The cylinder bushing should then be pushed out for cleaning. To remove the gate, turn out a screw in the lower side of the frame (hidden by the trigger guard), then the gate spring and catch can be withdrawn, and the gate can be pushed out.

To assemble the pistol, follow the directions for dismounting in reverse order. The mainspring is most conveniently mounted by turning in the screw part way, then swinging around the front end of the main spring until it bears against the under side of the friction roll. The cylinder bushing should be frequently removed for cleaning.

North's Patent Revolving Pistol.—To take the pistol apart, take out the screw in the forward end of the lock and barrel frame, which runs through the base-pin, then draw back the operating lever so as to bring the hammer to the half-cock, turn the cylinder round by hand until the mortise in the back end of the cylinder is found, which mortise connects the cylinder with the recoil shield; then unlock the rammer and draw it and the base-pin out; the cylinder is then left free to be taken out. When the cylinder is taken out be careful not to leave the spiral spring which lays in a recess made in the front end of the cylinder, and in putting together be careful to replace this spring.

To take the lock apart, first take out the main and lever springs which are both held by one screw; then take out the hammer, next the small screw connecting the lever with the link of the toggle-joint (this screw is in the lever on the outside of the pistol just back of the trigger). Next bend up the toggle-joint and take out the lever and trigger, which are both held by one screw; then take out the toggle-joint and revolving lever, which are connected together by two screws.

To put the lock together, first pnt in the toggle-joint, then the main and lever springs, next the hammer, then the lever and trigger; next screw the revolving lever to the toggle-joint.

To put the cylinder in its place, first put the recoil shield (the piece with ratchets made for turning the breech) into its place and draw back the operating lever so that the hammer will come to full cock, at the same time pressing back the recoil shield as far as it will go, still holding back the operating lever; see that the spiral spring is in place in front of the cylinder, put the cylinder in place, let the projecting pin on the recoil shield come into the mortise in back end of cylinder; then put base-pin and rammer to place and turn in the screw which holds it.

The Remington Revolver (*Smoot's Patent, made by E. Remington & Sons, Ilion, N. Y.*)—To load: Half-cock the hammer; then turn the cylinder around so as to bring the chambers in line with the opening in the recoil shield, in which position the cartridges can be inserted, or the empty shells extracted by means of the rammer on the side of the barrel.

To remove the cylinder: Half-cock the hammer, then slide forward the stud in front of the cylinder through which the extractor rammer operates. The cylinder is replaced in the same way, but it is generally necessary to turn it in its seat to get the pawl out of the way before the centre pin will enter the hole in the cylinder.

To take the arm apart for cleaning: Remove the

cylinder; then take out the two screws for holding the guard to the frame. When the guard is taken off, all the lock work is accessible for cleaning.

In order to keep a revolver in good condition, the cylinder should be taken out and oiled before putting it away after firing. The centre pin should be removed and cleaned to prevent it from rusting and impeding the rotation of the cylinder.

The Remington Magazine Pistol—(Rider's Patent. Made by E. Remington & Sons, Ilion, N. Y.)—To load: Draw the tube from the magazine; hold the pistol barrel upright; drop the cartridge, rim downwards, into the magazine; when full, insert the feeding tube in the magazine and lock in place by turning the caps and engaging catch in the notch under the barrel.

To fire: Grasp the pistol in the usual manner, press the thumb upon the breech-block, carrying the block downward until released from the recoil shoulder; then draw the block and hammer backward until the hammer engages in the cock notch; then let the block forward by an easy motion and the cartridge will be carried into the chamber; the pistol will remain at full cock and is discharged by pulling the trigger. In case the pistol should be loaded, and cocked, and not needed for use, the cartridge in the chamber may be returned to the magazine by simply drawing back the breech and pressing the carrier downward until the cartridge is in position to enter the magazine, then letting the block forward. This is to insure safety in carrying.

The principle of this arm is such that the same motion cocks the hammer and carries the charge from the magazine to the chamber.

Schofield, Smith & Wesson Revolver, cal. 45.—(*Made by Smith & Wesson, Springfield, Mass.*)—To dismount the pistol: The only part of the pistol which will ordinarily require removal is the cylinder, which can be taken out as follows: Turn the cylinder catch just 180 deg., as indicated by the notch on its head; open the pistol; press up the head of the catch until it clears the cylinder; draw out the cylinder; replace it in inverse order.

To remove the cylinder and ejector of the pocket pistols, open the pistol until the piston protrudes half way, raise the barrel catch and turn the cylinder *two* turns to the *left*.

To replace the cylinder and ejector, open the pistol to its full capacity, raise the barrel catch, *press* the cylinder forward upon the base pin and give it *two* turns to the *right*.

The Automatic (*Merwin, Hulbert & Co.*) is so simple in its arrangements as to need no directions for assembling or taking apart.

FINIS.